Cambodia

The Legacy and Lessons of UNTAC

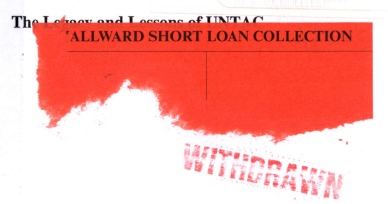

Cambodia

The Legacy and Lessons of UNTAC

SIPRI Research Report No. 9

Trevor Findlay

OXFORD UNIVERSITY PRESS

*This book has been printed digitally and produced in a standard specification
in order to ensure its continuing availability*

OXFORD
UNIVERSITY PRESS

Great Clarendon Street, Oxford OX2 6DP

Oxford University Press is a department of the University of Oxford.
It furthers the University's objective of excellence in research, scholarship,
and education by publishing world-wide in

Oxford New York

Auckland Bangkok Buenos Aires Cape Town Chennai
Dar es Salaam Delhi Hong Kong Istanbul Karachi Kolkata
Kuala Lumpur Madrid Melbourne Mexico City Mumbai Nairobi
São Paulo Shanghai Taipei Tokyo Toronto

Oxford is a registered trade mark of Oxford University Press
in the UK and in certain other countries

Published in the United States
by Oxford University Press Inc., New York

© SIPRI 1995

100501169 6

ISBN 0-19-829185-x

Printed in Great Britain by
Antony Rowe Ltd., Eastbourne

Contents

Final Act of the Paris Conference on Cambodia—Agreement on
a Comprehensive Political Settlement of the Cambodia Con-
flict—Agreement concerning the Sovereignty, Independence,
Territorial Integrity and Inviolability, Neutrality and National
Unity of Cambodia—Declaration on the Rehabilitation and
Reconstruction of Cambodia—Constitution of the Kingdom of
Cambodia

Preface

The United Nations peacekeeping operation in Cambodia between 1991 and 1993 is, so far, the most successful of the many such operations established by the UN since the end of the cold war. Although commonly called a peacekeeping operation, the Cambodia enterprise was much more. While comprising elements of traditional UN peacekeeping, such as monitoring a cease-fire, it was in fact a comprehensive plan to bring peace, democracy, constitutionality, human rights and the beginnings of reconciliation and reconstruction to Cambodia. It was the most ambitious and expensive such exercise the UN has ever undertaken, pushing the limits of peacekeeping even beyond those envisaged in 'second-generation' models and establishing new precedents in international law and practice. Despite its flaws, it provides new benchmarks for future UN operations.

This study is one of the first comprehensive assessments of the UN operation in Cambodia to be published. Based on research conducted over two years in Australia, Cambodia, Canada, Sweden and the USA, including interviews with key participants in the UN operation, it examines the peace process that led to the Paris Peace Accords, dissects the Accords themselves, discusses the establishment and operation of the UN Transitional Authority in Cambodia (UNTAC) and other elements of the peace process, and assesses the factors that contributed to the qualified success of the operation. Perhaps most important, it seeks to draw lessons from the Cambodia experience for future operations of similar size and nature. Finally it examines the troubling events that have occurred in Cambodia since the departure of UNTAC in late 1993 and the inferences that may be drawn about the durability of negotiated peace settlements once the UN blue helmets depart.

The study is the first published product of SIPRI's Project on Peacekeeping and Regional Security, established in mid-1993. It is also one of a series of studies of UN peacekeeping operations conducted by the Canadian Centre for Global Security in Ottawa as part of its International Peacekeeping Programme funded by the Ford Foundation. The Foundation's funding of the study is gratefully acknowledged.

SIPRI and the Canadian Centre for Global Security are delighted to be able to present Trevor Findlay's study jointly as a contribution to the present international debate on the future of multilateral peacekeeping.

Dr Adam Daniel Rotfeld
Director
SIPRI

Dr David Cox
Acting Director
Canadian Centre for Global Security

Acknowledgements

This study is based on research conducted in Australia and Sweden, a field trip to Cambodia from 21 to 27 May 1993, a workshop in Ottawa held on 19 November 1993 organized by the Canadian Centre for Global Security (CCGS), and subsequent interviews at UN headquarters in New York.

In Australia I spoke with Lieutenant-General John Sanderson, Military Commander of UNTAC; Susan Aitkin, Unesco; Terry-Anne O'Neil, Australian Defence Intelligence Organisation; and Simon Baker, Overseas Services Bureau.

In Cambodia, as well as visiting polling booths in Phnom Penh and Takhmau, UNTAC headquarters for press briefings and Cheung Ek (the 'killing fields' monument), I spoke with General and Mrs Sanderson; Nick Warner, Australian Mission; Stephen Marks, Basil Fernando and Jamie Medzel, UNTAC Human Rights Component; Mara Moustaphine, Telstra Overseas Telecommunications Corporation, Australia; Jennifer Ashton, UN High Commission for Refugees; Kwok Kwan Hung, Managing Director, *Rasmei Kampuchea* newspaper; Khoun Sodary, Deputy Editor, *Pracheachun* newspaper; Susan Aitkin, Unesco; Kim Wiesener, *Politiken,* a Danish newspaper; David Sporl, Canadian Mission; Sorasak Pan, Chief, EDP Section, UNTAC; Lieutenant-Colonel Damien Healy, UN Mixed Military Working Group Secretariat; Major John Flanagan, New Zealand Defence Force, Cambodian Mine Action Centre; Lieutenant-Colonel Marty Studdert, UNTAC Force Communications Unit; and Sek Barisoth, Unesco. In August 1992 in Shanghai I spoke with the Special Representative of the UN Secretary-General for Cambodia and head of UNTAC, Yasushi Akashi, and James Schear, UN Secretariat, New York.

The participants at the Ottawa workshop, which had the specific task of reviewing the first draft of this manuscript, were: Roohi Ahmed, UN Intern; Lieutenant-Colonel Lorne Bently, Head, Peacekeeping Section, Canadian Department of Foreign Affairs and Trade; Daniel Bon, Director-General, Policy Planning, Canadian Department of National Defence; Jane Boulden, Project Associate on Peacekeeping, CCGS; Colonel John Bremner, Director, Policy Operations, Canadian Department of National Defence; David Cox, CCGS; Commander James Dixon, Director, International Policy, Canadian Department of National Defence; David Henderson, Embassy of Japan; Carlton Hughes, Banksfield Consultants; Frank Ingruber, Australian High Commission; Arif Kamal, Embassy of Pakistan; Goran Kapetanovic, Distinguished Research Fellow, CCGS; Beverly Neufeld, CCGS; Craig Rickit, New Zealand High Commission; Dennis Snider,

Director, Arms Control Division, Canadian Department of Foreign Affairs and Trade; and Judy Thompson, Elections Canada.

In New York I again interviewed Yasushi Akashi, as well as Hisako Shimura, Director of the Department of Peace-keeping Operations (DPKO), United Nations; Richard Butler, Australian Ambassador to the United Nations; Michael Doyle, Deputy Director, International Peace Academy; and Lieutenant-Colonel Christian Hårleman, Military Advisor, DPKO, United Nations. In Sofia in October 1993 I spoke with General Stoyan Andreyev, Adviser on National Security and the Armed Forces to the President of Bulgaria. Kjell Engelbrekt of Radio Free Europe provided me with wire reports on the Bulgarian contingent in Cambodia.

Ian Anthony of SIPRI and Susan Aitkin kindly provided me with research materials on Cambodia. Colonel Bremner supplied a list of fact-finding missions to Cambodia, and Michael Maley of the Australian Electoral Commission provided information on the UNTAC Electoral Component. David Cox, CCGS, and Ramses Amer, Department of Peace and Conflict Research, Uppsala University, Sweden, made helpful comments on an early draft manuscript. The Australian Ambassador to Sweden and former Co-Chairman of the Third Committee of the 1989 Paris Conference, Dr Robert Merrillees, read a later version of the book and made many useful suggestions. Olga Hardardóttir and Jaana Kaarhilo of SIPRI's Project on Peace-keeping and Regional Security assisted with research and Olga Hardardóttir compiled the chronology and bibliography. The map was drawn by Billie Bielckus and the book edited by Eve Johansson.

I gratefully acknowledge the assistance of all the foregoing as well as that of the Peace Research Centre at the Australian National University, especially Helen Marshall; SIPRI, especially the library staff; the United Nations Secretariat; the Australian Department of Foreign Affairs and Trade, especially Allana Sherry and Jill Courtney; the Australian Embassy in Stockholm, especially Ambassador Merrillees and Hugh Borrowman; the Royal Cambodian Embassy in Paris; the Canadian High Commission in Canberra, especially the Deputy High Commissioner, Gardiner Wilson; the Australian and Canadian Missions in Phnom Penh; and the Canadian Centre for Global Security in Ottawa.

I owe a particular debt of gratitude to Susan Aitkin who opened doors in Phnom Penh that would otherwise have remained closed or unknown and who made my stay in that city both highly productive and enjoyable.

The opinions and judgements expressed in this study, notwithstanding the generous help I received from others, are entirely my own responsibility.

Trevor Findlay
October 1994

Acronyms

AEPU	Advance Electoral Planning Unit
ANKI	*Armée Nationale pour un Kampuchea Indépendent* (National Army of Independent Kampuchea)
ANS	*Armée Nationale Sihanoukiste*
ARF	ASEAN Regional Forum
ASEAN	Association of South-East Asian Nations
BLDP	Buddhist Liberal Democratic Party
CCGS	Canadian Centre for Global Security
CGDK	Coalition Government of Democratic Kampuchea
CivPol	Civilian Police
CMAC	Cambodian Mine Action Centre
CPAF	Cambodian People's Armed Forces
CPP	Cambodian People's Party
CPRAF	Cambodian People's Revolutionary Armed Forces
DES	District Electoral Supervisor
DK	Democratic Kampuchea
DPKO	UN Department of Peace-keeping Operations
EOD	Explosive ordnance disposal
FUNCINPEC	*Front Uni National Pour Un Cambodge Indépendent, Neutre, Pacifique et Coöpératif* (United National Front for an Independent, Neutral, Peaceful and Co-operative Cambodia)
GAO	US General Accounting Office
GDP	Gross domestic product
HIV	Human Immunodeficiency Virus
ICORC	International Committee on the Reconstruction of Cambodia
ICRC	International Committee of the Red Cross
IJA	Interim Joint Administration
IMF	International Monetary Fund
IPSO	International Polling Station Officer
JIM	Jakarta Informal Meeting
KPNLAF	Khmer People's National Liberation Armed Forces
KPNLF	Khmer People's National Liberation Front
KR	Khmer Rouge

MINURSO	*Mision de las Naciones Unidas para el Referendum del Sahara Occidental* (UN Mission for the Referendum in Western Sahara)
MMWG	Mixed Military Working Group
MP	Military police
NADK	National Army of Democratic Kampuchea
NGO	Non-governmental organization
NUPC	National Unity Party of Cambodia
ONUC	*Organisation des Nations Unies au Congo*
ONUMOZ	*Operación de las Naciones Unidas en Mozambique* (UN Operation in Mozambique)
ONUSAL	*Misión de Observadores de las Naciones Unidas en El Salvador* (UN Observer Mission in El Salvador)
PDK	Party of Democratic Kampuchea
PNGC	Provisional National Government of Cambodia
PRK	People's Republic of Kampuchea
RCAF	Royal Cambodian Armed Forces
QIP	Quick impact project
SNC	Supreme National Council
SOC	State of Cambodia
SRSG	Special Representative of the Secretary-General
UNAMIC	UN Advance Mission in Cambodia
UNAVEM II	UN Angola Verification Mission II
UNDP	UN Development Programme
UNFICYP	UN Peace-keeping Force in Cyprus
UNHCR	UN High Commissioner for Refugees
UNIFIL	UN Interim Force in Lebanon
UNIKOM	UN Iraq–Kuwait Observer Mission
UNMO	UN Military Observer
UNOSOM II	UN Operation in Somalia II
UNPROFOR	UN Protection Force (in the former Yugoslavia)
UNTAC	UN Transitional Authority in Cambodia
UNTAG	UN Transition Assistance Group (in Namibia)
UNTSO	UN Truce Supervisory Organization
UNV	UN Volunteer

The sun is rising, all Cambodians have
    to hurry up
UNTAC is holding an election that it
    wants to achieve soon
Secret polling is truly impartial.

All men and women of Cambodia will
    select their representatives with
    freedom
Democracy without coercion

Refrain:

An elected parliament
will draft a new constitution

Khmer electoral song by Eang Chanthana, used for the Kratie District's
civic education programme, published in *Free Choice*, UNTAC Electoral
Component Newsletter, Phnom Penh, 18 May 1993.

1. The Cambodian peace process

From the outset, the difficulties facing the achievement of peace in Cambodia[1] were clearly recognizable.[2] The country had suffered massive US bombing during the Viet Nam War, a right-wing coup by General Lon Nol in 1970 which had overthrown Prince Norodom Sihanouk's degenerating autocratic rule, and a civil war in which the radical communist Khmer Rouge (KR),[3] led by the infamous Pol Pot, had triumphed. Pol Pot's Democratic Kampuchea (DK), established in 1975, had been responsible for what has been described as attempted 'autogenocide'—the deaths of more than a million Cambodians through starvation, persecution and murder in the 'killing fields'.[4] A Vietnamese invasion followed in late 1978, which imposed another brand of communist regime on the country, the People's Republic of Kampuchea (PRK), known after 1989 as the State of Cambodia (SOC).

The PRK was led by former KR members Heng Samrin as President and later Hun Sen as Prime Minister. It was unable militarily to defeat the rump Khmer Rouge, which sought shelter along the Thai–Cambodian border, together with two less powerful anti-government guerrilla factions: the royalist FUNCINPEC,[5] founded by Sihanouk; and the republican Khmer People's National Liberation Front (KPNLF) led by Lon Nol's former Prime Minister Son Sann. The three factions—under considerable external pressure—established the so-called Coalition Government of Democratic Kampuchea (CGDK),

---

[1] Although 'Kampuchea' more accurately renders the Khmer name of the country in English, 'Cambodia' is used throughout this book because 'Kampuchea' is associated with the Khmer Rouge era, during which the country was known as Democratic Kampuchea, and because 'Cambodia' is the name used in the Paris Peace Accords and by the new government established under the Accords.

[2] For an excellent up-to-date history of Cambodia see Chandler, D. P., *A History of Cambodia*, 2nd edn (Westview Press: Boulder, Colo., 1993).

[3] The name Khmer Rouge, coined by Prince Norodom Sihanouk but not used by the group itself, is properly rendered in French in the plural as *Khmers Rouges*. English usage, however, has tended towards the singular. The Khmer Rouge began as the Communist Party of Kampuchea (PKK), later changing its name to the Party of Democratic Kampuchea (PDK). Some refer to it simply as the DK. Throughout this book 'Khmer Rouge' or 'KR' is used.

[4] Jackson, K. D., 'Introduction: the Khmer Rouge in context', ed. K. D. Jackson, *Cambodia 1975–1978: Rendezvous with Death* (Princeton University Press: Princeton, N.J., 1989), p. 3.

[5] *Front Uni National Pour un Cambodge Indépendant, Neutre, Pacifique et Coöpératif* (United National Front for an Independent, Neutral, Peaceful and Co-operative Cambodia). See table 1.1.

Table 1.1. The four Cambodian factions and their military forces

---

People's Revolutionary Party of Kampuchea (State of Cambodia—SOC)[a]
    Electoral name: Cambodian People's Party (CPP)
    Leader: Hun Sen, Prime Minister of Cambodia
    Armed force: Cambodian People's Armed Forces (CPAF)[b]

Front Uni National Pour Un Cambodge Indépendent, Neutre, Pacifique et Coöpératif (United National Front for an Independent, Neutral, Peaceful and Co-operative Cambodia—FUNCINPEC)
    Electoral name: FUNCINPEC
    Leader: Prince Ranariddh (replaced his father Prince Sihanouk in 1991)
    Armed force: *Armée Nationale pour un Kampuchea Indépendent* (National Army for an Independent Kampuchea—ANKI)[c]

Khmer People's National Liberation Front (KPNLF)
    Electoral name: Buddhist Liberal Democratic Party (BLDP)[d]
    Leader: Son Sann
    Armed force: Khmer People's National Liberation Armed Forces (KPNLAF)

Party of Democratic Kampuchea (PDK—Khmer Rouge or DK)
    Electoral name: National Unity Party of Cambodia (*Kana Mamakkhi Chet Kampuchea*—NUPC)[e]
    Leader: Khieu Samphan (nominal); Pol Pot (actual)
    Armed force: National Army of Democratic Kampuchea (NADK)

---

[a] Prior to May 1989, the People's Republic of Kampuchea (PRK).

[b] Formerly the Cambodian People's Revolutionary Armed Forces (CPRAF).

[c] Formerly *Armée Nationale Sihanoukiste* (Sihanoukist National Army—ANS).

[d] The Liberal Democratic Party (LDP), led by Suk Sutsakhan, was also a political party offshoot from the KPNLF.

[e] Launched on 30 Nov. 1992 for electoral purposes but seldom used thereafter.

Sources: UN, *Yearbook of the United Nations 1992* (United Nations: New York, 1993), p. 241; *Bangkok Post*, 5 Dec. 1992; *The Nation* (Bangkok), 1 Dec. 1992; *International Herald Tribune*, 22 Aug. 1988; *Jane's Defence Weekly*, 11 Nov. 1988, p. 1045; Carney, T. and Tan Lian Choo, Institute of Southeast Asian Studies, *Whither Cambodia? Beyond the Election* (ISEAS: Singapore, 1994), p. 4.

which received aid from China, Thailand and the West. It was also permitted to occupy the Cambodian seat at the United Nations, despite lacking the national attributes normally required for such international recognition. Meanwhile, the PRK, supported by Viet Nam and the Soviet Union, was isolated by the West, particularly the USA, and by the Association of South-East Asian Nations (ASEAN).[6]

---

[6] The members of ASEAN are Brunei, Indonesia, Malaysia, the Philippines, Singapore and Thailand.

On the ground the civil war reached something of a 'mutually hurting stalemate'.[7] The PRK could not defeat the KR and its coalition partners, nor could the coalition hope to bring down the Government by military means. The two smaller coalition factions, which according to Jarat Chopra and his colleagues never had 'the military strength or martial zeal to be a crucial factor in the war',[8] were suffering most from war-weariness and were therefore keenest to end armed conflict. The KR was having difficulty seizing and holding territory beyond its jungle redoubts against the greater military capability of the government forces. In Munck and Kumar's words, there emerged a 'classic lose-lose situation'.[9] Hence there were incentives for all sides to try diplomatic/political alternatives to achieve their goals—although undoubtedly both the KR and the PRK intended to resume military action if these alternatives failed.

There may also have been a 'mutually enticing opportunity' factor at work. Cambodia was now surrounded by states with either booming economies (such as China, Malaysia, Singapore and Thailand) or the potential to take advantage of such rapidly developing neighbours (in the case of Viet Nam). Cambodian political leaders would not have been unaware of the Asian economic miracle unfolding on their doorsteps.[10]

It was, however, only when outside powers decided that their own interests were no longer served by a continuation of Cambodia's sputtering conflict that the basis for a peace agreement emerged.[11] Viet Nam withdrew its troops in September 1989, leading to an improve-

---

[7] See Zartman, I. W., 'Regional conflict resolution', ed. V. A. Kremenyuk, Processes of International Negotiations (PIN) Project, *International Negotiation: Analysis, Approaches, Issues* (Jossey-Bass: San Francisco, Calif. and Oxford, 1991), p. 307.

[8] Chopra, J., Mackinlay, J. and Minear, L., Norwegian Institute of International Affairs, *Report on the Cambodian Peace Process*, Research Report no. 165 (NIIA: Oslo, Feb. 1993), p. 9.

[9] Munck, G. L., and Kumar, C., University of Illinois at Urbana-Champaign, Program in Arms Control, Disarmament, and International Security, *Conflict Resolution Through International Intervention: A Comparative Study of Cambodia and El Salvador*, Occasional Paper (ACDIS: Urbana, Ill., Apr. 1993), p. 6.

[10] Cambodia's per capita gross domestic product (GDP) in 1994 was one-sixth those of Malaysia and Thailand and the lowest in Asia, even including Laos and Viet Nam. In 1969, before the Khmer Rouge era, Cambodia had enjoyed a higher per capita GDP than Thailand. See Morgan Stanley, International Investment Research, *Cambodia: Dark History, Brighter Future*, Letters from Asia no. 6 (Morgan Stanley: Tokyo &c., 1994), p. 3.

[11] Alagappa, M., 'The Cambodian conflict: changing interests of external actors and implications for conflict resolution', *Pacific Review*, fall 1990.

ment of relations with China.[12] The dissolving Soviet Union and Warsaw Pact ended aid to both their long-standing ally Viet Nam and the PRK, while Thailand and other members of ASEAN concluded that Indo-China was more lucrative as a market-place than as a battle-field. China, the Khmer Rouge's principal foreign supporter, and the Soviet Union began a slow *rapprochement*, hastened by the Soviet withdrawal from Afghanistan. The USA and other Western countries began to fear a return to power of the KR. Following the Vietnamese withdrawal, the guerrilla group had gained financial autonomy by seizing large areas of relatively uninhabited Cambodian territory in the north-west and by engaging in gem and timber smuggling across the Thai border (with the active involvement of the Thai military).[13] The KR was believed to control at least 400 000 of Cambodia's 8 million people and about 15 per cent of the country, mainly in the west adjacent to Thailand,[14] and to field 10 000–20 000 'shooters' and 35 000 'operators'.[15] The USA stepped up pressure on China and Thailand to end their support for the KR (although unofficial Thai support continues to this day), began overtures to Viet Nam and the PRK, and withdrew support for the occupation of Cambodia's UN seat by the CGDK.

Several attempts had been made to negotiate peace in Cambodia in the 1980s. An International Conference on Kampuchea convened by the UN General Assembly in 1980 was boycotted by Viet Nam and the Soviet bloc. A good offices mission undertaken by the UN Secretary-General's Special Representative for Humanitarian Affairs in South-East Asia, Rafeeuddin Ahmed, did succeed in fostering a dialogue between the various Cambodian factions.[16] Following historic meetings between Prince Sihanouk and Hun Sen in late 1987 and early 1988, brokered by India and Indonesia,[17] the latter convened two meetings in Jakarta called the Jakarta Informal Meetings (JIMs) in July 1988 and February 1989. These were attended by all four Cam-

---

[12] According to Michael Leifer, the conflict over Cambodia was 'above all, an expression of Chinese–Vietnamese enmity'. See Leifer, M., 'Cambodia: the obstacle is in Beijing', *International Herald Tribune*, 16 Aug. 1988, p. 4.

[13] See Abuza, Z., 'The Khmer Rouge quest for economic independence', *Asian Survey*, vol. 33, no. 10 (Oct. 1993), pp. 1010–21. The other guerrilla factions also engaged in smuggling, although to a lesser extent.

[14] *International Herald Tribune*, 14–15 Nov. 1992, p. 4.

[15] Interview with Lt-Gen. John Sanderson, UNTAC military commander, Canberra, 24 Mar. 1993.

[16] Chopra *et al.* (note 8), p. 15.

[17] *Financial Times*, 10 Dec. 1987.

bodian factions meeting together for the first time and by Laos, Viet Nam and the ASEAN member states.

The first JIM, billed modestly as a 'cocktail party', was followed by a crucial Sino-Soviet meeting in Beijing in September 1988 which provided the impetus for an eventual lowering of tension between China and Viet Nam.[18] Talks between China and Viet Nam and between the PRK and Thailand in January 1989[19] produced a key breakthrough in the shape of Viet Nam's offer to withdraw its troops by the end of 1989 or 1990 and agreement to an international monitoring force. All external aid to the Cambodian parties would be halted and a political settlement implemented.[20]

In April 1989 Viet Nam announced that it would withdraw its troops from Cambodia by September 1989, several months ahead of schedule.[21] Encouraged by this and by further meetings between Sihanouk and Hun Sen, France and Indonesia jointly convened the Paris Conference on Cambodia in July 1989.[22] The conference, which lasted a month, from 30 July to 30 August, attempted to map out a comprehensive peace settlement for Cambodia. Progress was registered in a few areas, but the conference became deadlocked over demands by Sihanouk, Son Sann and the KR for a quadripartite power-sharing arrangement with Hun Sen's Government, now the State of Cambodia, to govern Cambodia under Prince Sihanouk's leadership pending the holding of an election.

Hun Sen categorically rejected any genuine power-sharing arrangement with the KR.[23] Both Australian Foreign Minister Gareth Evans and the Ambassador of Singapore, Tommy Koh, argued that this was the crucial issue which caused the conference to fail. Had it been resolved, agreement on other issues would have fallen into place.[24] According to Robert Merrillees, co-chair of the Third Committee of

---

[18] *The Independent*, 2 Sep. 1988, p. 10.

[19] *Financial Times*, 20 Jan. 1989, p. 3; *International Herald Tribune*, 21–22 Jan. 1989, p. 1.

[20] *International Herald Tribune*, 30 Jan. 1989, p. 2 and 31 Jan. 1989, p. 2; *Time* (Australia), 30 Jan. 1989, pp. 31–32.

[21] *Canberra Times*, 6 Apr. 1989.

[22] The conference involved, besides the four Cambodian factions, the five permanent members of the UN Security Council (China, France, the Soviet Union, the UK and the USA), the six ASEAN states (see note 6), the other Indochinese states (Laos and Viet Nam), Australia, Canada, India, Japan and Zimbabwe as then chair of the Non-Aligned Movement.

[23] Evans, G. and Grant, B., *Australia's Foreign Relations in the World of the 1990s* (Melbourne University Press: Carlton, 1991), p. 210.

[24] Evans and Grant (note 23), p. 210; Koh, T., 'The Paris Conference on Cambodia: a multilateral negotiation that "failed"', *Negotiation Journal*, vol. 6, no. 1 (Jan. 1990), p. 86.

the Paris Conference, the real reason for its failure was the unrelenting insistence of the KR that participants accept its allegations that Vietnamese forces were still in Cambodia and agree to ensure their withdrawal.[25]

The idea of some form of transitional arrangement was generally agreed, but its 'composition, powers and relationship to the existing Hun Sen Government were disputed',[26] as was the precise role of the UN in supervising the settlement.[27]

Over the whole proceedings hung the morally and politically tortuous question of how to handle Khmer Rouge responsibility for mass murder during the Pol Pot era. Some participants advocated war crimes trials, but most argued for putting the issue aside in the interests of Cambodian unity, some in the hope that a new, popularly elected government would deal with the issue. In the event, national reconciliation was judged to be of a higher priority than justice. Similar logic has been applied in the case of peace settlements in Nicaragua, South Africa and elsewhere. Meanwhile the KR at first denied that its holocaust had ever happened and then described it as a 'mistake'.[28]

With the adjournment of the Paris Conference, intensive efforts were made by Australia, France, Indonesia, Japan and the five permanent members of the UN Security Council to restart the negotiations. The key conceptual breakthrough was an idea originally proposed by US Congressman Stephen Solarz to Foreign Minister Evans in response to suggestions made by Prince Sihanouk in March 1981 and subsequently for some form of UN trusteeship over Cambodia.[29] The proposal envisaged that, instead of a quadripartite power-sharing arrangement, the UN itself would temporarily take over the administration of Cambodia, canton and demobilize the armed forces of the various parties and conduct the election, after which it would transfer power to a new Cambodian government. The Australians fashioned this idea into the 'Red Book', a detailed array of options for a UN transitional role in Cambodia, complete with cost and personnel esti-

---

[25] Conversation with the author, Stockholm, 16 Sep. 1994.

[26] Schear, J. A., 'The case of Cambodia', eds D. Daniel and B. Hayes, *Beyond Traditional Peacekeeping* (Macmillan: London, forthcoming 1995), p. 287.

[27] *Financial Times*, 30 Aug. 1989, p. 1.

[28] Solarz, S., 'Cambodia and the international community', *Foreign Affairs*, spring 1990, p. 106.

[29] Solarz mentioned the idea to Evans during discussions at the 1989 UN General Assembly. See Solarz (note 28); and *Far Eastern Economic Review*, 20 Apr. 1989, p. 11.

mates and proposed electoral system.[30] This document was tabled as a negotiating 'resource' at a February 1990 meeting in Jakarta which became known, confusingly, as the Informal Meeting on Cambodia (IMC).[31] This was attended by the JIM participants, the co-chairs of the Paris Conference and Australia as a 'resource' delegation.[32] Prior to the meeting a 'diplomatic marathon' had been run by Australian diplomat Michael Costello[33] between mid-December 1989 and mid-January 1990, involving around 30 major meetings in 13 countries, to sell the Australian plan to the Paris Conference participants.[34]

Japan, meanwhile, convened the Tokyo Conference on Cambodia on 4–5 June 1990, its first major effort to become involved in the Cambodia peace process. Tokyo's initiative unfortunately backfired when the Khmer Rouge failed to attend.[35]

After extensive further consultations based on the Australian initiative, in August 1990 the Permanent Five adopted a Framework Document for a Cambodian settlement.[36] This was accepted almost in its entirety at a final Jakarta meeting in September 1990, during which

[30] Australian Department of Foreign Affairs and Trade, *Cambodia: An Australian Peace Proposal* (Australian Government Printing Service: Canberra, Feb. 1990). The document was based on the findings of an Australian technical mission to Bangkok, Cambodia and the Thai–Cambodian border to assess conditions on the ground. The mission was led by Robert Merrillees and included representatives of the Department of Foreign Affairs and Trade, the Department of Defence and the Australian Electoral Commission. It was so detailed and densely packed with information that one critic described it as an 'indigestible brick'. For further background to the Australian initiative see Sturkey, D., 'Cambodia: issues for negotiation in a comprehensive settlement', Paper presented to the Fourth Asia–Pacific Roundtable on Confidence Building and Conflict Reduction in the Pacific, Kuala Lumpur, 17–20 June 1990. See also *International Herald Tribune*, 9 Jan. 1990; and *The Age* (Melbourne), 11 Sep. 1990.

[31] The reason for describing the proposal thus was not modesty, but to avoid accusations that Australia was attempting to foist Western solutions onto Asian problems. Gareth Evans' July 1990 proposal for a Conference on Security and Co-operation in Asia (CSCA) encountered just such criticism.

[32] Evans and Grant (note 23), p. 215.

[33] Currently Secretary of the Australian Department of Foreign Affairs and Trade.

[34] Evans and Grant (note 23), p. 214.

[35] Tomoda, S., 'Japan's search for a political role in Asia: the Cambodian peace settlement', *Japan Review of International Affairs*, vol. 6, no. 1 (spring 1992), pp. 47, 52. Tokyo's initiative also failed to meet with the full approval of China, the USA and ASEAN.

[36] For details see the Statement by the Permanent Five of 28 Aug. 1990, published as an Annex to UN, The situation in Kampuchea: Question of peace, stability and co-operation in South-East Asia, Letter dated 90/08/30 from the permanent representatives of China, France, the Union of Soviet Socialist Republics, the United Kingdom of Great Britain and Northern Ireland and the United States of America to the United Nations addressed to the Secretary-General, UN document A/45/472, S/21689, 31 Aug. 1990; and UN, Security Council Resolution 668, UN document S/RES/668, 20 Sep. 1990; and UN, General Assembly Resolution 45/3, UN document A7RES/45/3, 15 Oct. 1990.

all factions came under sustained international pressure to reach agreement. The Framework Document was endorsed and its acceptance welcomed by the Security Council on 20 September 1990[37] and by the General Assembly on 15 October.

The factions also agreed immediately to form the Supreme National Council (SNC) envisaged in the Framework Document. The idea was a watered-down variant of an earlier proposal by Hun Sen for a National Reconciliation Council, which would have supervised the election and handled political matters, while his Government remained intact to manage social and economic affairs during a transitional period.[38] The SNC, by contrast, would be largely symbolic and advisory. It would comprise 12 'individuals' representing the major political tendencies—six from the Hun Sen Government and two each from the three resistance factions. It was envisaged that Sihanouk would chair it. The early formation of the SNC, in advance of the peace settlement being finalized, was intended to bring the parties into a working relationship to help maintain the peace process and, in particular, to enable them to select a unified Cambodian delegation to the UN General Assembly.

Subsequently there was backtracking by the parties, among other things over the composition of the SNC: Sihanouk wished to become the 13th member of the SNC, while the Hun Sen Government argued that he should be one of the two FUNCINPEC members.[39] Later Viet Nam and the Hun Sen Government raised new concerns over military and sovereignty issues and revisited the question of KR responsibility for genocide. President Heng Samrin claimed that for his Government the peace plan embodied in the Framework Document was an 'invitation to commit suicide'.[40]

By February 1991 fierce conflict had resumed on the ground[41] and was not halted until all sides accepted a voluntary cease-fire, called for by the UN, on 1 May.[42] A four-man observation team led by the

---

[37] UN, Security Council Resolution 668 (note 36).

[38] *Financial Times*, 26 July 1988, p. 20; *Canberra Times*, 14 Apr. 1989.

[39] Sihanouk eventually did become the 12th SNC member, taking one of the two FUNCINPEC places. In Jan. 1993 the SNC admitted a third FUNCINPEC member, bringing its membership to 13. See UNTAC XII, Information/Education Division, *Brief*, no. 16 (25 Jan. 1993), p. 1; and chapter 4 of this volume.

[40] *The Australian*, 26–27 Jan. 1991.

[41] *Time* (Australia), 15 Apr. 1991, p. 24.

[42] *Far Eastern Economic Review*, 30 May 1991, p. 15.

UN military advisor, Ghanaian General Timothy Dubuama, was dispatched by the UN and confirmed that the cease-fire was holding.[43]

A meeting of the SNC, together with France, Indonesia and a UN representative, was convened in Jakarta in June 1991 but failed to reach agreement. The three outstanding issues were: the relationship between the SNC and the UN authority which would oversee the peace process; the pace and nature of the disarmament process faced by all the Cambodian parties; and the perennial problem of how to deal with past KR crimes against humanity and prevent their recurrence.[44]

At this point the SNC, cajoled by Prince Sihanouk, took the reins of the peace process. Meeting in Pattaya, Thailand, from 24 to 26 June for the first time without outside sponsorship, the SNC agreed on an unlimited cease-fire, a cut-off of all external military support and the establishment of an SNC presence in Phnom Penh as a 'super-government' over the whole of Cambodia.[45] Sihanouk invited foreign governments to accredit diplomatic representatives to the SNC, an invitation swiftly taken up by Australia, followed by the ASEAN states.[46]

These *ad hoc* SNC agreements, although consonant with some aspects of the Framework Document of September 1990, appeared to sideline others. Attempts were subsequently made to marry the SNC agreements with the plan of the Permanent Five. Meeting in informal session under unprecedented Chinese sponsorship in Beijing, the SNC in July 1991 approved an agreement between Sihanouk and Hun Sen whereby the former would become a neutral conciliator and drop his party affiliation, in return for the latter dropping his demand to become deputy chairman of the SNC.[47] Sihanouk, formally elected chairman of the SNC, would hence become *de facto* head of state of Cambodia pending the holding of the election. One French observer noted that: 'Prince Sihanouk has thus been made king again, under the title of president, by a consensus encouraged by the big powers and helped by a budding reconciliation between Beijing and Hanoi 12

[43] *Jane's Defence Weekly*, 1 June 1991, p. 903.

[44] *Financial Times*, 1–2 June 1991, p. 3.

[45] *Far Eastern Economic Review*, 4 July 1991, p. 13.

[46] *Sydney Morning Herald*, 20 July 1991. Australia was seen by some in the region as acting in 'indecent haste' in granting recognition to the SNC.

[47] Deron, F., 'Cambodian factions reach agreement', *Le Monde*, republished in *Guardian Weekly*, 28 July 1991, p. 14.

years after the Vietnamese invasion of Cambodia.'[48] The SNC also agreed to establish itself in Phnom Penh in November 1991 and to send an SNC delegation led by Sihanouk to occupy Cambodia's seat at the UN General Assembly. In addition, it requested the UN to send a mission to Cambodia to determine the size of the UN operation required to monitor the cut-off of external assistance to the parties and the cease-fire.

Meanwhile the Security Council amended the Framework Document to provide for only 70 per cent demobilization of the forces of each party, rather than complete disarmament.[49] This was intended to ease the SOC's fears of a Khmer Rouge take-over after its forces had been disarmed and demobilized, and was agreed to by the factions at a further SNC meeting in Pattaya in late August.[50] The 30 per cent of the forces remaining after demobilization would be cantoned and placed under UN supervision. Agreement was also reached at Pattaya on the relationship between the SNC and the UN body which would be established to guide the country through the peace settlement and the electoral process.[51] Finally, the Pattaya meeting agreed on wording relating to Khmer Rouge culpability for attempted genocide—without actually using the word itself or mentioning those responsible. Instead, reference was made to ensuring 'the non-return to the policies and practices of the past'.[52] No provision would be made for war crimes trials or other means of achieving justice.

In further talks in New York with the Permanent Five at the end of September, final agreement was reached on military arrangements and the electoral process.[53] With all the pieces of a settlement in place, it only remained for a resumed three-day Paris Conference from 21 to 23 October 1991 to adopt and sign the Paris Peace Accords formally.

---

[48] Deron (note 47), p. 14.

[49] *International Herald Tribune*, 20–21 July 1991, p. 5.

[50] *International Herald Tribune*, 28 Aug. 1991, p. 2.

[51] *Canberra Times*, 29 Aug. 1991.

[52] Agreement on a Comprehensive Political Settlement of the Cambodia Conflict, Paris, 23 Oct. 1991. Published as an annex to UN document A/46/608, S/23177, 30 Oct. 1991; reproduced in the appendix to this volume. See the Preamble, final paragraph and Article 15. The Accords also provided for the new Cambodian Constitution to prohibit the retroactive application of criminal law: see Annex 5, para. 2.

[53] *East Asia and Pacific Wireless File* (United States Information Service, Canberra), 2 Oct. 1991, p. 13.

2. The Paris Peace Accords

The Paris Peace Accords were signed on 23 October 1991 by the four contending Cambodian factions[1] acting together under the rubric of the Supreme National Council. They were also signed by the Permanent Five and 12 other states involved in the Paris Conference,[2] and comprised four documents: (*a*) the Final Act of the Paris Conference on Cambodia; (*b*) the Agreement on a Comprehensive Political Settlement of the Cambodia Conflict; (*c*) the Agreement Concerning the Sovereignty, Independence, Territorial Integrity and Inviolability, Neutrality and National Unity of Cambodia; and (*d*) the Declaration on the Rehabilitation and Reconstruction of Cambodia.[3] All entered into force upon signature. The two agreements had treaty status; the Declaration on Rehabilitation was not legally binding.[4]

The Accords committed the four Cambodian factions to a ceasefire, an end to their acceptance of external military assistance, the cantonment and disarmament of their military forces, the demobilization of at least 70 per cent of such forces prior to the completion of electoral registration, demobilization of the remaining 30 per cent or their incorporation into a new national army immediately after the election, and the release of all prisoners of war and civilian political prisoners. Each faction would retain its own administration and territory pending the election and the formation of a new national government. The non-Cambodian parties pledged to withdraw any remaining foreign forces from Cambodian territory, end military assistance to any of the Cambodian parties, assist in implementing the Accords and recognize and respect the sovereignty, independence, territorial integrity, inviolability, neutrality and national unity of Cambodia.

---

[1] See table 1.1, chapter 1.

[2] Australia, Brunei, Canada, India, Indonesia, Japan, Laos, Malaysia, the Philippines, Singapore, Viet Nam and Yugoslavia which had replaced Zimbabwe as the chair of the Non-Aligned Movement.

[3] Final Act of the Paris Conference on Cambodia, Paris, 23 Oct. 1991; Agreement on a Comprehensive Political Settlement of the Cambodia Conflict, Paris, 23 Oct. 1991; Agreement Concerning the Sovereignty, Independence, Territorial Integrity and Inviolability, Neutrality and National Unity of Cambodia, Paris, 31 Oct. 1991; and Declaration on the Rehabilitation and Reconstruction of Cambodia, Paris, 23 Oct. 1991: all published as annexes to UN document A/46/608, S/23177, 30 Oct. 1991 and reproduced in the appendix to this volume.

[4] Ratner, S. R., 'The Cambodia settlement agreements', *American Journal of International Law*, vol. 87, no. 1 (Jan. 1993), p. 8.

As envisaged in the Australian proposal, the UN would impose its authority over Cambodia during a transitional period between the entry into force of the Accords and the formation of a new government. An election for a constituent assembly, conducted by secret ballot and using proportional representation for a single national constituency, would be conducted by the UN. The assembly would write a new constitution for Cambodia before becoming the national legislature from which the new Cambodian government would be drawn. The UN would then relinquish its powers to the new Government.

The process would rest on two key institutions, both unprecedented in international practice and law: the SNC and the United Nations Transitional Authority in Cambodia (UNTAC).[5] The Paris Accords officially recognized the SNC as 'the unique legitimate body and source of authority in which, throughout the transitional period, the sovereignty, independence and unity of Cambodia are enshrined'.[6] The international community's acceptance of the SNC's unusual status was a new phenomenon in international law,[7] since the SNC would not become the Government of Cambodia or control any territory. Its purpose, in the absence of a reconciliation between the factions which might have produced a single Cambodian 'voice', was to 'embody' the will of the Cambodian nation. This would permit the UN to obtain Cambodian authorization to do what was necessary to implement the Paris Accords. Article 78 of the UN Charter otherwise prohibits the UN from placing a sovereign member state under trusteeship.

The SNC was required to delegate to UNTAC, which would be headed by a Special Representative of the Secretary-General (SRSG), 'all powers necessary' to implement the Accords.[8] UNTAC would not administer the country comprehensively—a venture that would have taken thousands more military and civilian personnel than were envisaged—but it would exercise 'direct supervision or control' over those aspects of government which could most readily influence the outcome of an election and 'supervision' of any aspects of administration that would ensure a return to 'normal day-to-day life'.[9] 'Special

---

[5] Ratner (note 4), p. 9.

[6] Agreement on a Comprehensive Political Settlement (note 3).

[7] See Ratner (note 4), pp. 10–11 and 22 for an interesting discussion of this point.

[8] Agreement on a Comprehensive Political Settlement (note 3), Article 6.

[9] Agreement on a Comprehensive Political Settlement (note 3), Annex 1, Section B, Articles 2 and 3. India had argued that these provisions exceeded the legal authority of the UN under the UN Charter. See Evans, G, 'The comprehensive political settlement to the

attention' would be paid to foreign affairs, national defence, finance, public security and information.[10]

The SRSG was also given two specific powers with respect to all government entities: the right to install UN personnel with 'unrestricted access to all administrative operations and information'; and the right to require the 'reassignment or removal' of any Cambodian personnel.[11] While in theory such control extended to the respective territories of all four factions, in practice it applied mainly to the SOC, which had the only fully functioning government.

James Schear, former adviser to the head of UNTAC, emphasizes that, contrary to popular myth, the mission was never designed to 'run' Cambodia but rather to 'prevent or correct for actions impeding UNTAC's operations' and to 'neutralize political bias in bureaucratic behaviour that could skew the environment for a free and fair election'.[12] Richard Solomon, US Secretary of State for Asian and Pacific Affairs, told the US Congress in early 1991 that no one envisaged 'dismantling' the Phnom Penh administration during the interim period, since the UN had neither the manpower nor the detailed expertise necessary to run the country. The UN would do 'only that which is necessary to bring about a free and fair election in a neutral political environment and thus establish a legitimate government—the most basic expression of Cambodia's sovereignty'.[13] Such distinctions were, however, sometimes lost sight of, both by UNTAC and by its critics, in the heady months to follow.

Between the SNC and UNTAC the balance of authority overwhelmingly lay with UNTAC. However, the SNC was empowered to 'offer advice' to UNTAC, which was obliged to comply with such advice provided there was consensus among SNC members and provided the

Cambodia conflict: an exercise in cooperating for peace', ed. H. Smith, Australian Defence Force Academy, Australian Defence Studies Centre, *International Peacekeeping: Building on the Cambodian Experience* (ADSC: Canberra, 1994), p. 8.

[10] Agreement on a Comprehensive Political Settlement (note 3), Article 6. China was responsible for enumerating these specific details.

[11] Agreement on a Comprehensive Political Settlement (note 3), Annex 1, Section B, Article 4.

[12] Schear, J. A., 'Beyond traditional peacekeeping: the case of Cambodia', Paper presented to the workshop on Beyond Traditional Peacekeeping, US Naval War College, Newport, R.I., 24 Feb. 1994, p. 9.

[13] *Effects of the Continued Diplomatic Stalemate in Cambodia*, Hearing before the Sub-committee on East Asian and Pacific Affairs of the Committee on Foreign Relations, US Senate, 102nd Congress (US Government Printing Office: Washington, DC, 11 April 1991). Statement of Richard H. Solomon. Reproduced in *East Asia and Pacific Wireless File* (United States Information Service: Canberra), 11 Apr. 1991.

advice was consistent with the Paris Accords. If there was no consensus, Prince Sihanouk could tender his own advice to UNTAC, again provided it was consistent with the Accords. If he were to be unable to render such advice, for whatever reason, his power would devolve on the SRSG.[14] Whether or not the SNC's advice on a particular matter was consistent with the Accords was to be determined by the SRSG. These provisions emphasized the 'depth' of UNTAC's powers.[15]

UNTAC was to be the most ambitious operation in the history of UN peacekeeping. 'Peacekeeping' indeed seemed a highly inadequate term to describe the totality of the UN role envisaged: the UNTAC operation is better described as a mixture of a peacekeeping, peacemaking and peace building.[16] In its complexity and comprehensiveness it remains the epitome of what have become known as 'second-generation' multinational operations.[17]

Although the UN had in the past been responsible for former colonial territories under the trusteeship system, as in the case of Namibia, or those in transition from the suzerainty of one power to another, as in the case of West Irian, UNTAC's 'supervision and control' of a sovereign, independent UN member state, qualified and limited though it may have been, was unprecedented.[18] Besides the traditional

[14] Agreement on a Comprehensive Political Settlement (note 3), Annex 1, Section A, Article 2.

[15] Ratner (note 4), p. 12.

[16] For a discussion of the problem of characterizing and categorizing UNTAC, see chapter 9 in this volume. For a discussion of the differences between these concepts, including from the UN perspective, see Findlay, T., 'Multilateral conflict prevention, management and resolution', SIPRI, *SIPRI Yearbook 1994* (Oxford University Press: Oxford, 1994), pp. 14–19.

[17] Mackinlay, J. and Chopra, J., 'Second generation multinational operations', *Washington Quarterly*, summer 1992, pp. 113–31.

[18] In 1962–63 the UN had taken over the administration of West Irian (Irian Jaya or West New Guinea) from the Netherlands in anticipation of the territory's incorporation into Indonesia. Its population was tiny, there was no civil war as there was in Cambodia, and the UN's role was somewhat limited compared to its intrusive presence in Cambodia. As Ratner notes (note 4, p. 13), the UN Temporary Executive Authority (UNTEA) operation was 'politically little more than a face-saving device for the Netherlands'. It was also a tiny operation compared to UNTAC, was supported and paid for by the two parties and only operated for 7 months. See Durch, W. J., 'The UN Temporary Executive Authority', ed. W. J. Durch, *The Evolution of UN Peacekeeping: Case Studies and Comparative Analysis* (St Martin's Press for the Henry L. Stimson Center: Washington, DC, 1993), pp. 285–98. In Namibia in 1989–90 the UN had supervised a cease-fire and the conduct of military and police authorities and conducted an election but had not taken over administration from the South African authorities. Moreover Namibia had never been an independent state but a UN trusteeship in theory and a South African colony in practice. Ratner (note 4, p. 13) notes several other unfulfilled plans for UN administration of territories, including the Free Territory of Trieste

UN peacekeeping role of monitoring and supervising the cease-fire, UNTAC's mandate included: (*a*) supervision, monitoring and verification of the withdrawal and non-return of foreign military forces; (*b*) cantonment, disarmament and demobilization of the four factions; (*c*) location and confiscation of caches of weapons and military supplies; (*d*) the conduct of a free and fair election (not only monitoring and supervision as in Angola, Haiti, Namibia and Nicaragua);[19] (*e*) promotion and protection of human rights; (*f*) oversight of military security and civil administration and of the maintenance of law and order; (*g*) repatriation and resettlement of Cambodian refugees and displaced persons; (*h*) assistance with mine clearance (de-mining) and establishment of training programmes in mine clearance and mine awareness; and (*i*) rehabilitation of essential infrastructure and the commencement of economic reconstruction and development.

To implement the military aspects of the mission and act as a first level of response to suspected infractions, the Paris Accords established a Mixed Military Working Group (MMWG) composed of senior military representatives of each faction, chaired by the chief of UNTAC's Military Component and supported by a secretariat. It was the only quadripartite body established by the Accords apart from the SNC and its secretariat.

Unlike earlier peace settlements for Indo-China that set up 'free-standing (and ineffectual) supervisory mechanisms', the Paris Accords envisaged a sizeable military force to oversee their implementation.[20] They did not, however, specifically provide for enforcement or any kind of sanction in the event of non-compliance by one or more of the Cambodian parties. They were 'premised on a good-faith implementation by all the parties concerned'.[21] Other observers have described the Accords as 'all carrots and no stick'. In the event of violation or threat of violation, the Accords simply provided for the two co-chairs of the Paris Conference, France and Indonesia, to

and Jerusalem. Recent proposals for UN administration of Sarajevo under a Bosnian peace plan have a similar ring to them.

[19] Ratner (note 4), p. 22 notes that the UN envisages a role in the Western Saharan referendum similar to that which it played in Cambodia.

[20] Ratner (note 4), pp. 17–18. Laos, Viet Nam and the Hun Sen Government had at one stage proposed a reactivation of the International Control Commission, comprising Canada, India and Poland, which had monitored implementation of the 1954 Geneva Agreements on Indo-China, with the addition of Indonesia and a UN representative. This idea was superseded by the Australian plan. See *International Herald Tribune*, 7 Apr. 1989, p. 6.

[21] Akashi, Y., 'The challenges faced by UNTAC', *Japan Review of International Affairs*, summer 1993, p. 186.

engage in consultations 'with a view to taking appropriate steps'.[22] Implicit in this was the likely involvement of the Security Council, especially given that it had played such a significant role in producing the Paris Accords in the first place.

UNTAC itself was apparently regarded by at least some UN officials as having enforcement powers beyond those specified in the Paris Accords.[23] Since its mandate did not refer to any chapter of the UN Charter, it might be assumed that, as in the case of many past peacekeeping operations, 'Chapter 6 1/2' rules were applicable—that is, UNTAC's powers would fall somewhere between Chapter 6's focus on peaceful settlement and Chapter 7's emphasis on peace enforcement. The traditional reading of the '6 1/2' rules of peace-keeping was in fact that they abjured enforcement by military means, limiting the use of force to self-defence and 'defence of the mission' and emphasizing the need for the continuing consent of the parties and the importance of maintaining the neutrality and impartiality of the UN operation. As in previous UN peacekeeping operations, popular misconceptions about UNTAC's enforcement powers were to prove both useful on occasions in implementing the Paris Accords and a frustrating source of unfulfillable expectations about UNTAC's role.

The agreements between the Cambodians which the Paris Accords embodied were extremely fragile, not only because of the bitterness and animosities aroused by decades of civil war but also because fundamentally they were the product of efforts made by the international community rather than by Cambodians themselves. To a great extent the Accords were pressed on a mostly reluctant Cambodian political élite by an international community eager to be rid of the Cambodian problem. According to Chopra and colleagues, 'The factions, particularly the Khmer Rouge, were instinctively suspicious and emotionally unprepared for a settlement which they felt had been

---

[22] Agreement on a Comprehensive Political Settlement (note 3), Article 29.

[23] *UN Peacekeeping: Observations on Mandates and Operational Capability,* Statement of Frank C. Conahan, Assistant Comptroller General, National Security and International Affairs Division, testimony before the Subcommittee on Terrorism, Narcotics, and International Operations, Committee on Foreign Relations, US Senate, 9 June 1993, GAO/T-NSIAD-93-15, p. 1. The mandate for UNTAC was not specified in the Security Council resolution which established it (Resolution 745 (1992), 28 Feb. 1992), but was drawn from Annex 1 of the Agreement on a Comprehensive Political Settlement, with specific elements drawn from other annexes and from the Declaration on the Rehabilitation and Reconstruction of Cambodia. See UN, Report of the Secretary-General on Cambodia, UN document S/23613, 19 Feb. 1992, para. 4, p. 2.

imposed on them. At a time of exhaustion and lack of resources in the field, enormous political and economic pressure placed on them spurred their co-operative behaviour'.[24] Although it had seemed at the outset of the 1989 session of the Paris Conference that the Cambodian parties wanted a settlement,[25] thereafter this assumption became increasingly untenable. If it had been left to the Cambodians themselves there would have been no Paris Accords.

This is not to say that the Accords were against the best interests of the vast majority of Cambodians, that they had been crafted against Cambodian wishes or that the international community lacked altruism in pursuing the peace process; but it is clear that among the external powers involved the prime motivation was national self-interest in removing the Cambodia issue from their domestic, regional and international agendas. If this could be done by bringing genuine peace and reconciliation to Cambodia then so much the better, but they would be satisfied with the de-internationalization of the conflict and its removal from the international agenda. On this there was an extraordinary convergence of view among the international players at Paris.[26]

The momentum behind the Jakarta and Paris negotiating processes came largely from an unusual chemistry between Indonesian Foreign Minister Ali Alatas and Gareth Evans, who together persisted with the Cambodian parties when others would have given up. Australia provided Indonesia with diplomatic support and 'resources' in the form of key working papers, cost estimates and logistical plans, while Indonesia provided the Asian diplomatic skills and perspicacity. Indonesia brought ASEAN along with it, while Australia, to some extent, brought its ally the United States.

For Australia, as for all the Western countries involved in the Cambodia settlement, one of the principal motivations was the need to excise a political sore that had troubled successive governments as a result of their support for an anti-Vietnamese coalition which included the Khmer Rouge. Australia's annual vote in favour of KR diplomats occupying the Cambodian seat at the UN was a particular bone of

[24] Chopra, J., Mackinlay, J. and Minear, L., Norwegian Institute of International Affairs, *Report on the Cambodian Peace Process*, Research Report no. 165 (NIIA: Oslo, Feb. 1993), p. 16.

[25] Koh, T., 'The Paris Conference on Cambodia: a multilateral negotiation that "failed"', *Negotiation Journal*, vol. 6, no. 1 (Jan. 1990), p. 86.

[26] Ambassador Koh, Singapore's representative to the Paris conferences, concurs: see Koh (note 25), pp. 84–86.

contention. There was constant public pressure on Australian governments from human rights and aid organizations to reject the CGDK
and troubling reverberations within Australia's sizeable Indochinese
migrant community as a result of Australian policy. Australia, like
other Western states, would have found it difficult to recognize the
Hun Sen Government. It also realized that ASEAN, whose lead on
Cambodia it had followed as an expression of regional solidarity,
would never be able to focus its attention on broader regional issues
until Cambodia was removed from its preponderant place on the
ASEAN agenda. Australia's drive to take its appropriate place as a
regional power politically and economically in Asia could only benefit from Canberra's patient, low-key efforts to resolve a major Asian
imbroglio.

For Indonesia, the other regional prime mover of the Cambodian
settlement, the motivation was almost entirely regional. As the most
influential member of ASEAN and the one furthest removed geo-
graphically from Indo-China, it could also see the inhibiting effect
that the Cambodian situation was having on ASEAN's evolution,
including on its relations with Viet Nam and China, and its attempts
to tackle broader security issues in the Asia–Pacific region.

Of the other major players, France provided the grand diplomatic
setting of Paris, a European connection and its long-standing colonial
links to Indo-China.[27] The USA added diplomatic weight, obtained
Security Council endorsement and ensured UN involvement at a time
of stretched resources. China brought the Khmer Rouge along,
motivated by the desire to divest itself of a political liability at a time
when it was seeking international respectability. Among the Permanent Five, China, France and the USA were the most proactive, with
the UK and the Soviet Union tagging along. Japan, with an eye on
future Security Council membership and eager to expand its international horizons, offered strong if sometimes misguided support.
From an international perspective the Paris Accords represented an
unusually robust and unified commitment to peace in Cambodia
which was followed through to the end of the transitional period and
beyond.

---

[27] Koh reports that the two co-chairs of the Paris Conference worked well together,
although there were occasions when France acted unilaterally, to the 'considerable embar-
rassment and resentment of Indonesia': see Koh (note 25), p. 83.

It was against this unlikely background—international solidarity and Cambodian equivocation—that the United Nations was to pursue the implementation of the Paris Accords.

Critics of the Paris Accords, often motivated by distaste for involving the Khmer Rouge in any peace agreement, argued that the alternative was to throw the support of the UN and the international community behind the Hun Sen Government.[28] There are six points to be made against this view. First, it would never have been acceptable to China, which needed a face-saving device to enable it to withdraw its support from the KR[29] and would thus have prevented the Hun Sen Government from gaining universal recognition and the right to occupy Cambodia's seat at the UN. The Cambodia issue would therefore have continued seriously to divide the international community. Second, there was a danger that even with broad international support and recognition the Hun Sen Government might not withstand an intensified KR military campaign without further Vietnamese intervention.[30] Third, the refugee situation on the Thai–Cambodian border would not have been resolved without a comprehensive peace settlement. Fourth, ASEAN would not have been able to get off its Cambodia 'hook'—its virtual obsession with the Cambodia problem—while a pro-Viet Nam government remained in Phnom Penh. Fifth, the USA would not have been able easily to end its support for the pro-Western coalition forces, including Sihanouk. Stephen Solarz argued in 1990 that building political support for US recognition of the Hun Sen Government, even on anti-Khmer Rouge grounds, would not have been easy:

Hun Sen's party remains a Leninist party both organizationally and ideologically. The PRK's leaders are tainted, moreover, by a sordid past. Most of the members of the PRK politburo are former Khmer Rouge who were part of the killing machine established by Pol Pot. They defected to Vietnam not for reasons of principle but because they were about to be devoured themselves. Having ridden into Phnom Penh on Vietnamese tanks, they then

---

[28] Pilger, J., 'Cambodia: return to year zero', *New Internationalist*, no. 242 (Apr. 1993), pp. 4–7; and 'The return to year zero', *The Bulletin* (Sydney), 11 May 1993, pp. 32–37.

[29] Evans, G., 'Conflict of interests', *The Bulletin* (Sydney), 18 May 1993, p. 20.

[30] Sheridan, G., 'Peace plan critics fail to see erosion of Khmer Rouge position', *The Australian*, 26 Jan. 1993, p. 8.

engaged in human rights abuses that, according to Amnesty International, included the execution, incarceration and torture of thousands.[31]

The Hun Sen Government's commitment to Marxism–Leninism was by 1990 suspect and by 1991 officially abandoned in favour of a free market economy under authoritarian government (not unlike most South-East Asian countries),[32] and the USA recognizes and deals with governments with similar or worse human rights records (Burma and China, for example); none the less, political realities in the USA would have made movement on the issue slow and painful.

Finally, Sihanouk himself, perhaps the only credible purveyor of Cambodian national identity and unity, would have remained at loggerheads with the Phnom Penh Government. If the Paris Accords were imperfect, the alternative was even more unsatisfactory.

---

[31] Solarz, S., 'Cambodia and the international community', *Foreign Affairs*, spring 1990, p. 114.

[32] Vickery, M., Institute of Southeast Asian Studies, 'The Cambodian People's Party: where has it come from, where is it going?', *Southeast Asian Affairs 1994* (ISEAS: Singapore, 1994), p. 110.

3. Implementation of the Paris Peace Accords

Quite apart from the fragility of the agreements arrived at, implementation of the Paris Peace Accords was destined to be difficult. Cambodia was by this time one of the poorest of the developing countries, economically ruined by decades of war and neglect, denied assistance by the West because of its Vietnamese-installed government, lacking basic infrastructure and industry, and probably more heavily sown with anti-personnel mines than any other country in the world.[1] Operationally, especially in terms of logistics, the planned UN operation faced enormous challenges. Psychologically, the country was also in poor shape. In addition to mistrust between the factions, fear and loathing of the Khmer Rouge and of Pol Pot, the former KR leader still believed to be its guiding light despite his official 'retirement', remained strong.[2]

Some observers argued that the peace settlement and the UN mission were doomed to failure because of abiding cultural factors. Pierre Lizée contended that 'the particular trajectory of state and capitalist development in Cambodia, combined with other factors such as the influence of Buddhism and Brahmanism' had 'instilled in Cambodians a deep mistrust toward any institutionalization of politics'—the very thing that the UN was now mandated to attempt. The importance of patronage and the family network and the absence of a 'public sphere' in the Cambodian psyche would, he argued, impede the development of notions of political participation and legitimacy.[3] Others, more simplistically, saw the Paris Accords as ill-fated because they represented a conspiracy to impose Western values on an uncomprehending and unwilling populace.[4] Still others saw the lumbering

---

[1] Aitkin, S., Getting the message about mines: towards a national public information strategy and program on mines and mine safety, vol. 1: Report (UNESCO: Phnom Penh, Sep. 1993), pp. 2–3.

[2] For a biography of Pol Pot see Chandler, D. P., *Brother Number One: A Political Biography of Pol Pot* (Westview Press: Boulder, Colo., 1992).

[3] Lizée, P., 'Peacekeeping, peace building and the challenge of conflict resolution in Cambodia', ed. D. A. Charters, University of New Brunswick, Centre for Conflict Studies, *Peacekeeping and the Challenge of Civil Conflict Resolution* (CCS: Fredericton, 1991), pp. 141–43. See also Chandler, D., 'The tragedy of Cambodian history revisited', *SAIS Review*, vol. 14, no. 2 (summer–fall 1994), pp. 84–85.

[4] Pilger, J., 'Peace in our time?', *New Statesman and Society,* 27 Nov. 1992, p. 10.

United Nations as simply incapable of carrying out the complex and sensitive tasks the Paris Peace Accords had assigned to it. All these spectres were to haunt but not deter the UN mission in the months to come.

I. UNAMIC, the 'interim period' and Phase I of the cease-fire

Although implementation of the Paris Accords was meant to begin as soon as they were signed on 23 October 1991, UN Secretary-General Javier Perez de Cuellar recognized that the UN would be unable to mobilize itself speedily enough to deploy UNTAC immediately. On 30 September 1991 he recommended to the Security Council that it should instead authorize the establishment of a UN Advance Mission in Cambodia (UNAMIC), which would be dispatched as soon as signature had taken place. This was done on 16 October.[5] UNAMIC was apparently intended to represent the 'good offices' of the Secretary-General, vaguely detailed in the Paris Accords, which would 'assist' the parties in their observance of the cease-fire.[6]

UNAMIC was headed by Ataul Karim of Bangladesh, with its Military Component under the command of French Brigadier-General Jean-Michel Loridon.[7] Its mandate was extremely limited and its personnel resources slim. Apart from helping the warring parties establish the cease-fire, Phase I of which had begun with the signing of the Paris Accords, it was to begin a mine-awareness programme among the civilian population.[8] The Security Council later expanded UNAMIC's mandate to include the training of Cambodians in mine

---

[5] UN, Security Council Resolution 717, UN document S/RES/717, 16 Oct. 1991.

[6] Agreement on a Comprehensive Political Settlement of the Cambodia Conflict, Paris, 23 Oct. 1991, Annex 2, Article 1.2. Published as an annex to UN document A/46/608, S/23177, 30 Oct. 1991; reproduced in the appendix to this volume. See also *East Asia and Pacific Wireless File* (United States Information Serice, Canberra), 2 Oct. 1991, pp. 13–14.

[7] *Canberra Times*, 7 Nov. 1991. The appointment of the military commander of UNAMIC was reportedly delayed by a dispute between France and the USA, which was opposed to any permanent member of the Security Council filling the position and only approved the appointment of Loridon on condition that Lt-Gen. Sanderson, an Australian, be appointed military commander of UNTAC. Akashi notes that Australia and France were particularly active with regard to the military aspect of UNTAC, although 'they may at times have been at odds with each other'. See Akashi, Y., 'The challenges faced by UNTAC', *Japan Review of International Affairs*, summer 1993, p. 199.

[8] UN, *United Nations Focus: Cambodia: United Nations Transitional Authority in Cambodia*, New York, Feb. 1993, pp. 1–2.

clearance and the initiation of a mine-clearance programme, after a plea by the Secretary-General for such a programme to begin before the deployment of UNTAC.[9] Initially with just 268 personnel, but authorized to reach 1504, UNAMIC consisted of civil and military liaison staff, some of whom would be attached to the Cambodian factions' military headquarters, mine-awareness experts and logistics and support personnel.[10] It was formally established in Phnom Penh on 9 November 1991 with the arrival of Karim.[11] The first national military contingent, 37 Australian signallers who were to provide the communications system for both UNAMIC and UNTAC, arrived on 10 November.[12] Initially there was popular euphoria as the first peace-keepers arrived and when Prince Sihanouk returned on 14 November after more than two decades. The peace settlement seemed to be advancing as 17 new diplomatic missions were opened, and the three opposition factions installed themselves in Phnom Penh as members of the SNC.[13]

However, UNAMIC's prolonged tenure and the hiatus in power resulting from the delay in deploying UNTAC led to a serious deterioration of the situation in Cambodia, touching off a factional struggle within the Hun Sen Government, allowing violations of the cease-fire to occur unchecked, encouraging lawlessness in the cities and banditry in the countryside and creating uncertainty and cynicism about the peace process and the UN role. There was, moreover, a growing fear that the KR would take advantage of the situation to make military gains or even seize the capital. Instability in Phnom Penh was heightened by the political free-for-all which developed after the Hun Sen Government announced in November that Cambodia would become a multi-party state.[14] Corrupt officials seized the opportunity to sell state assets for personal gain, while ordinary Cambodians began voicing their dissatisfaction with official malpractice and cor-

[9] UN, Security Council Resolution 728, UN document S/RES/728, 8 Jan. 1992. See also Asia Watch, *Political Control, Human Rights, and the UN Mission in Cambodia* (Asia Watch: New York, Sep. 1992), pp. 61–62.

[10] UN, *United Nations Peace-keeping* (United Nations: New York, 31 May 1993), p. 52. The states contributing military personnel were: Algeria, Argentina, Australia, Austria, Bangladesh, Belgium, Canada, China, France, Germany, Ghana, India, Indonesia, Ireland, Malaysia, the Netherlands, New Zealand, Pakistan, Poland, Russia, Senegal, Thailand, Tunisia, the UK, Uruguay and the USA.

[11] *Canberra Times*, 7 Nov. 1991.

[12] *International Herald Tribune*, 12 Nov. 1991, p. 2.

[13] Thayer, N., 'Unsettled land', *Far Eastern Economic Review*, 27 Feb. 1992, p. 23.

[14] Thayer (note 13), p. 26.

ruption. In January 1992 anti-corruption riots against the Government resulted in bloodshed and there was an attempted assassination of one of Cambodia's best-known dissidents, Oung Phan.[15]

Sihanouk decried UNTAC's absence in this crucial early phase as leaving the four Cambodian factions without a neutral mediator to ease the inevitable political and military tensions between them.[16] Immediately upon his return to Cambodia in mid-November, however, he himself had launched into unabashed politicking, attempting to form an alliance between FUNCINPEC and the Hun Sen Government, presumably to outmanœuvre both the KR and the Accords by installing a coalition government with all the advantages of incumbency before elections took place. As part of this ploy, the Government on 20 November 1991 recognized Sihanouk as its 'legitimate head of state'.[17] Since Heng Samrin was already President, the move gave Cambodia, in effect, two heads of state.

Lieutenant-General Sanderson, the UNTAC Military Commander, argues that this was the first major infraction of the Paris Accords.[18] In a functioning, established democracy such behaviour would not be frowned upon; in Cambodia, where the whole peace process was dependent on a free, fair and equal electoral contest between the existing factions, it could have been disastrous. Certainly it would have antagonized the Khmer Rouge. Fortunately, Sihanouk and Hun Sen shelved their plans for a coalition government by early December.

The second major infraction, in Sanderson's view, was the SOC-orchestrated riots against the KR on 27 November. The nominal Khmer Rouge leader, Khieu Samphan, was nearly lynched only hours after his return to Phnom Penh from 13 years in exile to head the newly-opened KR office and lead the KR delegation to the SNC.[19] He and his entourage fled back to Bangkok, while the KR office was ransacked. Before it would return the KR called for the immediate deployment of between 800 and 1000 peacekeepers to provide security in the capital and a neutral political environment for the SNC to begin its work.[20] At a meeting of the SNC in Pattaya, at which the

[15] *The Independent*, 11 Mar. 1992.

[16] *International Herald Tribune*, 21 Nov. 1991, p. 2; Thayer (note 13), p. 23.

[17] *International Herald Tribune*, 21 Nov. 1991, p. 3.

[18] Sanderson, J. M. (Lt-Gen.), 'A review of recent peacekeeping operations', Paper presented to the Pacific Armies Management Seminar (PAMS) XVIII Conference, Dacca, Jan. 1994, p. 6.

[19] *International Herald Tribune*, 29 Nov. 1991, p. 7.

[20] *International Herald Tribune*, 4 Dec. 1991, p. 2; Thayer (note 13), p. 28.

Permanent Five and the co-chairs of the Paris Conference attempted to convince the guerrilla group to return to Phnom Penh, the Government agreed to guarantee the security of the KR delegation, it was given offices in a UN building for extra protection and Sihanouk once more agreed to play a neutral rather than a partisan role as SNC chairman and Cambodian head of state.[21]

More worrying than the situation in Phnom Penh was the faltering of Phase I of the peace plan—an end to the fighting. KR violations of the cease-fire were numerous and continuing.[22] On 30 December the SNC, including the Khmer Rouge, appealed to the UN to accelerate the deployment of UNTAC[23] even though the KR had restricted UNAMIC's freedom of movement at an early stage.[24] From January 1992 the KR also engaged Government forces in Kompong Thom province, Pol Pot's birthplace, seeking to control this strategic area between Phnom Penh and the north-east of the country. It also withheld co-operation from UNAMIC by failing to attend the 14 February meeting of the MMWG,[25] alleging the presence of Vietnamese forces in the country, citing foreign assistance being channelled to the Phnom Penh Government and complaining of the late deployment of UNTAC. In late February an Australian officer became the first UN casualty in Cambodia when he was wounded in a KR attack on a UNAMIC helicopter.[26]

Not only had UNAMIC not been foreseen in the Paris Accords; neither had the length of time for which it would need to 'hold the fort' pending the deployment of UNTAC. According to Sanderson, the establishment of UNAMIC 'appeared to lull the UN bureaucracy into a false sense of security'.[27] One diplomat involved in drafting the Paris Accords was reported as saying that 'there was a major screwup in this whole process—and that is UNAMIC. UNAMIC was only an afterthought when the peace accord was drawn up. No one believed it would take so long for UNTAC to be deployed and no one

---

[21] *International Herald Tribune*, 5 Dec. 1991, p. 2.

[22] Asia Watch (note 9), p. 9.

[23] *Disarmament Newsletter*, Feb. 1992, p. 10.

[24] *East Asia and Pacific Wireless File* (United States Information Service, Canberra), 20 Feb. 1992, p. 23.

[25] *East Asia and Pacific Wireless File* (United States Information Service, Canberra), 27 Feb. 1992, p. 11.

[26] *International Herald Tribune*, 6 Mar. 1992, p. 5.

[27] Sanderson, J. M. (Lt-Gen.), 'UNTAC: successes and failures', ed. H. Smith, Australian Defence Force Academy, Australian Defence Studies Centre, *International Peacekeeping: Building on the Cambodian Experience* (ADSC: Canberra, 1994), p. 18.

took this interim period as seriously as, in hindsight, we should have'.[28] UNAMIC was particularly plagued by a troubled relationship between its civil and military elements and by language difficulties among its personnel and between them and Cambodians.

Some of the military officers at UNAMIC attempted to engage in detailed planning in the field for UNTAC's arrival[29] but tended to be distracted by UNAMIC's inability to handle the deteriorating situation in the country or even to fend for itself. In retrospect, UNAMIC should have been fully mandated and equipped to prepare for UNTAC's arrival. It was reportedly anxious to do so but was held back by the UN Secretariat until late January. According to Chopra and colleagues, 'competing for attention with the more visible and demanding events in Croatia, there seemed to be no staff available in New York to meet the UNAMIC team and a reluctance to respond to their enquiries'.[30] To its credit, UNAMIC did succeed in establishing a UN presence under 'extremely difficult conditions' and was able to alert the UN to some urgent requirements, such as the need for extensive mine clearance.[31] By the time UNTAC finally arrived, however, the peace settlement was in considerable jeopardy.

II. Planning for UNTAC

While UNAMIC was struggling to maintain the semblance of a UN presence in Cambodia, the UN Secretariat in New York at the request of the Security Council was preparing a detailed plan for deploying UNTAC.[32] Yasushi Akashi[33] of Japan, head of the then UN Department of Disarmament Affairs, was appointed SRSG and head of UNTAC on 9 January 1992.[34] Lieutenant-General John Sanderson of

[28] Thayer (note 13), p. 22.

[29] UN, Report of the Secretary-General on Cambodia, UN document S/23613, 19 Feb. 1992, p. 20.

[30] Chopra, J., Mackinlay, J. and Minear, L., Norwegian Institute of International Affairs, *Report on the Cambodian Peace Process*, Research Report no. 165 (NIIA: Oslo, Feb. 1993), p. 19.

[31] Chopra et al. (note 30), p. 17. Curiously the authors also criticize UNAMIC for 'creating unrealistic expectations amongst the Cambodian population'. It is hard to see how this could have been avoided and it would probably have been exacerbated by more thorough investigative activities by UNAMIC.

[32] UN, Security Council Resolution 718, UN document S/RES/718, 1 Nov. 1991.

[33] In Japan he would be known as Akashi Yasushi. This book uses the Westernized order of his name.

[34] The Deputy SRSG was an American, Behrooz Sadry.

Australia was appointed Commander of UNTAC's military forces.[35] The election was set for April/May 1993 and the deadline for agreement on a new Constitution and the establishment of a new government for August 1993.

A peacekeeping force of approximately 15 900 military personnel at its peak was envisaged.[36] In addition there would be 3600 Civilian Police (CivPols) and 2000 civilians.[37] UNTAC would also see the widespread use of UN Volunteers (UNVs): 450 low-paid, mostly young volunteers from a wide variety of countries were to assist in electoral and information tasks.[38] UNTAC's international personnel— military, police and civilian—would peak at approximately 22 874 and be drawn from over 100 countries.[39] Troops and police would be provided by 46 countries, the largest contingents by France, India and Indonesia. In terms of the total number of UN personnel, it was to be the biggest UN operation since the 20 000-strong ONUC (*Organisation des Nations Unies au Congo*) force sent to the Congo in the early 1960s[40] and the most international of all UN missions. A number of contributor states had never previously participated in peacekeeping operations, among them Brunei, Bulgaria, Germany (medical personnel only), Japan (an engineering battalion), Namibia and Uruguay. In addition to its international staff, UNTAC would be supported by an estimated 7000 locally-recruited Cambodians, including some 2500 interpreters and 4000 electoral staff.[41]

[35] The Cambodians would have preferred an Indonesian because of their cultural affinities. See Lao, M. H., 'Obstacles to peace in Cambodia', *Pacific Review*, vol. 6, no. 4 (1993), p. 391.

[36] Infantry battalions would be provided by 11 countries: Bangladesh, Bulgaria, France, Ghana, India, Indonesia (2 battalions), Malaysia, the Netherlands, Pakistan, Tunisia and Uruguay. See UN, *Yearbook of the United Nations 1992* (United Nations: New York, 1993), p. 245.

[37] UN, *Yearbook of the United Nations 1992* (note 36), p. 245; Akashi (note 7), p. 187.

[38] UN, *Yearbook of the United Nations 1992* (note 36), p. 246; UN, *The United Nations in Cambodia: A Vote for Peace* (United Nations: New York, 1994), p. 74. The UNV programme began in 1971 under the auspices of the UN Development Programme (UNDP) to assist in international aid projects. The total cost of one UNV, including travel and salary, was, according to Nick Warner, less than the Mission Subsistence Allowance of a staff member recruited from within the UN system: see Warner, N., 'Cambodia: lessons of UNTAC for future peacekeeping operations', Paper presented to an international seminar on UN Peacekeeping at the Crossroads, Canberra, 21–24 Mar. 1993, p. 10.

[39] *UN Chronicle*, June 1993, p. 23.

[40] Durch, W. J., 'The UN operation in the Congo: 1960–64', ed. W. J. Durch, *The Evolution of UN Peacekeeping: Case Studies and Comparative Analysis* (St Martin's Press for The Henry L. Stimson Center: Washington, DC, 1993), p. 315.

[41] Details of the strengths and roles of the various components in this section are taken from UN, *Yearbook of the United Nations 1992* (note 36), pp. 244–46; and UN, UNTAC

Table 3.1. States providing military personnel and civil police to UNAMIC/UNTAC

	Military	CivPols		Military	CivPols
Algeria	x	x	Japan	x	x
Argentina	x		Jordan		x
Australia	x	x	Kenya		x
Austria	x	x	Malaysia	x	x
Bangladesh	x	x	Morocco		x
Belgium	x		Namibia	x	
Brunei	x	x	Nepal		x
Bulgaria	x	x	Netherlands	x	x
Cameroon	x	x	New Zealand	x	
Canada	x		Nigeria		x
Chile	x		Norway		x
China	x		Pakistan	x	x
Colombia		x	Philippines	x	x
Egypt		x	Poland	x	
Fiji		x	Russia	x	
France	x	x	Senegal	x	
Germany	x	x	Singapore	x	x
Ghana	x	x	Sweden		x
Hungary		x	Thailand	x	
India	x	x	Tunisia	x	x
Indonesia	x	x	UK	x	
Ireland	x	x	Uruguay	x	
Italy		x	USA	x	

Sources: UN, *The United Nations in Cambodia: A Vote for Peace* (United Nations: New York, 1994), p. 105; Personal communication with the UN Department of Peace-Keeping Operations, New York.

UNTAC was to be structured into seven components—human rights, electoral activities, military, civil administration, civil police, repatriation and rehabilitation. The UN Field Administration, which serviced and supported these components, was to comprise the Division of Administration and the Information and Education Division.[42]

The Human Rights Component would be given responsibility for fostering an environment in which respect for human rights and fun-

Cambodia: United Nations Transitional Authority in Cambodia, UN document DPI/1218-92542, June 1992.
[42] UN, *The United Nations in Cambodia: A Vote for Peace* (note 38), pp. 60–69.

damental freedoms was ensured. Its principal activities would be: (*a*) a human rights education campaign; (*b*) general human rights oversight of all existing administrative structures; and (*c*) establishment of a mechanism for investigating allegations of human rights abuses during the transitional period. A human rights office at headquarters in Phnom Penh would be the central policy-making and co-ordinating body, with specialists in human rights advocacy, civic education and investigation and liaison.[43]

The Electoral Component was entrusted with organizing and conducting a free and fair election. Among its responsibilities was the drafting, in consultation with the SNC, of a legal framework for the election, including an electoral law, regulations to govern the electoral process and an electoral code of conduct.[44] Other aspects included civic education and training, registration of voters and political parties and the polling process itself. The Electoral Component would consist of 72 international personnel operating from headquarters and 126 personnel at 21 provincial and municipal centres.[45] Under their supervision more than 400 UNVs would operate from each of the 200 districts. Electoral personnel would be supplemented by 800 Cambodian teams (4000 personnel) during the three- to four-month voter registration period, and, for the polling process, by 1000 International Polling Station Officers (IPSOs) and 8000 Cambodian electoral teams (56 000 personnel). The Electoral Component would be phased out shortly after the election.

The largest component of UNTAC, the Military Component, was charged with 'stabilizing the security situation and building confidence among the parties to the conflict'. It would have the following specific functions:[46] (*a*) verification of the withdrawal from Cambodia and non-return of all categories of foreign forces and their arms and equipment (by posting military observers at 24 fixed entry/exit points and deployment of mobile monitoring teams);[47] (*b*) supervision of the cease-fire and related measures, including regroupment, cantonment,

---

[43] UN, *Yearbook of the United Nations 1992* (note 36), p. 244.
[44] UN, UNTAC Cambodia: United Nations Transitional Authority in Cambodia (note 41).
[45] UN, *Yearbook of the United Nations 1992* (note 36), p. 246.
[46] UN, UNTAC Cambodia: United Nations Transitional Authority in Cambodia (note 41); UN, *Yearbook of the United Nations 1992* (note 36), p. 244.
[47] Military liaison officers were also stationed in Bangkok, Vientiane and Hanoi.

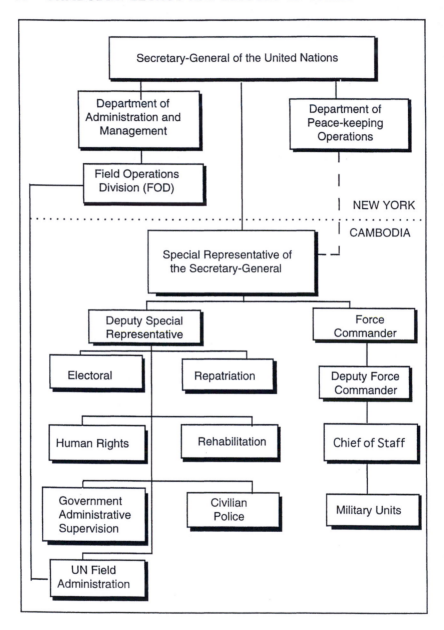

Figure 3.1. UNTAC organizational chart

Source: United Nations.

disarmament and demobilization of the armed forces of the Cambodian parties; (c) weapons control, including monitoring the cessation of outside military assistance, locating and confiscating caches of weapons and military supplies, and storing the arms and equipment of the cantoned and demobilized armed forces; and (d) assisting with mine clearance, including training and mine-awareness programmes.

The Military Component was also charged with investigating allegations of non-compliance with the provisions of the Paris Accords relating to military arrangements, either following complaints by one or more of the parties or on its own initiative. It would also assist in the release of prisoners of war and the repatriation of Cambodian refugees and displaced persons. The scale of its task is indicated by the fact that it would be required to canton and disarm an estimated 450 000 regular and irregular troops, supervise the demobilization of 70 per cent of these, secure more than 300 000 weapons of all types and some 80 million rounds of ammunition, and monitor the security of Cambodia's borders and territorial waters.[48]

The Military Component would comprise:[49] (a) a military observer group (UNMOs) of 485; (b) a force headquarters and sector headquarters staff of 204; (c) 12 enlarged infantry battalions of all ranks totalling 10 200; (d) an engineer element of 2230; (e) an air support group of 326 to operate and maintain 10 fixed-wing aircraft (2 communication and liaison aircraft, 4 short take-off and landing aircraft and 4 heavy transport aircraft) and 26 helicopters (2 heavy transport, 6 medium and 18 utility helicopters); (f) a signals unit of 582; (g) a medical unit of 541; (h) a composite military police company of 160; (i) a logistic battalion of 872; and (j) a naval element of 376 to operate 6 sea patrol boats, 9 river patrol boats, 3 landing craft and 12 specialized boats, all except the 12 special boats to be provided by Cambodia. These figures included the personnel and equipment already deployed and planned for UNAMIC. It was intended that the infantry and observer elements would be reduced from 10 200 and 485 respectively to 5100 and 300 by 30 September 1992, after cantonment and

---

48 UN, Report of the Secretary-General on Cambodia, 19 Feb. 1992 (note 29), p. 14. These estimates, which were based on information provided by the four factions, proved to be vastly inflated.

49 UN, Report of the Secretary-General on Cambodia, 19 Feb. 1992 (note 29), p. 19.

demobilization of 70 per cent of the Cambodian parties' military forces.

The role of the Civil Administration Component was to exercise direct control over Cambodia's existing administrative structures in the fields of foreign affairs, national defence, finance, public security and information. It would also receive and investigate complaints. Together, the Human Rights and Civil Administration components would comprise some 224 specialists, assisted by 84 international support staff, and would operate at UNTAC headquarters, from offices in the 21 provincial and municipal centres and, especially in regard to the dissemination of information and civic education, from offices in all the estimated 200 districts in Cambodia. Specific tasks of the Component would include identifying the agencies, bodies and offices of existing administrative structures, training Cambodian administrative personnel in codes of conduct and management guidelines and setting up complaints mechanisms and investigation procedures. Offices would be established to deal with each of the five areas identified for direct control.

The Police Component, comprising civil police monitors (CivPols), was given the task of supervising or controlling the estimated 50 000 local civil police to ensure that law and order were maintained effectively and impartially and human rights and fundamental freedoms fully protected. It would operate throughout Cambodia from offices to be established in the 21 provincial and municipal centres and the 200 district offices. The latter would operate as mobile teams.

The Repatriation Component would work with the UN High Commissioner for Refugees (UNHCR), designated the lead agency, in the repatriation and resettlement of Cambodian refugees and displaced persons. Its tasks would include the movement of returning refugees, the provision of immediate assistance and food and the establishment of a reintegration programme. Appropriate border crossing points and routes would be designated and cleared of mines and other hazards. Repatriation was expected to be completed within nine months. A memorandum of arrangements between UNHCR and Thailand was intended to 'define the modalities' of all aspects of the repatriation programme.

The Rehabilitation Component was charged with attending to food security, health, housing, training, education, the transport network and the restoration of Cambodia's basic infrastructure and public utilities. The efficient and effective co-ordination of this effort was to be ensured by the UNTAC Co-ordinator for Rehabilitation.

The cost of UNTAC (including UNAMIC) was estimated to be over $1.6 billion.[50] This was exclusive of the refugee repatriation programme, estimated to cost $92.5 million, and rehabilitation, both of which were to be funded by voluntary contributions.[51] This made UNTAC at the time the most expensive peacekeeping operation ever undertaken by the UN.[52] It was to be funded by contributions from all UN member states according to the usual UN scale of assessments. In view of the size of the operation and the need for early deployment, the General Assembly took the unusual step of approving a relatively large advance of $200 million for start-up costs prior to the UNTAC budget being approved.[53]

III. Deployment of UNTAC

UNTAC was created by the Security Council on 28 February 1992.[54] Akashi arrived in Phnom Penh on 15 March, five months after the Paris Accords had entered into force. Battalions from nearby countries—Indonesia, Malaysia and Thailand—were asked to deploy rapidly to establish a UN military presence for his arrival.[55] The rest of UNTAC barely existed. As Akashi diplomatically put it, UNTAC would have been 'more effective had its deployment in Cambodia been expedited by a more prompt arrival of military and civilian personnel and a more rapid dispatch of vehicles, prefabricated housing, office and communication equipment, and other necessary infrastructure'.[56]

On the military side, all contributing battalions were required to arrive with 60 days' self-sufficiency without resupply.[57] Not all of them did so.[58] Support units arrived after infantry battalions, reversing

---

[50] UN, *Yearbook of the United Nations 1992* (note 36), p. 248. Unless otherwise indicated, values are given in US$.

[51] UNHCR, *Information Bulletin*, Phnom Penh, no. 8 (Mar. 1993), pp. 3–4.

[52] UN, *United Nations Focus: Cambodia: The United Nations Transitional Authority in Cambodia*, New York, Apr. 1993, p. 14.

[53] UN, *Yearbook of the United Nations 1992* (note 36), p. 247.

[54] UN, Security Council Resolution 745, UN document S/RES/745, 28 Feb. 1992.

[55] Chopra *et al.* (note 30), p. 20.

[56] Akashi (note 7), p. 188.

[57] Chopra *et al.* (note 30), p. 20.

[58] *UN Peacekeeping: Observations on Mandates and Operational Capability,* Statement of Frank C. Conahan, Assistant Comptroller General, National Security and International

the natural military order.[59] Considerable difficulty was experienced in emplacing and securing necessary equipment.[60] According to Karl Farris, it

quickly became apparent that the rate at which the Military Component could pursue its tasks . . . depended on how fast infrastructure improvements could be made—the military needed repaired roads, operational airfields and ports, an adequate fuel supply, storage and distribution capacity, electrical power, an effective communications network, warehouse space, and adequate personnel accommodations.[61]

Of the 24 checkpoints planned to monitor withdrawal of foreign forces and verify that new military equipment and supplies were not entering the country, only three, on the border with Viet Nam, had been established by the end of April 1992.[62]

No formal troop contributors' meeting was held until April, just two months before full troop deployment was scheduled. After the meeting the UN decided to recruit more troops from French-speaking countries, thereby adding to the delay.[63] The military force's 12 battalions were still not fully deployed by June 1992, when cantonment and disarmament of the factions was scheduled to commence.[64] Deployment was 'almost complete' by mid-July.[65]

The CivPols were not fully in the field until October 1992. For more than two months after the deployment of UNTAC, the Electoral

Affairs Division, Testimony before the Subcommittee on Terrorism, Narcotics, and International Operations, Committee on Foreign Relations, US Senate, 9 June 1993, GAO/T-NSIAD-93-15, p. 7. For example, some units did not deploy with equipment to purify water from surface sources, even though the UN had asked them to do so.

[59] Chopra et al. (note 30), p. 20.

[60] UN, Yearbook of the United Nations 1992 (note 36), p. 250.

[61] Farris, K., 'UN peacekeeping in Cambodia: on balance, a success', Parameters, vol. 24, no. 1 (1994), pp. 43–44.

[62] UN, Yearbook of the United Nations 1992 (note 36), p. 250. They were to be along the borders with Thailand (7), Viet Nam (9) and Laos (2), at Kompong Som and Phnom Penh ports (one each) and at the airports at Phnom Penh, Battambang, Siem Reap and Stung Treng (one each). By late May all those along the border with Viet Nam had been established: see Amer, R., 'The United Nations' peacekeeping operation in Cambodia: overview and assessment', Contemporary Southeast Asia, vol. 15, no. 2 (Sep. 1993), p. 214.

[63] UN peacekeeping: observations on mandates and operational capability (note 58), p. 7.

[64] UN, Special report of the Secretary-General on the United Nations Transitional Authority in Cambodia, UN document S/24090, 12 June 1992, p. 4. The planned date for completion of deployment was the end of May 1992: see UN, Report of the Secretary-General on Cambodia, 19 Feb. 1992 (note 29), p. 23.

[65] UN, Second special report of the Secretary-General on the United Nations Transitional Authority in Cambodia, UN document S/24286, 14 July 1992, p. 3.

Component (as distinct from the Advance Electoral Planning Unit (AEPU), which arrived with UMAMIC) consisted of only a handful of people.[66]

On the administrative side, even by May 1992 most UNTAC departments were only beginning to be established. Three of the five section heads of the Administrative Division did not arrive until August, while only 20 per cent of its staff were in Cambodia for the first three months of UNTAC's existence. The Information Division was still without a Deputy Director a year after it was established. UNTAC as a whole was not fully operational until July or August 1992.[67] All components were hampered in their work by the late arrival of staff, and particularly by their late deployment outside Phnom Penh.[68]

In the view of Nick Warner, Counsellor at the Australian Mission in Phnom Penh, the delay in UNTAC's deployment was critical, 'cutting into the timetable outlined in the peace agreement, and chipping away at UNTAC's credibility in the eyes of the Cambodian people and the four factions'.[69] With characteristic understatement Akashi says the delay 'affected the perceptions of Cambodians regarding UNTAC's efficiency'.[70]

Worst of all, it emboldened the Khmer Rouge to defy the UN. The most publicized case occurred after the Dutch battalion attempted to deploy to a sensitive KR area near Pailin. This was allegedly done 'in the manner of an administrative move', without the full weight of UNTAC behind it.[71] The Dutch were turned back. By the time a more impressive convoy accompanied by Akashi and Sanderson arrived, the KR position had 'irrevocably hardened' and they were halted by KR police at a bamboo-pole checkpoint between Pailin and the Thai border on 30 May.[72] Critics claim that this was a turning-point in Cambodians' perceptions of UNTAC's effectiveness.[73] On 9 June the

[66] Maley, M., 'Reflections on the electoral process in Cambodia', ed. H. Smith (note 27), p. 90.

[67] Warner (note 38), pp. 4, 9.

[68] Maley (note 66), p. 90.

[69] Warner (note 38), p. 4.

[70] Akashi (note 7), p. 188.

[71] Chopra *et al.* (note 30), pp. 20–21.

[72] UN, Special report of the Secretary-General, 12 June 1992 (note 64), p. 3.

[73] Asia Watch (note 9), p. 9.

KR told Akashi by letter that it would not allow UNTAC forces to deploy in its areas.[74]

IV. Phase II

While Phase I of the peace plan had been difficult enough, real trouble began when UNTAC attempted to move into Phase II—the cantonment, disarmament and demobilization of the four factions. In May Sanderson, anxious to bring some order back into the peace process, and despite the fact that only two of UNTAC's 12 battalions were fully deployed in the field (those from Indonesia and Malaysia), announced that regroupment and cantonment would begin on 13 June and be completed in four weeks.[75] To achieve this, UNTAC's Military Component was deployed to 84 out of 103 planned cantonment sites and to 20 checkpoints.[76] Assurances were obtained from each of the four parties that they would (a) grant freedom of movement to UNTAC personnel, vehicles and aircraft; (b) mark minefields in areas they controlled; (c) provide information by 20 May on their troops, arms, ammunition and equipment; and (d) adhere to the Paris Peace Accords, in particular by not interfering with other factions' troops moving to regroupment and cantonment areas and by informing their own troops of the regroupment and cantonment plan.[77]

The KR, however, continued to violate the cease-fire, refused to allow UNTAC forces to deploy in its areas, failed to provide UNTAC with an accounting of its troops and *matériel* or to assist in mine clearance, and, finally, refused to allow its troops to be cantoned and disarmed.[78] It made several demands of UNTAC before it would participate in Phase II, including: (a) UN verification that all Vietnamese troops had left Cambodia and would not return (later widened to a demand that all Vietnamese leave Cambodia); (b) establishment by UNTAC of full control over the SOC Government (later broadened to

---

[74] UN, Special report of the Secretary-General, 12 June 1992 (note 64), p. 3.

[75] By 13 June, 4 UNTAC battalions were fully deployed to their sectors with all equipment ready to start cantonment.

[76] Sanderson, J. M. (Lt-Gen.), 'Preparation for, deployment and conduct of peacekeeping operations: a Cambodia snapshot', Paper presented at a conference on UN Peacekeeping at the Crossroads, Canberra, 21–24 Mar. 1993, p. 8. Of the cantonment sites, 15 were for the NADK, 5 for ANKI, 4 for the KPNLAF and the remainder for the CPAF.

[77] UN, *Yearbook of the United Nations 1992* (note 36), p. 251.

[78] UN, *Yearbook of the United Nations 1992* (note 36), p. 251.

a demand for its complete dissolution);[79] (c) changes to the role and powers of the SNC and UNTAC to enable the SNC to become the 'sole source of power in Cambodia during the transitional period';[80] and (d) a redrawing of the border between Cambodia and Viet Nam.[81]

The Ministerial Conference on the Rehabilitation and Reconstruction of Cambodia, held in Tokyo on 22 June 1992, in addition to securing pledges of aid for Cambodia, attempted to address KR concerns.[82] To meet its allegations about Vietnamese forces still being in the country, UNTAC increased the number and stepped up the operations of its border checkpoints and Strategic Verification Teams and investigated reports of Vietnamese still serving in the SOC military. UNTAC initially discovered three, all Vietnamese-Cambodians associated with the SOC, one of them retired, and later another four.[83] The KR was unable to produce evidence of any other Vietnamese military personnel still in Cambodia.

The KR remained unmollified by UNTAC's measures. Discussions in the SNC also failed to resolve their difficulties. The NADK, the KR's military force, meanwhile withdrew from the MMWG, returning to it only in September 1992.[84] In July the Security Council warned the KR that no reconstruction aid would go to parties not cooperating in the peace process.[85]

In July 1992, General Loridon, former Military Commander of UNAMIC and then Deputy Military Commander of UNTAC, was relieved of his position after advocating the use of force against the KR.[86] This was also the opinion of the 'large and vocal nongovernment organization community in Cambodia, whose work was significantly hampered by the worsening security situation'.[87] Loridon was

[79] *Phnom Penh Post*, 24 July 1993, p. 3.

[80] Rowley, K., 'UN has an active option open to it in Cambodia', *Canberra Times*, 29 June 1992, p. 13.

[81] Asia Watch, 'Cambodia: human rights before and after the elections', *Asia Watch*, vol. 5, no. 10 (May 1993), p. 7.

[82] Akashi (note 7), p. 190; and UN, Second special report of the Secretary-General, 14 July 1992 (note 65), Proposal for Discussion, Annex, pp. 6–7.

[83] UN, Fourth progress report of the Secretary-General on the United Nations Transitional Authority in Cambodia, UN document S/25719, 3 May 1993, p. 11; *Bangkok Post,* 2 Mar. 1993. Viet Nam refused to take them back, arguing that they were civilians and Cambodian citizens.

[84] UN, Second progress report of the Secretary-General on the United Nations Transitional Authority in Cambodia, UN document S/24578, 21 Sep. 1992, p. 5.

[85] UN, Security Council Resolution 766, UN document S/RES/766, 21 July 1992.

[86] *The Age* (Melbourne), 24 July 1992; *The Independent*, 5 Aug. 1992.

[87] Farris (note 61), p. 45.

Table 3.2. Cantoned and disarmed forces of the Cambodian factions as of 10 September 1992

Cambodian People's Armed Forces	42 368
Armée Nationale pour un Kampuchea Indépendent	3 445
Khmer People's National Liberation Armed Forces	6 479
National Army of Democratic Kampuchea	–
Total	**52 292**

Source: UN, Second progress report of the Secretary-General on the United Nations Transitional Authority in Cambodia, UN document S/24578, 21 Sep. 1992, p. 5.

quoted as suggesting that he would accept the deaths of up to 200 soldiers, including his own, to end the KR threat once and for all. On his departure he told the press that he was leaving Cambodia 'frustrated by my inability to implement the UN mandate. Here was our chance to deal with the Khmer Rouge, push them to implement the accords they have signed. But I haven't succeeded in getting my superiors to agree with me'.[88] Akashi said he was startled by the General's remarks, since a military plan that cost 200 lives would be 'a failure, a bankruptcy, of a peacekeeping operation'.[89] It is notable, however, that Akashi did not completely rule out the use of force but said rather: 'It's premature to consider military enforcement. That would change the rules of the game so completely. Some of the countries that have contributed might try to remove their troops. It is not a decision that should be made lightly.'

In the face of lack of KR co-operation in cantonment and disarmament, the UN had the choice of suspending the process or proceeding with it. It decided to proceed with the three factions that were co-operating, but with safeguards to ensure that they would not be disadvantaged militarily—an acknowledgement that such a process could not proceed indefinitely without surrendering the country to the KR. By 10 September 1992, UNTAC had cantoned more than 52 000 troops of these co-operating parties and taken custody of approximately 50 000 weapons.[90]

---

[88] Chanda, N., 'Cambodia: UN divisions', *Far Eastern Economic Review*, 23 July 1992, p. 8. One UN official was quoted as saying that Loridon was sacked because he was a 'loose cannon'. He was replaced by another Frenchman, General Robert Rideau.

[89] Quoted in Shenon, P., 'A Japanese envoy's impossible job: keeping the peace in Cambodia', *New York Times*, 4 Oct. 1992, p. IV-8.

[90] UN, *United Nations Focus: Cambodia* (note 8), p. 9.

These comprised roughly 50 per cent of FUNCINPEC's and the KPNLF's total strength and 25 per cent of the SOC's regular forces.[91] Only about 200 KR troops ever came in to cantonment centres[92] and UNTAC was eventually forced to call a halt to the entire process. Many of the soldiers already cantoned were sent on 'agricultural leave' to harvest the wet-season rice crop.[93] The end result was that, while the two smaller factions had mostly disarmed,[94] the SOC kept the best part of its army intact and the KR suffered no impairment of its fighting capacity whatsoever. This left two credible fighting forces in Cambodia—the Government's army, between 100 000 and 150 000 strong, and the KR, estimated to have about 12 000 seasoned fighters.

With the failure of the cantonment and disarmament phase of the peace plan and the burgeoning threat to the neutral political environment which UNTAC was supposed to establish, the UN Security Council now had to decide whether or not to proceed with the election in May 1993. The alternatives were to proceed, to postpone it until the KR's co-operation was secured or to cancel it and effectively scuttle the Paris Accords.[95] Abandonment of Cambodia was seen by the Secretary-General as unacceptable, given all that had been achieved up to that point.[96] Putting the process on hold was also rejected as an option since, according to the UN, 'neither the political nor economic situation in Cambodia would sustain a prolonged transitional period. Moreover, it would require the international community to maintain indefinitely a large and very costly operation, whose recurrent costs ran at almost $100 million per month'.[97]

[91] Akashi (note 7), p. 196. According to Raoul Jennar, almost all KPNLF forces were cantoned, leading to its elimination as a military force of any consequence. See Jennar, R., *Cambodian Chronicles*, V (7 Sep. 1992), p. 4, cited in Klintworth, G., Australian National University, Research School of Pacific Studies, Strategic and Defence Studies Centre, *Cambodia's Past, Present and Future*, Working Paper no. 268 (SDSC: Canberra, 1990), p. 8.

[92] Schear, J. A., 'The case of Cambodia', eds D. Daniel and B. Hayes, *Beyond Traditional Peacekeeping* (Macmillan: London, forthcoming 1995), p. 291.

[93] *Bangkok Post*, 20 Aug. 1992. Their release was on condition that they be recallable in 14 days; that their weapons remain in UNTAC custody; and that their respective armies pay them in advance and issue an agricultural leave pass. See Sanderson (note 76), pp. 6–7.

[94] Asia Watch reported that even before the arrival of UNTAC the KPNLF and FUNCINPEC militaries in some areas were disintegrating into small armed gangs. See Asia Watch (note 9), p. 38.

[95] The option of conducting by-elections in contested areas after the main elections was later considered but rejected: see UN, Report of the Secretary-General on the implementation of Security Council Resolution 783 (1992), UN document S/24800, 15 Nov. 1992, p. 7.

[96] UN, Second progress report of the Secretary-General, 21 Sep. 1992 (note 84), p. 15. For a discussion of these achievements, see chapter 4.

[97] UN, *United Nations Focus: Cambodia* (note 8), p. 4.

Other factors favouring proceeding with the election included the facts that electoral enrolment had proceeded spectacularly well, that the international consensus behind UNTAC was holding firm and that the KR seemed intent only on boycotting rather than disrupting the election. Moreover, according to Schear, the election was perceived as a 'gateway' to the emergence of an internationally recognized government in Phnom Penh that could secure broad support, including that of former KR supporters, in the task of national reconstruction.[98]

UNTAC's situation perfectly illustrated the contention of Michael Doyle that as soon as the UN begins to invest money and resources in a peacekeeping mission the bargaining relationship with the contracting parties dramatically alters. While the UN holds all the cards at the outset, thereafter the parties increase their leverage as the success of the mission comes to depend increasingly on their co-operation. As Akashi acknowledged, 'I cannot afford not to succeed'.[99]

On 13 October 1992 the Security Council unanimously accepted the Secretary-General's recommendation to proceed with the election.[100] The resolution also, for the first time, named the Khmer Rouge as the obstacle to peace in Cambodia. Cynics and a number of human rights advocates saw the decision to proceed as a move by the West and the Security Council to be rid of the Cambodian 'problem' once and for all, regardless of the fairness of the electoral process. Whatever the justice of this interpretation, the decision to proceed was a high-risk strategy, since the holding of a free and fair election had always been predicated on an end to the civil war and the creation of a peaceful atmosphere during the election campaign. The creation of a neutral political environment was dependent on the creation of a neutral security environment. Neither was now possible.

In an effort to counteract these unfavourable circumstances, UNTAC made several significant adjustments to its operations.

First, it redeployed its Military Component towards direct support of the electoral process, a vital move in keeping a 'reasonable line of distance', both physically and psychologically, between areas of KR operation and those where electoral preparations were taking place.[101]

---

[98] Schear (note 92), pp. 293–94.

[99] Doyle, M. W., 'UNTAC: sources of success and failure', ed. Smith (note 27), p. 97.

[100] UN, Security Council Resolution 783, UN document S/RES/783, 13 Oct. 1992.

[101] The country had originally been divided into military sectors, some with sub-sectors and with Phnom Penh as a 'Special Zone' where the Force Headquarters was located. Sector boundaries were redrawn and infantry battalions that had been deployed around cantonment areas were reassigned to establish a protective presence in medium- and high-risk areas where

Military sectors were redrawn to correspond to provincial boundaries and infantry battalions redeployed accordingly.[102] The new military deployment would serve as a deterrent, make more effective the protection of UNTAC activities through escort and patrol operations, ensure rapid reaction at potential trouble-spots and permit direct contact and negotiation with those threatening the electoral process.[103] In addition to establishing 12 local area mobile reserves, Sanderson also created a Force Commander's Mobile Reserve 'on 60 minutes' notice to move'.[104]

Initially these measures increased the number of peacekeepers in contested areas, leading the KR to initiate a 'cat-and-mouse game of taking peacekeepers hostage and then releasing them'.[105] General Sanderson records that he had a major task in convincing diplomats of contributing countries (although not the military contingents themselves) of the need for UNTAC to deploy deeper in the countryside.[106] UNTAC also decided to allow the SOC and the other two parties to repulse KR forces to secure the safety of polling stations.[107] In April 1993, the MMWG reached agreement with these parties on cooperative arrangements for the use of minimum force and proportionate response in providing security during the election, thus binding them to the process.[108] At the request of these parties UNTAC was then obliged to return to them some of the weapons in cantonment. General Sanderson emphasized, however, that the changed deployment of the Military Component did not greatly change its mission:

---

electoral preparations were under way. See UNTAC Electoral Component, Phnom Penh, *Free Choice: Electoral Component Newsletter*, no. 11 (15 Jan. 1993), pp. 12–14; Schear (note 92) pp. 294, 298.

[102] UN, *The United Nations in Cambodia: A Vote for Peace* (note 38), p. 40.

[103] Sanderson (note 76), p. 12.

[104] Sanderson (note 76), p. 12.

[105] See Schear (note 92), p. 294; *The Nation* (Bangkok), 6 Dec. 1992; *Bangkok Post*, 6 Dec. 1992; *International Herald Tribune*, 17 Dec. 1992, p. 7; *Financial Times*, 18 Dec. 1992, p. 5. These incidents were resolved mostly through the MMWG and faction liaison officers, proving, says Sanderson, 'the power of patience and negotiation': see Sanderson (note 76), p. 12. Much of the kidnapping appears to have been initiated by the infamous one-legged KR military 'warlord', Ta Mok, also called 'the Butcher' because of atrocities he committed during the KR rule of Cambodia. See *Sydney Morning Herald*, 9 Apr. 1993, p. 5. In one case Uruguayan peacekeepers were held hostage after landing in a KR village unannounced.

[106] Sanderson (note 27), p. 21.

[107] Akashi (note 7), p. 197.

[108] Sanderson (note 27), p. 27.

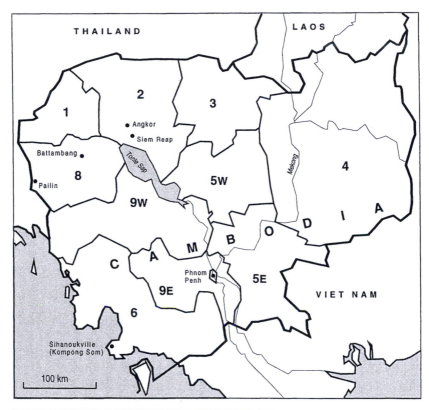

Military sector	Infantry battalion	Province
1	Netherlands	Banteay Manchey
2	Bangladesh	Sim Reap
3	Pakistan	Preah Vihear
4	Uruguay	Kratie, Mondolkiri, Ratanakiri, Stung Treng
5E	India	Kompong Cham, Prey Veng, Syay Rieng
5W	Indonesia	Kompong Thom
6	France	Kampot, Koh Kong, Sihanoukville (Kompong Som), Takeo
8	Malaysia	Battambang
9E	Bulgaria	Kandal, Kompong Speu
9W	Tunisia	Kompong Chhnang, Pursat
PPSZ	Ghana	Phnom Penh Special Zone

Figure 3.2. UNTAC infantry deployments in Cambodia after October 1992

Source: UNTAC Electoral Component, *Free Choice*, no. 11 (15 Jan. 1993), p. 8.

The mission is not defending Cambodia. Therefore the UNTAC Military Component will not be drawn into internal security operations. Nor is the mission to defend the political process but we are in Cambodia to defend an electoral process. We, the military, are responsible for the provision of a secure framework for the UN components to conduct activities which will result in election of the next generation of Cambodian leaders.[109]

Second, UNTAC took stronger measures to deal with political intimidation and violence.[110] Third, it greatly intensified its media and civic education programmes, especially through Radio UNTAC, the core message being to assure voters of the secrecy of their votes.[111]

In the meantime, diplomatic efforts were pursued to convince the KR to co-operate, first by France and Indonesia, the co-chairs of the Paris Conference, and second by Japan and Thailand.[112] The KR continued to violate the Accords and denigrate UNTAC. Khmer Rouge radio quoted criticism of Akashi as lacking 'common sense, courage, far-sightedness and political will' and called for his resignation.[113]

In response, the Security Council in November 1992 imposed a non-mandatory embargo on petroleum supplies to the KR—a move that was deliberately not described as a sanction in order to avoid a Chinese veto and the alienation of Thailand.[114] It commended the SNC on its 22 September decision to impose a moratorium on exports of uncut logs and called on it to enact additional measures, namely bans on the export of minerals and gems. While these were described as 'natural resource preservation measures', they were in effect veiled sanctions on the KR, which drew a major source of its income from such exports, either directly or by selling permits to Thai companies.[115] The measures, however, applied to all parties, including the

---

[109] Sanderson (note 76), p. 10.

[110] Schear (note 92), p. 294 for details.

[111] UNTAC distributed nationwide nearly 300 000 radios donated by a Japanese non-governmental organization (NGO). Although this increased radio penetration, it also caused some security problems in its own right. See Schear (note 92), p. 295.

[112] See UN, Report of the Secretary-General, 15 Nov. 1992 (note 95), which includes documents prepared by Japan and Thailand and the two Paris co-chairs respectively on their negotiating efforts with the KR.

[113] New York Times, 4 Oct. 1992, p. IV-8.

[114] UN, Security Council Resolution 792, UN document S/RES/792, 30 Nov. 1992; UN, Report on the implementation of Security Council Resolution 792 (1992), UN document S/25289, 13 Feb. 1993.

[115] Towards the end of Dec. 1992, Laos, Thailand and Viet Nam all announced that they would impose a complete ban on the import of Cambodian logs beginning on 1 Jan. 1993. This was only after the Thai military had clumsily attempted to pressure the UN to delay

Hun Sen Government, which was estimated to be responsible for a far greater amount of uncontrolled logging than the KR.[116] The Council also threatened further measures, such as freezing KR assets outside Cambodia. The resolution was a compromise between the hard-line approach of the USA and the UK, a softer-line French draft, and the opposition of the UN Secretary-General to any type of sanctions at that stage.[117]

The petroleum embargo and export bans were, in the event, more symbolic than effective.[118] In February 1993 UNTAC reported 'numerous and large-scale violations' of all the embargoes by both land and sea routes.[119] Sanderson noted in March that:

UNTAC has been unable to establish the 30 border checkpoints deemed necessary to fulfil our obligations. The denial of freedom of movement through NADK-controlled zones has prevented full deployment. At the 21 locations we have been able to access, UNTAC has established a team of 5 UNMOs, a protection party of 6 soldiers and a communicator. A system of aerial surveillance and special patrolling by UNTAC battalions complements the monitoring conducted by border checkpoints.[120]

The Thai Government did apparently close the border completely for a brief period and thereafter restricted some border traffic, but its enforcement of the embargoes was erratic at best.[121] It also refused to allow UNTAC to establish checkpoints on Thai territory.[122] The Thai military had such a large financial stake in the cross-border trade—through its own commercial activities and those of protected Thai companies in logging, gem mining and drug-running—that any government-level co-operation with UNTAC and the peace process

implementation of the ban by forcing UN supply flights to give 3 days' notice before entering Thai airspace. See *The Australian*, 2 Dec. 1992.

[116] *The Age* (Melbourne), 8 Feb. 1993, p. 8. UNTAC officials later noted that the Government, not the KR, was the main violator of the logging ban.

[117] *Bangkok Post*, 20 and 30 Nov. 1992. See also UN, Report of the Secretary-General, 15 Nov. 1992 (note 95), p. 6.

[118] According to Asia Watch, there was no UN monitoring of the Thai–Cambodian border in KR areas: see Asia Watch (note 85), p. 7. UNTAC claimed that it originally had 17 checkpoints on the Thai–Cambodian border. Additional checkpoints were to be established along the Thai border with the KR zone after the moratoria were imposed: see UN, *United Nations Focus: Cambodia* (note 8), p. 9.

[119] UN, Report on the implementation of Security Council Resolution 792, 13 Feb. 1993 (note 114), p. 5. See also Klintworth (note 91), pp. 9–10.

[120] Sanderson (note 76), p. 13.

[121] *International Herald Tribune*, 2–3 Jan. 1993, p. 2.

[122] *The Nation* (Bangkok), 10 Dec. 1992.

was badly undercut.[123] UNTAC made several representations to Bangkok about such issues, but found itself in the uncomfortable position of trying to pressure a government whose goodwill was required for diplomatic efforts to bring the KR back into the peace process. Moreover the Thai civilian Government was so fragile and its relationship with the military so finely balanced that it would have been unable to withstand the type of pressure required to ensure compliance. None the less, Thailand was clearly in breach of its obligations under the Paris Accords in providing succour to the KR.

Far from returning to the peace process, the KR, exploiting the long history of Vietnamese–Cambodian enmity, began attacking Vietnamese villages and businesses as part of an anti-Vietnamese campaign apparently designed to win popular Cambodian support. More than 200 000 Vietnamese were believed to be resident in Cambodia.[124] The Vietnamese population had increased after the Paris Accords were signed as craftspersons, restaurateurs, traders and prostitutes from the south of Viet Nam, attracted by the boom conditions, came to Phnom Penh.[125] The KR was not the only party to indulge in anti-Vietnamese activity. FUNCINPEC and KPNLF leaders, including Prince Ranariddh and Son Sann, also engaged in verbal attacks. In the words of Asia Watch, 'Three centuries of political subjugation and loss of territory by [sic] Vietnam lies behind the almost pathological fear and hatred that Cambodians bear their dominant neighbour'.[126]

Meanwhile the SOC and its political party, the CPP, began harassing opposition political parties, especially FUNCINPEC, intimidating voters, bombing electoral offices and even murdering candidates and party officials. This occurred increasingly in the provinces as the opposition parties began establishing offices in what had formerly been exclusively SOC areas. In early November the first attack on a party office, a drive-by shooting at a BLDP office in Koh Kong province, took place, followed by a grenade attack on a FUNCINPEC office in Battambang 10 days later.[127] The situation was exacerbated by the unwillingness of the SOC police to arrest those accused of infringements of electoral law, especially murders and bombings, since most such incidents were connected with the Government

---

[123] Asia Watch (note 85), p. 7.
[124] *Asian Recorder*, 30 Sep.–6 Oct. 1992, p. 22609.
[125] *The Independent*, 14 Oct. 1992, p. 12.
[126] Asia Watch (note 9), pp. 57–59.
[127] UN, *The United Nations in Cambodia: A Vote for Peace* (note 38), p. 29.

itself.[128] Using a mirror image of KR reasoning, the SOC justified its behaviour by citing the failure of UNTAC—which it described as a 'paper tiger'—to control the KR.[129] While the KR was clearly the first faction to begin systematic and blatant violation of the Paris Accords, violations by the KR and the SOC fed on each other, creating a downward spiral of chicanery and malfeasance.

In early January 1993 Prince Sihanouk announced from Beijing, where he had been seeking medical treatment since November, that he was ending his co-operation with UNTAC and resigning from the SNC because of the escalating violence. Akashi rushed to Beijing and succeeded in placating him. Sihanouk none the less continued to criticize UNTAC, alleging that 'In order to be able to tell the UN and the world that they have succeeded in their mission, UNTAC is going to have an election despite the fact that none of the conditions for the election have been met. None. It is a hideous comedy'.[130]

The situation was made worse by the general ineptness of UNTAC's Civilian Police Component, which constituted neither a deterrent nor an enforcement mechanism. Gareth Evans has described the CivPols as being 'with conspicuous exceptions, ineffective'.[131] Unsure of their role, many CivPols ended up either doing very little or becoming involved in corrupt activities. Some treated the local population heavy-handedly, sometimes in a racist fashion. Tunisian police were accused of child molestation, others of rape. Philippine police were arrested on their return to Manila for smuggling out arms. While a small minority of the military forces was also ill-disciplined (particularly the Bulgarians), it was the CivPols who gave UNTAC its worst public relations problem.[132]

---

[128] UNTAC, Statement by the Director of the UNTAC Human Rights Component on Political Violence, Phnom Penh, 23 May 1993. In 1993 UNTAC launched a series of 'control team' no-notice inspections of provincial offices which confirmed widespread suspicions of SOC complicity in such activities. See UN, Fourth progress report of the Secretary-General, 3 May 1993 (note 83).

[129] Akashi (note 7), p. 196.

[130] *Far Eastern Economic Review*, 4 Feb. 1993, p. 21. UNTAC's true feelings about Sihanouk may have been betrayed by one UN official's remark to Reuters in Phnom Penh: 'if the old man really cared for the Cambodian people, maybe he would get his royal behind over here instead of throwing mud at us from Peking': see *The Independent*, 6 Jan. 1993, p. 10.

[131] Evans, G., *Cooperating for Peace: The Global Agenda for the 1990s and Beyond* (Allen & Unwin: Sydney, 1993), p. 108.

[132] Schear (note 92, p. 297) notes 'a small but steady stream of reports of personal misconduct on the part of UNTAC soldiers and civilians'.

Law and order deteriorated steadily in early 1993 as local bandits and criminals began taking advantage of the hiatus in state power caused by UNTAC's presence. The SOC Government also launched offensives against the KR in at least 10 provinces in February.[133] Some of this activity was attributed by Akashi to 'a ritual dry-season offensive' that the Cambodian parties have traditionally undertaken.[134] None the less, UNTAC officially described the attacks as the 'largest cease-fire violation' it had registered and as going 'beyond the SOC's right to defend itself against any hostile action by the PDK'.[135] Akashi reportedly proposed to UN headquarters the stationing of UNTAC troops in a buffer zone between the two sides to end the fighting.[136] General Sanderson was subsequently reported as responding that it was impossible for his troops to fulfil such a role.[137] New York apparently did not respond positively to the idea either.[138]

A confidential UNTAC report of 18 January 1993 obtained by the *Far Eastern Economic Review* noted 'a very serious erosion of public confidence in UNTAC and the peace process in general'.[139] It stated that 'a Khmer Rouge return is seen as a very real threat, especially after UNTAC departs' and that 'the population believes that the SOC/ Cambodian People's Party have undertaken a full-fledged campaign of violent repression, thereby making it impossible for other provisionally registered political parties to seriously conduct legitimate political activities'. Most depressing for UNTAC, the report detailed what the *Review* called 'popular outrage at UNTAC and their personnel', concluding that Cambodians now refer to UNTAC soldiers as 'mercenaries' who 'come here only to collect their salaries'. While the *Review*'s account may have exaggerated the conclusions, and in any case the document may have represented the view of only one part of UNTAC, such reports undoubtedly fed KR propaganda about UN powerlessness and lack of control over the SOC.

In February the UN Secretary-General suggested that, contrary to the original plan, all UNTAC forces might have to remain in Cambodia after the May election to prevent an escalation of instability

---

[133] *Bangkok Post,* 2 Feb. 1993.
[134] *International Herald Tribune,* 4 Jan. 1993, p. 2.
[135] *UN Chronicle,* June 1993, pp. 23, 25.
[136] *The Australian,* 4 Feb. 1993, p. 8.
[137] *The Age* (Melbourne), 5 Feb. 1993, p. 8.
[138] *Weekend Australian,* 6 Feb. 1993, p. 15.
[139] Thayer, N. and Chanda, N., 'Cambodia: shattered peace', *Far Eastern Economic Review,* 11 Feb. 1993, p. 11.

prior to the formation of a new government.[140] The Security Council noted the suggestion and invited specific recommendations from the Secretary-General.[141] Significantly, China backed the resolution, which also reaffirmed that the election should proceed without the participation of the Khmer Rouge.

By March new massacres of Vietnamese were occurring, causing a flood of over 21 000 refugees across the border into Viet Nam.[142] Many fled on floating villages which drifted from the Tonle Sap (Great Lake) into the Mekong River which flows into Viet Nam. UNTAC naval units scrambled to protect the refugees in what became known as Operation Safe Passage. There were also hand-grenade attacks on bars in Phnom Penh. Over 100 people were killed in anti-Vietnamese incidents throughout Cambodia during March. Sihanouk did not help matters by declaring that 'the only reasonable alternative left to [the Vietnamese] is to leave Cambodia straight away and go and live in Viet Nam'.[143] The latter part of March was also marked by a comparative increase in the number and violent character of election-related incidents.[144] By early April, Dennis McNamara, Head of the Human Rights Component, was reported as saying that the 'spiral of violence' in recent weeks had 'overwhelmed us, and we cannot even investigate all the killings properly'.[145]

During March and April the KR also stepped up its attacks, abductions and murders of UN peacekeepers and others.[146] In late March a Bangladeshi soldier became the first UN peacekeeper to die in Cambodia from enemy fire when the KR launched a three-hour attack on his unit in the district of Angkor Chum in the north-west.[147] On 2 April the KR cold-bloodedly murdered three Bulgarian peacekeepers and wounded six others in Kompong Speu.[148] On 4 April

[140] UN, Report on the implementation of Security Council Resolution 792 (1992), 13 Feb. 1993 (note 114).

[141] UN, Security Council Resolution 810, UN document S/RES/810, 8 Mar. 1993.

[142] The Age (Melbourne), 26 Mar. 1993, p. 7. For details see UN, Fourth progress report of the Secretary-General, 3 May 1993 (note 83), pp. 14, 25.

[143] Sunday Age (Melbourne), 4 Apr. 1993, p. 10.

[144] UN, Fourth progress report of the Secretary-General, 3 May 1993 (note 83), p. 25.

[145] The Independent, 6 Apr. 1993, p. 11.

[146] Peacekeepers were sometimes apparently killed accidentally when UN forces were in the vicinity of engagements between the KR and SOC troops. Some incidents allegedly carried out by the KR were later found to have been perpetrated by others.

[147] Phnom Penh Post, 9–22 Apr. 1993, p. 3.

[148] Phnom Penh Post (note 147), p. 3; Sunday Age, 4 Apr. 1993 (note 143), p. 10. In contrast to Somalia, where UNOSOM II sought to arrest the leadership of the suspected

Khieu Samphan formally announced that his party would not participate in the election because 'Vietnamese forces of aggression' continued to occupy Cambodia and because a neutral political environment did not exist.[149]

UNTAC implemented several new security measures, including a ban on the possession and carrying of firearms and explosives by unauthorized persons and the guarding of party offices and officials by UNTAC CivPols. To control the possession of illegal firearms, checkpoints staffed by CivPols and local police were established in Phnom Penh in March and throughout the rest of the country thereafter.[150] The number of violent incidents fell markedly by the end of April.[151] Raoul Jennar, a harsh critic of UNTAC, observes that the 'impressive security measures' taken by UNTAC in the lead-up to the election had the effect—attested to by KR defectors—of deterring the KR from attempting to sabotage the electoral process.[152]

Explanations of why the Khmer Rouge decided blatantly to violate the Paris Accords, boycott the election and undermine the peace process vary. One theory is that it had never intended to comply but was simply buying time to regroup in preparation for a resumption of military hostilities. As Pol Pot is reported to have said of his strategy in 1988, 'the fruit remains the same; only the skin has changed'.[153] Hence the justifications the KR gave for not co-operating with UNTAC were simply a pretext for acting as it had always intended.

A second theory is that the KR genuinely believed that UNTAC would dismantle the SOC administration to a point where a KR takeover, either before or after the election, would be possible. When it became clear that UNTAC could not and would not completely control (much less dismantle) the SOC Government and that it could not even prevent SOC elements from violating the Accords, the KR reneged on its undertakings. It may have been encouraged to do this by the UN's failure to curb Serbian aggression in the former Yugo-

---

perpetrators, UNTAC issued arrest warrants for the soldiers immediately responsible and their platoon leader. See Schear (note 92), p. 301.

[149] UN, Fourth progress report of the Secretary-General, 3 May 1993 (note 83), p. 3.

[150] UN, *The United Nations in Cambodia: A Vote for Peace* (note 38), p. 31.

[151] UN, Fourth progress report of the Secretary-General, 3 May 1993 (note 83), p. 19.

[152] Jennar, R. M., 'UNTAC: "international triumph" in Cambodia?', *Security Dialogue*, vol. 25, no. 2 (1994), p. 148.

[153] Etcheson, C., 'Pol Pot and the art of war', *Phnom Penh Post*, 13–26 Aug. 1993, p. 7.

slavia.[154] Sanderson recalls that the KR Commander-in-Chief, General Son Sen, told him that unless UNTAC acted promptly to control the SOC he would not be able to control his own forces.[155]

Another explanation is that the KR had calculated its electoral prospects as being good until the political landscape began to change after the Accords were signed. Munck and Kumar speculate that

[since] the Khmer Rouge never really had an agenda upon which to construct a political party . . . its ability to transform itself from a military to a political force could be doubted. With the break-up of the CGDK coalition, the Khmer Rouge increasingly saw its electoral possibilities diminish. This led it to renege on its promise to participate in . . . and to take steps to undermine a process in which it would inevitably end up a loser. Making matters worse, the rising popularity of Prince Sihanouk [and his son's FUNCINPEC party] . . . led the former Phnom Penh government forces, increasingly dubious of their electoral prospects, to resort to force.[156]

A final theory is that the KR was playing for time, extending its network into the villages, moving repatriated settlers into its own districts, repositioning its forces, testing UN resolve rather than attempting to derail the peace process altogether, and aiming to effect a long-planned transition from military to political action.[157] According to the transcript of a Pol Pot speech supplied by KR defectors, he told a meeting that cadres must try to win the hearts and minds of the people to gain popular strength: 'Possession of popular strength translates into possession of political administration in the villages. It also begets representation in the parliament, which means persons belonging to us will be in the assembly'.[158]

A common thread running through all these explanations is one that often applies to parties to agreements ending long and bitter civil wars: the KR, like the Hun Sen Government, signed the Accords hop-

---

[154] It was reported that KR leaders could watch the 1 pm news broadcast by the French television channel *Antenne 2* daily on local Cambodian television. See *Guardian Weekly*, 21 June 1992, p. 11.

[155] Presentation by Lt-Gen. Sanderson at the Swedish Armed Forces Staff and War College, Stockholm, 29 Sep. 1994.

[156] Munck, G. L. and Kumar, C., University of Illinois at Urbana-Champaign, Program in Arms Control, Disarmament, and International Security, *Conflict Resolution through International Intervention: a Comparative Study of Cambodia and El Salvador*, Occasional Paper (ACDIS: Urbana, Ill., Apr. 1993), pp. 12–13.

[157] Branegan, J., 'Cambodia: up against a wall', *Time* (Australia), 29 June 1992, p. 64; *The Independent*, 5 Aug. 1992; Hornik, R., 'Sympathy for the devil', *Time* (Australia), 21 Sep. 1992, p. 43.

[158] Hornik (note 157), p. 43.

ing that the peace process might work to its advantage but remained ready to resume the armed struggle at any time if it did not. KR behaviour during the early days of implementation supports this interpretation. In late 1991 and early 1992 the KR was pressing strongly for the full and rapid deployment of UNTAC.[159] When UNTAC was finally deployed, the KR initially adopted a posture of cautious co-operation, despite engaging in numerous cease-fire violations.[160] It was represented actively at SNC meetings in Phnom Penh by Khieu Samphan, its nominal president, it accepted UNHCR's repatriation programme and the presence of UNTAC civilians in contested areas,[161] it concurred in the SNC's accession to international human rights instruments[162] and it joined UNTAC's police training programme.[163] It even allowed a small number of UN military observers into its territory to reconnoitre regroupment and cantonment areas—although 'circumscribing their movements so closely that at times they seemed to be more hostages than monitors'.[164]

Akashi confirms that at the outset 'there was still a distinct impression' that the KR was willing to co-operate with UNTAC.[165] Some local KR commanders gave UNTAC military observers the impression that they were simply awaiting instructions on cantonment,[166] although it was not clear at the time whether UNTAC was being manipulated or whether there was disunity within KR ranks. It is now known that there was a high-level dispute within the group in May 1992 about whether it should withdraw from the Paris Accords. General Son Sen, one of two KR members of the SNC, was sacked as KR Commander-in-Chief and Defence Minister and his membership of the party's standing committee was terminated after he argued in favour of entering into Phase II of the Accords.[167]

[159] Warner (note 38), p. 3.

[160] Schear (note 92), p. 290.

[161] UN, First progress report of the Secretary-General on the United Nations Transitional Authority in Cambodia, UN document S/23870, 1 May 1992, p. 2.

[162] *Bangkok Post*, 24 Sep. 1992.

[163] *Bangkok Post*, 29 Nov. 1992. In Nov. 1992, 24 KR constables graduated.

[164] Asia Watch (note 85), p. 6. UNTAC personnel at KR headquarters at Pailin were essentially placed under house arrest and only allowed to shop at the market under armed escort after Jan. 1993: see *Bangkok Post*, 2 Feb. 1993.

[165] Akashi (note 7), p. 189.

[166] One of many instances, he says, where the UNTAC military was misled about KR intentions. See Akashi (note 7), p. 190.

[167] Thayer, N., 'Shake-up in KR hierarchy', *Phnom Penh Post*, 28 Jan.–10 Feb. 1994, p. 1.

4. Other pre-election aspects of implementation

I. Repatriation

One particularly impressive aspect of the UNTAC operation was the repatriation programme carried out by the Office of the UN High Commissioner for Refugees. It began inauspiciously, according to Nick Warner, with unrealistic and overly sophisticated planning and the failure of a $650 000 satellite photo-mapping of Cambodian territory.[1] It was also threatened in its early stages by the Cambodian factions' attempts to repatriate refugees to their own areas by force.[2] Fortunately they largely complied with subsequent UN warnings to desist.

The first convoy of returning refugees crossed into Cambodia on 30 March 1992 and within a year all the 360 000 refugees camped along the Thai–Cambodian border had been repatriated and the camps closed. The last of them, the infamous Site 2 at Aranyaprathet, once the largest Cambodian community outside Phnom Penh, was declared closed by the High Commissioner, Mrs Sadako Ogata, on 30 March 1993.[3] A remaining 600 or so refugees were deported by Thailand.[4] A small number of Cambodian refugees was also repatriated from Hong Kong, Indonesia, Malaysia, Singapore and Viet Nam.[5] The closure of the border camps effectively emasculated the support bases of the three anti-Government Cambodian factions in Thailand, ended the virtual imprisonment of thousands of innocent Cambodians, and removed a refugee problem which had had an impact throughout South-East Asia and further afield for Australia, Hong Kong, Japan and the USA.

A poignant tidying-up of the loose ends of history occurred when a group of 398 Vietnamese Montagnards calling themselves the *Front*

[1] Warner, N., 'Cambodia: lessons of UNTAC for future peacekeeping operations', Paper presented to an international seminar on UN Peacekeeping at the Crossroads, Canberra, 21–24 Mar. 1993, p. 12.

[2] *Asian Recorder*, no. 50 (9–15 Dec. 1991), p. 22049.

[3] *The Australian*, 31 Mar. 1993, p. 5.

[4] UNTAC XII, Information/Education Division, *Brief*, no. 31 (20 May 1993), p. 7.

[5] UN, Fourth progress report of the Secretary-General on the United Nations Transitional Authority in Cambodia, UN document S/25719, 3 May 1993, p. 20.

Uni de Libération des Races Opprimées (United Front for the Liberation of Oppressed Races), who had been living in the forests of Mondolkiri Province for more than 15 years since the end of the Viet Nam War, laid down their arms on 10 October 1992 and were transported to an UNTAC transit centre near Phnom Penh.[6] After being screened by US officials, all were accepted for resettlement in North Carolina.

A major problem encountered by UNHCR in resettling repatriated refugees was the lack of sufficient mine-free arable land in the areas where refugees were choosing to settle to enable the agency to grant them the two hectares per family originally promised.[7] Acting creatively and flexibly, UNHCR instead offered refugees a range of four options, a mix of cash, food rations, agricultural land, a household plot, housing kits and employment.[8] Most chose the cash option ($50 per adult and $25 per child). Jarat Chopra and colleagues note that this change of policy 'was positive and quickened the pace of repatriation'.[9] They none the less question the priority in effort and resources given to the repatriation of refugees compared with their resettlement and integration.

The Chopra report also expresses concern about the extent to which political factors speeded up the repatriation timetable. The UN view was that speed was essential to permit all Cambodians to participate in the electoral and peace processes and that most refugees were eager to return to Cambodia anyway—UNHCR was simply ensuring their orderly departure. In any event, since the repatriation programme was only possible because of a 'political' process, it is unrealistic to expect that politics would not have influenced the timetable.

Part of the reason for the success of the repatriation programme was the UNHCR's long involvement in and familiarity with the Cambodian refugee situation and its participation in the Paris Conference of 1989 and subsequent meetings. It was the first time in the UNHCR's history that a field operation was totally managed from the field, with authority and financial arrangements delegated to the

[6] UN, Third progress report of the Secretary-General on the United Nations Transitional Authority in Cambodia, UN document S/25124, 25 Jan. 1993, p. 18.

[7] Asia Watch, *Political Control, Human Rights, and the UN Mission in Cambodia* (Asia Watch: New York, Sep. 1992), p. 9.

[8] UNHCR, *Information Bulletin*, no. 7, Phnom Penh (28 Oct. 1992), p. 4.

[9] Chopra, J., Mackinlay, J. and Minear, L., Norwegian Institute of International Affairs, *Report on the Cambodian Peace Process*, Research Report no. 165 (NIIA: Oslo, Feb. 1993), p. 27.

Phnom Penh office.[10] General Sanderson adds that the programme was successful because the Thais wanted it to be.[11]

II. Electoral enrolment

Voter registration was planned for a three-month period beginning in October 1992.[12] It was to take place at fixed, temporary or mobile registration stations and, for military personnel, at cantonments[13] and be based on a demographic survey conducted by the AEPU, which had begun work in March 1992.[14] Over 450 UNVs acting as District Electoral Supervisors (DES) would supervise an estimated 4000 local registration personnel working in five-member teams which would canvass all districts in Cambodia.[15] Despite the tardy deployment of the Electoral Component, the three-month registration period began on 5 October 1992. It was later was extended to 31 January 1993, partly because it was discovered that the electorate was larger than expected,[16] but also because political problems were preventing access to the entire country, because the 1992 rainy season had left the roads in a poor state and because of the late enactment of the Electoral Law.[17]

The Electoral Law, submitted by UNTAC on 1 April 1992, was not approved by the SNC until 5 August, because of continuing Khmer Rouge objections.[18] Akashi persisted in seeking SNC agreement to the law although he could have promulgated it under his own authority in accordance with the Paris Accords. As finally agreed, the Electoral Law differed from the provisions of the Paris Accords in order to meet the concerns of the resistance factions that only 'Cambodian persons', meaning no Vietnamese, would be permitted to vote. While

---

[10] Warner (note 1), p. 12.

[11] Interview with the author, Canberra, 24 Mar. 1993.

[12] UN, *Yearbook of the United Nations 1992* (United Nations: New York, 1993), p. 244.

[13] Polling stations would be in the same location as registration stations.

[14] UN, *The United Nations in Cambodia: A Vote for Peace* (United Nations: New York, 1994), p. 74.

[15] UN, *The United Nations in Cambodia: A Vote for Peace* (note 14), p. 74.

[16] UN, *United Nations Focus: Cambodia: The United Nations Transitional Authority in Cambodia,* New York, Mar. 1993, p. 8.

[17] Maley, M., 'Reflections on the electoral process in Cambodia', ed. H. Smith, Australian Defence Force Academy, Australian Defence Studies Centre, *International Peacekeeping: Building on the Cambodian Experience* (ADSC: Canberra, 1994), p. 93.

[18] UN, Second progress report of the Secretary-General on the United Nations Transitional Authority in Cambodia, UN document S/24578, 21 Sep. 1992, pp. 3–4.

agreeing that recent Vietnamese settlers should not be entitled to vote, UNTAC refused to disenfranchise ethnic Vietnamese who had lived in Cambodia for several generations. Hence, while the Paris Accords had intended to enfranchise any person over the age of 18 born in Cambodia *or* with one parent born in Cambodia, the revised law restricted the franchise to those over 18 born in Cambodia *and* with at least one parent born in Cambodia. In addition, the law enfranchised all over 18, wherever born, who had at least one parent and one grandparent born in Cambodia. Any Cambodian resident overseas could vote at one of the three polling stations to be established in Europe, North America and Australia provided they had enrolled personally in Cambodia. In December, Akashi rejected further proposals from FUNCINPEC and the BLDP, which would have benefited them electorally, that all Cambodians resident overseas be allowed to vote, as well as 'Khmer Krom'—ethnic Khmers born or with a parent born in southern Viet Nam and now resident in Cambodia.[19]

Meanwhile voter registration proceeded spectacularly well, an incredible 4.6 million Cambodians having enrolled by the time voting rolls closed.[20] Their details were stored on a specially designed Khmer-language computer system. Thousands registered in Khmer Rouge-controlled areas, including KR soldiers and even some commanders, despite the fact that UNTAC's access to such territory was limited. 'At the end of the day', according to Reginald Austin, chief of the UNTAC Electoral Component, the KR 'was able to tolerate' the registration process.[21]

Credit for the success of the process must go to the Electoral Component, especially the AEPU. It drew skilfully on previous UN electoral experience in Namibia, the experience of national electoral organizations such as Elections Canada, and the options outlined by the Australian Electoral Commission in the Australian 'Red Book', some of which were based on Australian experience in Namibia.[22] The draft electoral law for Cambodia was largely based on the Election (Constituent Assembly) Proclamation which had governed

[19] UN, Fourth progress report of the Secretary-General, 3 May 1993 (note 5), p. 6.

[20] *Phnom Penh Post*, 29 Jan.–11 Feb. 1993, p. 16.

[21] *Phnom Penh Post* (note 20), p. 16.

[22] See Hayes, M., 'UN advance team sets stage for elections', *Phnom Penh Post*, 24 July 1992, p. 1; Chopra *et al.* (note 9), p. 25; and Sturkey, D., 'Cambodia: issues for negotiation in a comprehensive settlement', Paper presented to the Fourth Asia–Pacific Roundtable on Confidence Building and Conflict Reduction in the Pacific, Kuala Lumpur, 17–20 June 1990, pp. 7–8.

the conduct of the 1989 Namibian election and which had been accepted by the UN Security Council as embodying 'internationally recognized norms of electoral administration'.[23] This is one case where the UN learned from previous experience, something that cannot be said for other aspects of the Cambodian operation.

Warner describes the AEPU as 'one of the great successes of UNTAC'.[24] On the ground, the use of UN Volunteers proved to be inspired. They were able to penetrate remote areas in a non-threatening manner and quietly convince Cambodians of the value of enrolling and voting. Armed with materials produced by UNTAC's Information and Education Division—videos, cassettes, posters, brochures and comic books—civic education teams held community meetings in villages across the country. Austin also applauds the role played by the 4000 Khmer registrars, who 'were on the front lines of the registration process' and who 'did their job with real quality'.[25]

The distribution of laminated voter identity cards, complete with coloured photograph and fingerprint, also proved to be an incentive to enrol. For many Cambodians this was the most modern object they had ever owned, a portent of future national modernity, a harbinger of political change and a tangible sign of the UN's presence.[26] Asia Watch also notes, more soberly, that identity cards for many Cambodians signify both political protection and control.[27]

On 27 January 1993, 20 political parties which had previously registered provisionally for the election now did so officially by submitting a list of at least 5000 registered voters who were party members.[28] The KR's political party, whether under its old name, the PDK, or under its new name, the National Unity Party of Cambodia (NUPC), was not among them.

Sihanouk, meanwhile, toyed with the idea of a presidential election, before, during or after the general election. The new Secretary-General of the United Nations, Boutros Boutros-Ghali, endorsed holding the elections simultaneously, being aware of the costs involved.[29]

[23] Maley (note 17), p. 88.

[24] Warner (note 1), p. 7.

[25] *Phnom Penh Post* (note 20), p. 16.

[26] The SOC had also issued laminated identity cards with fingerprints and photographs: see Asia Watch (note 7), p. 21.

[27] Asia Watch, 'Cambodia: human rights before and after the elections', *Asia Watch*, vol. 5, no. 10 (May 1993), p. 36.

[28] UN, *United Nations Focus: Cambodia* (note 16), p. 8.

[29] *The Nation* (Bangkok), 30 Jan. 1993.

ASEAN, backed by China and Japan, proposed a presidential election before the general election to permit Sihanouk to unify the country under a quadripartite interim government.[30] The KR rejected the idea of a presidential election outright.[31] After obtaining the support of the Security Council for such a substantial alteration of the arrangements envisaged by the Paris Accords, Sihanouk abandoned the idea, presumably to allow him to seek to return to the throne at some future point.[32] On 8 March 1993 the Security Council unanimously passed a resolution endorsing an election for a constituent assembly only.[33]

III. The Supreme National Council

During UNTAC's tenure, the SOC held a total of 30 meetings, including special sessions in Tokyo and Beijing and working sessions at UNTAC headquarters which were chaired by Akashi in the absence of Prince Sihanouk.[34] At the signing ceremony for the Paris Accords the then UN Secretary-General, Perez de Cuellar, had expressed the hope that the SNC would go beyond being simply the embodiment of Cambodian sovereignty as provided for in the Accords and help 'fashion genuine national reconciliation based on the higher interest of Cambodia and its people'.[35] The Permanent Five, on the other hand, appeared to assume that factional differences would prevent the SNC from making any significant decisions.

Despite the high hopes of the UN Secretary-General, the SNC was in fact plagued from the outset by disagreement between the factions and Sihanouk's machinations to the point where Steven Solarz described it as a 'meaningless body' playing only a 'symbolic role'.[36] Akashi noted in mid-1993 that 'the SNC has not in reality exercised much power'.[37] It was left to UNTAC to make proposals and negotiate. This had, however, been anticipated by the Paris negotiators: it

[30] *The Nation* (Bangkok), 16 and 22 Jan. 1993.

[31] *Bangkok Post*, 14 and 17 Jan. 1993.

[32] *Far Eastern Economic Review*, 4 Feb. 1993, p. 21. By this stage a number of items for a presidential election had been ordered by the Electoral Component, and it was possible to cancel them. See Maley (note 17), p. 95.

[33] UN, Security Council Resolution 810, UN document S/RES/810, 8 Mar. 1993.

[34] UN, *The United Nations in Cambodia: A Vote for Peace* (note 14), p. 10.

[35] *Asian Recorder* (note 2), p. 22049.

[36] Quoted in Peang-Meth, A., 'The United Nations peace plan, the Cambodian conflict and the future of Cambodia', *Contemporary Southeast Asia*, vol. 14, no. 1 (June 1992), p. 38.

[37] Akashi, Y., 'The challenges faced by UNTAC', *Japan Review of International Affairs*, summer 1993, p. 187.

Table 4.1. Membership of the Supreme National Council, January 1993

HRH Prince Norodom Sihanouk	Head of State and President of the SNC
Hun Sen	CPP
Hor Namhong	CPP
Tea Banh	CPP
Dith Munty	CPP
Im Chhun Lim	CPP
Sin Sen	CPP
HRR Prince Norodom Ranariddh	FUNCINPEC
Sam Rainsy	FUNCINPEC
Son Sann	KPNLF/BLDP
Ieng Mouly	KPNLF/BLDP
Khieu Samphan	PDK
Son Sen	PDK

Source: UNTAC XII, Information/Education Division, *Brief*, no. 16 (25 Jan. 1993).

was the very reason why executive power was vested in UNTAC rather than the SNC. Had agreement between the factions been possible, the UN stewardship of Cambodia during the transitional phase would have been unnecessary.[38] As Richard Solomon told the US Congress in 1991, 'if the SNC is paralyzed' UNTAC would keep the process 'moving forward to that ultimate exercise of Cambodian sovereignty—free and fair elections'.[39]

What had not been anticipated by the Paris Accords was the determination of Akashi to engage the SNC in decision making and his refusal to use its impotence as 'a green light for his own independent action'.[40] He thus sought to avoid being seen as dictatorial, to strengthen UNTAC's hand in managing the peace process and to encourage the Cambodians to take responsibility for the future of their country. Paradoxically, this allowed the Permanent Five and other interested states to exercise 'much influence' over SNC decision making through their diplomatic representatives accredited to the Council.[41]

[38] Sturkey (note 22), p. 7.
[39] *Effects of the Continued Diplomatic Stalemate in Cambodia*, Hearing before the Subcommittee on East Asian and Pacific Affairs of the Committee on Foreign Relations, US Senate, 102nd Congress (US Government Printing Office: Washington, DC, 11 Apr. 1991). Statement of Richard H. Solomon. Reproduced in *East Asia and Pacific Wireless File* (United States Information Service, Canberra), 11 Apr. 1991.
[40] Ratner, S., 'The United Nations in Cambodia: a model for resolution of internal conflicts?', ed. L. F. Damrosch, *Enforcing Restraint: Collective Intervention in Internal Conflicts* (Council on Foreign Relations Press: New York, 1993), p. 255.
[41] Doyle, M. W., 'UNTAC: sources of success and failure', ed. Smith (note 17), p. 86.

The Khmer Rouge complained constantly that the SNC had not been given enough power to control the SOC Government. This was a deliberate misreading of the intent of the Paris Accords, which had considerably watered down, with the agreement of all parties, the original proposal for a governing coalition during the interim period. The emasculated SNC was never intended to 'govern' Cambodia. That was to be left to the individual Cambodian parties under the supervision and control of UNTAC. The irony is that, had the KR been more co-operative in the SNC, it could have exercised considerably more influence over the peace process than it did.

In July 1992 Boutros-Ghali attempted to breathe new life into the SNC by inviting it to meet more frequently and investing it with greater responsibilities—presumably in an effort to make Cambodians share the burden of difficult decisions facing UNTAC. This included involving the SNC in questions related to verification of the alleged presence of Vietnamese forces in Cambodia, as demanded by the KR, and the handling of cease-fire violations.[42] The SNC, however, remained as factious as ever.

IV. Control of the civil administration

In theory UNTAC was to 'supervise and control' the civil administrative structures of all four Cambodian parties. In practice only the SOC had a fully-fledged government with all its appurtenances: FUNCINPEC and the KPNLF had virtually none, while the Khmer Rouge refused to allow UNTAC access to its zones to determine the extent of its administrative control. Having the largest and most accessible civil administration, conveniently centralized in Phnom Penh, the SOC authorities naturally viewed UNTAC's attempts at control as discriminatory, which to a great extent they were. On the other hand, control of the SOC administration had been one of the major inducements for the KR to sign the Paris Accords, and UNTAC

---

[42] The SNC was also tasked with validating passports, travel documents and identity cards of Cambodians, meeting high-level guests and advising UNTAC on the issuing of visas to foreigners. See *East Asia and Pacific Wireless File* (United States Information Service, Canberra), 22 July 1992, p. 6. Technical Advisory Committees, chaired by senior UNTAC officials, had been established as subsidiary organs of the SNC to recommend specific courses of action. One initiative taken at the request of the SNC was the establishment of a 'hot line' linking Akashi and the UNTAC Military Commander with a representative of each of the four factions. See UN, First progress report of the Secretary-General on the United Nations Transitional Authority in Cambodia, UN document S/23870, 1 May 1992, pp. 2–3.

was obliged to make every effort to effect such control even if the KR would not permit itself to be similarly supervised and controlled. UNTAC's abject failure to establish even the degree of control over the SOC envisaged in the Paris Accords, let alone the higher standards demanded by the KR, fed KR propaganda about UNTAC's inadequacies and alleged bias and provided a convenient excuse for the guerrilla group to withhold further co-operation from the UN.

Most threatening to the neutral political environment that was required for the holding of the election was UNTAC's failure to assert adequate control over the SOC security forces and police. UNTAC, for instance, neglected to deal at an early stage with the dossiers that the Government kept on all citizens applying for identity cards, an important element of SOC political control.[43] The Hun Sen security forces reportedly went underground, using mobile telephones to communicate with each other. UNTAC investigators concluded that these forces were being used to 'try to reverse early opposition party successes, with a view to assuring a CPP electoral victory'.[44]

Shadowy groups called 'Reaction Forces' were allegedly tasked with the overt disruption of legitimate political activity through verbal and physical attacks on opposition party members and offices and by preventing opposition figures from canvassing freely. So-called 'A' Groups—including A-92 groups under the direct control of the Ministry of National Security, which was supposed to be under UNTAC supervision—were tasked with infiltrating opposition parties to create internal dissension and disruption. A secret UNTAC report later concluded that a directive from the SOC/CPP leadership to the Reaction Forces to curb excesses of violence had led to the decline in the level of political violence after January 1993, even though the overall frequency of incidents of intimidation changed little.[45] This implies either that UNTAC's intensified security efforts may not have been as effective as was thought at the time or that those running the

---

[43] Asia Watch (note 7), p. 3. Applicants for SOC identity cards were required to submit extensive biographical data on themselves and their extended family, including their political affiliations and activities in various periods of Cambodia's history. This information was recorded in a dossier kept in a government office at the district of residence, where it could be consulted by officials wishing to evaluate an individual's political background. See Asia Watch (note 7), p. 20.

[44] Thayer, N., 'Cambodia: shot to pieces', *Far Eastern Economic Review*, 20 May 1993, p. 11.

[45] The text of the report on undercover units formed by the Phnom Penh regime to oppose political rivals was published as part of Asia Watch, 'An exchange on human rights and peace-keeping in Cambodia', *Asia Watch*, vol. 5, no. 14 (23 Sep. 1993), Part II.

covert forces felt that such efforts might have led to their being unmasked if levels of violence were maintained.

As to UNTAC's supervision and control of the rest of the SOC administration, Akashi admits that it was 'less than effective at the beginning', while time was spent developing control concepts and methodologies and recruiting staff to accomplish this unprecedented task.[46] Lyndall McLean, Deputy Director of the Civil Administration Component, says that the lack of precedents was the biggest problem facing the Component: 'While the mandate clearly stated what we should be controlling, there were no guidelines as to *how* we should exercise control. The promised codes of conduct and guidelines . . . had to be drafted in the course of the mission. Numerous redrafts and refinements meant that many were not finalised. For the most part, those that were came too late.'[47]

Such difficulties were exacerbated by the archaic, heavily politicized and rudimentary Cambodian legal system with which the Component had to deal. The Component's tasks were rendered even more difficult by the familiar litany of poor advance planning, an acute lack of resources and staff, the recruitment of unqualified or unsuitable staff and the overlapping responsibilities of UNTAC's various components in the civil administration area. According to McLean, the Component recognized from the start that it would not be able to fulfil the mandate as written:

The extent of the mandate—with its demands to monitor all aspects of the media, scrutinise all sources of information, examine and control all financial records, judicial and administrative decisions, let alone deal with the queues of complainants lining up on a daily basis to present their allegations against officials—was totally unrealistic purely from the point of [view of] language skills alone.[48]

Hence, according to McLean, 'selective application was necessary'.

Despite UNTAC's protests and the occasional removal of recalcitrant officials, the SOC's co-operation with UNTAC's civil administrative control was, according to James Schear, never more than

---

[46] Akashi (note 37), p. 192.

[47] McLean, L., 'Civil administration in transition: public information and the neutral political/electoral environment', ed. Smith (note 17), p. 52.

[48] McLean (note 47), p. 52.

'partial and begrudging'.[49] The SOC particularly objected to UNTAC having *a priori* control or prior review of instructions and directives issued by its ministries. As a result UNTAC had particular difficulty implementing 'direct control' over the areas of foreign affairs and information.[50] One startling example of this was the negotiation by the Foreign Ministry of an aviation agreement with Malaysia without the involvement of the SNC or UNTAC.[51] Financial control, McLean says, 'failed abjectly', being beyond UNTAC's human resources.[52] While the Component had little effect on the content of public information disseminated by the four factions, it did, somewhat belatedly, improve access to the media for all opposition political parties.[53]

Overall control of the SOC administration also gradually improved, with UNTAC overseers eventually stationed not only in Phnom Penh but in all 21 provinces. Various bodies were established to facilitate the Component's work, including a Complaints Clarification Committee, joint Cambodian–UNTAC Implementation Teams to see that judicial or administrative decisions in line with the Paris Accords were actually carried out, and a Joint Standing Committee on Public Security to authorize action to be taken to improve security and public order.[54] In January 1993 UNTAC established a roving Control Team to conduct in-depth random checks to verify that at the provincial, district and village levels administration was being conducted in a politically neutral manner. Analysis of SOC documents to which the Team gained access indicated 'widespread and persistent use of the SOC state apparatus to conduct political campaign activities of the Cambodian People's Party (CPP)'.[55]

In late February 1993, the French head of UNTAC administration, Gérard Porcell, resigned, increasingly frustrated with UNTAC's failure to deal more firmly with the KR and the SOC. In an interview in

[49] Schear, J. A., 'The case of Cambodia', eds D. Daniel and B. Hayes, *Beyond Traditional Peacekeeping* (Macmillan: London, forthcoming, 1995), p. 292.

[50] UN, *The United Nations in Cambodia: A Vote for Peace* (note 14), p. 29.

[51] Doyle (note 41), p. 93.

[52] McLean (note 47), p. 56. Curiously, the assessments of Doyle and McLean are contradicted by the findings of a conference organized by the Institute for Policy Studies and UNITAR, the United Nations Institute for Training and Research, in Aug. 1994. It concluded that UNTAC was 'successful in carrying out its mandate in some ministries, e.g. Finance and Foreign Affairs, and less successful in the case of others, e.g. Interior, Security and Defence': see Institute for Policy Studies and UNITAR, International Conference on UNTAC: debriefing and lessons, Singapore, 2–4 Aug. 1994, p. 3.

[53] McLean (note 47), p. 56.

[54] McLean (note 47), p. 54.

[55] UN, Fourth progress report of the Secretary-General, 3 May 1993 (note 5), p. 14.

January Porcell had criticized the lack of enforcement powers: 'When we don't have the political will to apply the peace accords, the control cannot but be ineffective'.[56] According to Akashi, however, so great was UNTAC's intrusiveness by March 1993 that Hun Sen complained to him that its methods resembled those of Pol Pot.[57] McLean points to the near impossibility of accurately assessing or quantifying the real impact of UNTAC on the SOC administration, but notes that, while 'control' may not have been achieved, UNTAC 'certainly influenced the behaviour' of the SOC administrative structures.[58]

V. Human rights and law and order

Given the gross violations that had occurred under the Pol Pot regime, human rights were a critical issue in the Paris negotiations and remained so during the implementation period. Chopra and his colleagues argue that during the negotiation process the issue of human rights abuses in Cambodia was 'increasingly marginalized'.[59] However, the Paris Accords did require compliance by all parties with all 'relevant human rights instruments' and UNTAC was required to safeguard and promote human rights as an integral part of the peace process. In addition, the post-Accords planning for UNTAC considerably boosted its human rights responsibilities. According to the UN, the mandate of UNTAC in the area of human rights was the most extensive in the history of peacekeeping operations.[60]

Although slow in getting under way, once in place the UNTAC Human Rights Component did a commendable job in conducting human rights awareness courses, disseminating information, helping with the establishment of a wide range of Cambodian human rights groups (with a reported membership of 150 000),[61] investigating incidents and ensuring that Cambodia became party to international human rights conventions. In the promotion of human rights, as in other aspects of the civic education programme, creative use was

---

[56] *International Herald Tribune*, 27–28 Feb. 1993, p. 5; *Canberra Times*, 1 Mar. 1993, p. 12. Porcell later agreed to stay on through the May election: see UNTAC Electoral Component, Phnom Penh, *Free Choice: Electoral Component Newsletter*, no. 15 (12 Mar. 1993), p. 19.

[57] Akashi (note 37), p. 192.

[58] McLean (note 47), p. 57.

[59] Chopra *et al.* (note 9), p. 24.

[60] UN, *The United Nations in Cambodia: A Vote for Peace* (note 14), p. 54.

[61] Akashi (note 37), p. 195.

made of traditional Khmer cultural media—singers, puppets, comics and local artists—in addition to modern media such as radio, television and video.[62] In September 1992 UNTAC induced the SNC to adopt regulations relating to the judiciary and criminal law procedures during the transitional period before the election of a new Government.[63] It also established a Prisons Control Commission, leading to the release of political prisoners and prisoners detained without trial, improved gaol conditions and even the enrolment of prisoners to vote.

By October 1992, human rights officers had been deployed in all 21 provinces, but not in the KR zone.[64] In November 1992 an International Symposium on Human Rights in Cambodia was held in Phnom Penh, one of its main goals being to build international and regional support for Cambodian human rights groups in the post-UNTAC period. Another part of working towards long-term human rights protection in Cambodia was the establishment of a UN Human Rights Trust Fund, which was used to support international and regional non-governmental organizations (NGOs) in working with their Cambodian counterparts in a variety of education and training activities.[65]

Enforcement of human rights was, however, dilatory, sporadic and improvised. Under the Paris Accords UNTAC was invested with the responsibility for 'the investigation of human rights complaints, and, where appropriate, corrective action'.[66] Akashi interpreted the latter power narrowly, 'given the limited time period and resources and political and diplomatic constraints within which UNTAC functioned'.[67] He considered 'corrective action' to be largely limited to actions specified in the Paris Peace Accords, such as the dismissal or transfer of government officials. Even this he used sparingly, on the grounds that his 'use of threats to remove some of the government leaders

---

[62] For a full account of Human Rights Component activities to Jan. 1993, see UN, *The right of peoples to self-determination and its application to peoples under colonial or alien domination or foreign occupation: Situation in Cambodia*, Report of the Secretary-General, UN document E/CN.4/1993/19, 14 Jan. 1993.

[63] UN, *The United Nations in Cambodia: A Vote for Peace* (note 14), p. 28.

[64] UN, *United Nations Focus: Cambodia: The United Nations Transitional Authority in Cambodia*, New York, Feb. 1993, p. 7.

[65] UN, *The United Nations in Cambodia: A Vote for Peace* (note 14), p. 56.

[66] Agreement on a Comprehensive Political Settlement of the Cambodia Conflict, Paris, 23 Oct. 1991, Article 3. Published as an annex to UN document A/46/608, S/23177, 30 Oct. 1991; reproduced in the appendix to this volume.

[67] Letter from Akashi to Ms Sydney Jones, Executive Director, Asia Watch, New York, 11 June 1993, published in Asia Watch, 'An exchange on human rights and peace-keeping' (note 45), p. 4.

from their posts was often sufficient for them to mend their ways, making their actual removal unnecessary'.[68] In any event the SOC increasingly refused to remove officials at Akashi's request.[69]

The power to effect arrests or prosecute suspects was considered by Akashi to be the prerogative of the law enforcement authorities of the SOC and the other Cambodian factions in their respective territories.[70] 'Punishment', he believed, 'remains a State responsibility which the UN can promote or facilitate but cannot replace'.[71] The problem was that, despite the hundreds of investigations conducted by UNTAC, the SOC Government refused to make any arrests. The Preamble to the Criminal Law passed by the SNC recognized that UNTAC had 'the responsibility to assist in establishing such structures, laws and judicial institutions where they are absent and to improve them where they already exist in order to bring them up to the requirements of the Agreement'.[72] According to Mark Plunkett, UN Special Prosecutor in Cambodia, as far as the letter of the law was concerned there were 'adequate foundations upon which justice was to be established'.[73]

Human rights groups also contested Akashi's narrow view of UNTAC's powers and severely criticized UNTAC's performance.[74] Asia Watch argued that 'corrective action' encompassed a wide range of measures, including arresting and prosecuting perpetrators and publicly exposing and stigmatizing wrongdoers.[75] It alleged that UNTAC often viewed public condemnation of individuals responsible for abuses as being inimical to the peace process and peacekeeping. Chopra and his colleagues describe UNTAC's Human Rights Component as being 'marginalized'.[76] Plunkett cites lack of resources and competition within UNTAC for resources as part of the reason for the Component's difficulties: 'Although the Paris Agreement had many

---

[68] Akashi, Y., 'The challenges of peace-keeping in Cambodia: lessons to be learned', Paper presented to School of International and Public Affairs, Columbia University, New York, 29 Nov. 1993, p. 14.

[69] UN, *The United Nations in Cambodia: A Vote for Peace* (note 14), p. 30.

[70] Fernando, J. B., *The Inability to Prosecute: Courts and Human Rights in Cambodia and Sri Lanka* (Future Asia Link: Hong Kong, 1993).

[71] Letter from Akashi to Ms Sydney Jones (note 67).

[72] Quoted in Plunkett, M., 'The establishment of the rule of law in post-conflict peace-keeping', ed. Smith (note 17), p. 67.

[73] Plunkett (note 72), p. 67.

[74] Asia Watch (notes 7, 27). For the UN response, see UNTAC, Statement by the Director of UNTAC Human Rights Component on political violence, Phnom Penh, 23 May 1993; and Asia Watch, 'An exchange on human rights and peace-keeping' (note 45).

[75] Asia Watch, 'An exchange on human rights and peace-keeping' (note 45), p. 2.

[76] Chopra *et al.* (note 9), p. 25.

of the hallmarks of a Marshall Plan for Cambodia, it had to focus in the first instance on creating a political settlement rather than on nation-building'.[77]

Other members of the Component complained of failure on the part of UNTAC's leadership to lend political weight to their activities. There was in fact an ongoing dispute within UNTAC over the issue. Akashi refused to adopt the more 'radical' measures urged by the Component because, he said, of his concern about the UN's neutrality and because such measures 'seemed to be based on unrealistically high standards in the context of Cambodian reality'.[78]

The issue reached crisis proportions as a result of the escalating political and ethnic violence of November and December 1992. Foreign governments, NGOs, political parties and Cambodian human rights groups all protested to UNTAC about the situation. It was repeatedly raised in sessions of the SNC. Finally, matters came to a climax when Prince Sihanouk expressed his frustration at the situation.[79]

On 6 January 1993 Akashi announced the establishment, by administrative directive, of a Special Prosecutor's Office to press charges against and detain suspects for flagrant political and human rights crimes.[80] This step, described by Akashi as 'unusual and radical', could be regarded as verging on peace enforcement, since the CivPols, for the first time in a UN mission, now had the power of arrest.[81] Although such a function was not specifically envisaged in the Paris Accords, any question of the legality of Akashi's initiative was resolved by the Security Council's recognition of the Special Prosecutor's Office on 8 March.[82]

The next problem faced was the lack of a gaol, as the SOC gaol system was unlikely to be secure enough for SOC offenders and would be dangerous for others (even assuming that the gaols would accept custody of UNTAC's suspects in the first place). Ironically, given Cambodia's history, suitable detention facilities were in short supply.[83] In mid-1993 UNTAC finally established its own gaol (certified as four-star by the Red Cross). By then it had arrested two suspects

---

[77] Plunkett (note 72), p. 68.

[78] Akashi (note 68), p. 14.

[79] Fernando (note 70), p. 31.

[80] Akashi (note 68), p. 13.

[81] Warner (note 1), p. 13. This also raised the question of whether CivPols should be armed—they previously were not.

[82] UN, Security Council Resolution 810, UN document S/RES/810, 8 Mar. 1993.

[83] Plunkett (note 72), p. 68.

associated with the SOC and a member of the Khmer Rouge who had admitted helping to murder 13 civilians during one of the several massacres of ethnic Vietnamese that occurred in early 1993.[84]

The next challenge for UNTAC was the refusal of the SOC judiciary to bring those arrested and charged by UNTAC to trial. Plunkett was refused a hearing by the Phnom Penh Municipal Tribunal of Justice.[85] There were in any case serious doubts as to whether Cambodian courts had been appointed according to law and were therefore eligible to hear UN prosecutions.[86] A further difficulty was that the SOC courts represented the system of justice of only one of the four Cambodian factions, and could therefore be viewed as inherently biased. There was in fact no independent Cambodian judicial and penal system for UNTAC to call on. The Pol Pot regime had systematically removed most of Cambodia's judicial and legal expertise during its murderous reign, while the Hun Sen judiciary, such as it was, was an integral part of the executive and thereby subservient to government authority.[87]

While the Human Rights Component had conducted training courses for judges, defence lawyers and public prosecutors, UNTAC did not attempt to establish a complete new judicial system and the task was probably impossible given the time constraints. Foreign donors baulked at financing the construction of gaols. The idea of importing foreign judges and lawyers was never pursued, although it was considered within UNTAC in January 1993 when a list of retired judges from Australia, India, New Zealand, Papua New Guinea and other South Pacific states who were willing to serve on UN courts was prepared.[88] According to human rights groups, the failure to follow this through was the result of 'legalism' and timidity; according to Plunkett it was because of 'many other pressures on the mission'. Suspects detained by UNTAC were thus still awaiting trial

---

[84] *The Age* (Melbourne), 29 Apr. 1993, p. 10.

[85] Plunkett (note 72), p. 72.

[86] Plunkett (note 72), p. 73.

[87] By 1978 only 6–10 legal professionals remained in Cambodia. For a useful summary of the legal system under the Hun Sen regime see Chopra *et al.* (note 9), pp. 11–12. In 1994 it was estimated that Cambodia had only 15 trained lawyers: see Morgan Stanley, International Investment Research, *Cambodia: Dark History, Brighter Future*, Letters from Asia no. 6 (Morgan Stanley: Tokyo etc., 1994), p. 3.

[88] *The Nation* (Bangkok), 29 Jan. 1993; *The Guardian*, 4 Jan. 1993, p. 6; Plunkett (note 72), p. 75.

when UNTAC departed and prosecutions were left to be pursued by the new Government.[89]

VI. The economic situation

The economic impact of UNTAC, particularly in Phnom Penh, was decidedly mixed. The influx of large sums of US dollars, along with thousands of highly paid UN officials, soldiers and police, was accompanied by a dramatic drop in the value of the Cambodian currency, the riel, and its substitution in most transactions by the dollar. UNTAC boosted inflation by paying exorbitant rents for properties and by paying local employees wages far above the going rate. Robin Davies, Visiting Professor at the Institute of Economics in Phnom Penh, gives several reasons for UNTAC's impact on the riel, including 'cost push' (higher rents and wages paid by UNTAC and strains on local services) and 'demand pull' (including for locally available foods, such as rice and seafood, and trained staff).[90]

In January 1993 UNTAC belatedly recognized the need for more careful monitoring and handling of the economic situation by appointing the Director of the Rehabilitation Component, Roger Lawrence, as Economic Adviser to the SRSG.[91] In a report of December 1992 the Economic Adviser's Office denied the charge that UNTAC had been primarily responsible for high inflation, since UNTAC's outlays had 'not increased the cost of buying necessities for low income families'. It stated that inflation was the result of the SOC Administration's 'resort to the printing press to pay for an ever increasing budget deficit'.[92] The UN claimed that the 'fluctuation [*sic*] in the value of the riel was not due to UNTAC but to the lack of support for the currency by the three non-SOC factions'. In an attempt to reduce the price of rice, UNTAC introduced additional supplies onto the market.[93]

Davies concedes that a major problem was the SOC budget deficit, but argues that UNTAC should have propped the budget up with

[89] Plunkett (note 72), pp. 73, 75.
[90] Davies, R., 'UNTAC and the Cambodian economy: what impact?', unpublished manuscript, Phnom Penh, 14 Jan. 1993.
[91] UN, *The United Nations in Cambodia: A Vote for Peace* (note 14), p. 58.
[92] UNTAC Economic Adviser's Office, Impact of UNTAC on Cambodia's economy, Phnom Penh, 21 Dec. 1992, p. 1.
[93] UN, Fourth progress report of the Secretary-General, 3 May 1993 (note 5), para. 70 and p. 16.

financial support.[94] Here UNTAC faced an agonizing dilemma: it could either leave the SOC budget alone and see social services and government administration suffer further or provide budget support and risk new accusations from the KR of bias towards the Government. Since its choice of the former in any event helped validate KR propaganda to the effect that the SOC was collapsing and unable to look after the Cambodian people, UNTAC was in a no-win situation. UNTAC, however, also failed to help the SOC increase government revenue by other means such as reform of Cambodia's arcane customs and tax laws.[95]

A workshop held in July 1993 by the UN Research Institute for Social Development (UNRISD) in Geneva belatedly made a number of recommendations to UNTAC, including measures to minimize the distorting impact of aid; greater attention to budget support and reform of the tax regime; effective co-ordination between UNTAC and the hundreds of other agencies in Cambodia; improved impact assessments; better training and participation of Cambodians; improved data gathering and dissemination; and greater reliance on local knowledge and institutions.[96]

VII. Rehabilitation

Rehabilitation of Cambodia's infrastructure, ruined by decades of war, neglect and penury, was a massive undertaking. A World Bank mission visited in May 1992 and produced an 'Agenda for Rehabilitation and Reconstruction' which outlined Cambodia's development needs.[97] UNTAC could only hope to make a start on this agenda.

In April 1992 Boutros-Ghali launched an appeal to the international donor community to provide $593 million for Cambodia.[98] In June the Tokyo Ministerial Conference on the Rehabiliation and Reconstruc-

---

[94] This was done after the election and formation of a provisional government.

[95] This was achieved by the new Cambodian Government by the end of 1993: *Phnom Penh Post*, 31 Dec. 1993–13 Jan. 1994, p. 1.

[96] UN Research Institute for Social Development (UNRISD), The social consequences of the peace process in Cambodia, recommendations and findings from UNRISD Workshop, Geneva, 29–30 Apr. 1993 (UNRISD: Geneva, July 1993), pp. 2–3.

[97] UN, *The United Nations in Cambodia: A Vote for Peace* (note 14), p. 27.

[98] UN, *The United Nations in Cambodia: A Vote for Peace* (note 14), p. 27.

tion of Cambodia exceeded this amount by pledging $880 million[99] and established the International Committee on the Reconstruction of Cambodia (ICORC) as mandated by the Paris Accords.[100]

On the ground in Cambodia work moved slowly, partly because of the enormous infrastructural, supply and transport problems encountered. Engineering battalions from China, Japan and Thailand began repairing Cambodia's airfields, roads and bridges, although, according to one highly placed military source, much more could have been accomplished if the need for more such battalions had been foreseen. Commercial companies such as Australia's Telstra, which is handling Cambodia's international telephone communications, were contracted to repair or in some cases completely replace other elements of Cambodia's infrastructure.[101] The rehabilitation efforts in some instances had a significant effect in stimulating commercial activity in provincial towns.[102]

Quick Impact Projects (QIPs) were also initiated by UNHCR in cooperation with the UNDP and NGOs, in part to help communities absorb repatriated refugees.[103] Such projects included road and bridge repair, mine clearance, agricultural development, the digging of wells and ponds and the improvement and construction of sanitation, health and education facilities.[104] UNTAC's Military Component also worked closely with UNDP in administering or assisting reintegration and rehabilitation projects including those relating to functional literacy, entrepreneurship development, driver training and industrial employment.[105]

The rehabilitation operation, however, continued to suffer from logistical bottlenecks and financial delays. Some donors were reluc-

---

[99] The figure of US$880 million is somewhat misleading. Some pledges included commitments already made to the repatriation programme as well as funds that would be spent well beyond the transition phase in 1993. See Chopra *et al.* (note 9), p. 28.

[100] Declaration on the Rehabilitation and Reconstruction of Cambodia, para. 13. Published as an annex to UN document A/46/608, S/23177, 30 Oct. 1991; reproduced in the appendix to this volume.

[101] The Australian company Transfield, for instance, constructed six steel bridges under contracts issued by Australia, the UNDP and the Cambodian Roads and Bridges Department: see United Nations Association of Australia, Canberra, *Unity*, no. 41 (Aug. 1993).

[102] Schear (note 49), p. 297.

[103] For examples see *UNHCR Information Bulletin*, Phnom Penh, no. 7 (28 Oct. 1992), p. 8.

[104] UN, Fourth progress report of the Secretary-General, 3 May 1993 (note 5), p. 20.

[105] Sanderson, J. M. (Lt-Gen.), 'Preparation for, deployment and conduct of peacekeeping operations: a Cambodia snapshot', Paper presented at a conference on UN Peacekeeping at the Crossroads, Canberra, 21–24 Mar. 1993, pp. 7–8.

tant to proceed with funding development projects until after the election, a tendency sharply criticized by Akashi.[106] There were other difficult political considerations involved. It was logistically and administratively easiest to carry out reconstruction and rehabilitation in areas controlled by the SOC, especially in and around Phnom Penh, but to do so on too grand a scale would have fed KR accusations of UNTAC bias. The KR routinely obstructed the work of the SNC/UNTAC Technical Advisory Committee, which was required to approve development plans, to such an extent that such plans were subsequently cleared with the factions individually rather than discussed in the whole Committee.[107] The World Bank cancelled its planned $63 million loan because of KR and FUNCINPEC objections that it would have helped the SOC Government.[108] On the other hand, the Asian Development Bank did approve a $67.7 million loan in November 1992.[109]

Chopra and his colleagues allege that the Rehabilitation Component took too 'relaxed' an approach to co-ordinating various rehabilitation efforts, reflecting either the wishes of donors, deliberate UNTAC strategy, the limitations on its staff or the fact that of all UNTAC components it was the only one with no provincial representatives.[110] Davies blames 'donor political considerations, a lack of UNTAC boldness, and the complexities of UN bureaucratic control'.[111] Australian journalist Sue Downie argues that planning for rehabilitation and reconstruction would have been enhanced by the taking of a census during voter registration.[112]

As of June 1993, 51 rehabilitation and development projects worth $407 million had been approved and more than $230 million disbursed by UNTAC.[113] These projects included loan assistance, UNDP and United Nations Children's Fund (UNICEF) programmes, bilateral support of training institutions and a range of infrastructure, agricultural and social sector activities. The Rehabilitation Component

[106] *The Nation* (Bangkok), 26 Feb. 1993.

[107] Chopra *et al.* (note 9), p. 29. The KR's attitude reportedly improved after the pledge of $880 million by the Tokyo Ministerial Conference: see UN, Second progress report of the Secretary-General, 21 Sep. 1992 (note 18), p. 12.

[108] *The Nation* (Bangkok), 6 Mar. 1993.

[109] *The Nation* (Bangkok), 29 Jan. 1993.

[110] Chopra *et al.* (note 9), p. 29.

[111] Davies, R, 'Blue berets, green backs, what was the impact?', *Phnom Penh Post*, 22 Oct.–4 Nov. 1993, pp. 16, 17, 19.

[112] Private communication with the author, Phnom Penh, May 1993.

[113] UN, *The United Nations in Cambodia: A Vote for Peace* (note 14), p. 58.

reported that it maintained a data base of commitments, disbursements and needs, which helped to ensure that projects complemented rather than duplicated each other. Regular meetings were held with the donor community to keep them informed and to establish post-UNTAC mechanisms for co-ordinating aid. The Component also co-ordinated implementation of the moratoria on the exploitation of various natural resources and chaired the SOC Technical Advisory Committee on the Management and Sustainable Exploitation of Natural Resources.[114]

One controversy that raged towards the end of UNTAC's tenure was over how much equipment it would leave behind to assist in Cambodia's rehabilitation. Ultimately, while UNTAC did leave some resources and equipment behind, large amounts were shipped out to other UN peacekeeping operations in Somalia and the former Yugoslavia or to the UN storage facility at Pisa in Italy.[115]

VIII. Mine awareness and de-mining

Studded with mines of every variety from the past 25 years, Cambodia, as Asia Watch notes, has the 'dubious distinction of having the highest proportion of amputees of any population in the world'.[116] The de-mining of the country is a long-term operation involving the mapping of the thousands of square kilometres of minefields containing an estimated 6–10 million mines of various types,[117] the training of de-miners and the creation of national mine awareness. Experts have concluded that it will take 30–40 years to rid Cambodia of most of its mines, and that the country may never be completely clear of them.[118]

UNTAC's de-mining programme was subject to much criticism, some justified, some of it based on a misunderstanding of the scale of the undertaking.[119] Despite numerous studies warning of the extent of

---

[114] UN, *The United Nations in Cambodia: A Vote for Peace* (note 14), p. 59.

[115] UN, Further report of the Secretary-General pursuant to paragraph 7 of Resolution 840 (1993), UN document S/26360, 26 Aug. 1993, p. 4; *Phnom Penh Post*, 11–24 Jan. 1994, p. 17.

[116] Asia Watch (note 7), p. 61.

[117] Cambodian Mine Action Centre, Cambodia's future (CMAC: Phnom Penh [late 1992]), p. 1.

[118] Burslem, C., 'When the office is a minefield', *Phnom Penh Post*, 13–26 Aug. 1993, p. 13.

[119] For an excellent consideration of the complexities of the issue see Aitkin, S., Getting the message about mines: towards a national public information strategy and program on mines and mine safety, vol. 1: Report (UNESCO: Phnom Penh, Sep. 1993).

the problem[120] and the inclusion of de-mining in UNAMIC's mandate, the programme start was delayed because of lack of funds[121]—the fault of donor countries rather than the UN. The UN essentially provided only 'seed money' for the programme, which was reliant on voluntary donations from international organizations and individual states. In addition, most troop contributing countries were unwilling to authorize their forces to participate in the dangerous business of de-mining. The prevailing attitude, according to Asia Watch, seemed to have been that Cambodians had created the problem and should therefore shoulder the responsibility for solving it.[122] However, those advocating the diversion of scarce resources to the 'quick fix' of immediate mine clearance by foreigners tended to overlook the exponential and longer-term benefits of investing those resources in training Cambodians for mine clearance. It has also been argued that by conducting highly publicized mine-clearance programmes, organized, funded and carried out by foreigners, the UN risks creating disincentives for local parties in civil war situations to stop planting mines and engage or assist in their removal.[123]

In June 1992 the de-mining activities of UNTAC were taken over by the Cambodian Mine Action Centre (CMAC), established by the SNC. Based in Phnom Penh, it was principally staffed by foreign military personnel. By March 1993 CMAC had trained more than 1600 Cambodian de-miners and established 11 mine clearance training centres; by May it had compiled 80 per cent of a country-wide minefield data base, and by June it had assembled 40 de-mining teams, 10 mine marking teams and 10 explosive ordnance disposal (EOD) teams.[124]

One consequence of the failure of demobilization in Phase II of the peace plan was that large numbers of military personnel were not available for de-mining: their familiarity with the types and locations

---

[120] See Asia Watch and Physicians for Human Rights, *Land Mines in Cambodia: The Coward's War* (New York, Sep. 1991). The report (p. 2) warned that 'if the international community waits until a peace settlement is in place before it begins a mine surveying and eradication program, there will be a disaster. Refugees spontaneously returning will fall victim to mines, the clearance program in designated resettlement areas may be too hastily and cheaply put together, and the health care system will be unable to deal with the injuries'.

[121] Asia Watch (note 7), pp. 61–62.

[122] Asia Watch (note 7), p. 62. ·

[123] Presentation by Steve Biddle, Institute for Defense Analyses, Alexandria, Va., at SIPRI on 20 Oct. 1994.

[124] Cambodian Mine Action Centre, Phnom Penh, *CMAC Bulletin*, vol. 1, no. 1 (21 Apr. 1993), p. 3; UN, *United Nations Focus: Cambodia* (note 16), p. 10.

of mines they themselves had sown would have been especially useful. Initially there were problems in paying Cambodian de-miners because of lack of funds (subsequently they were well paid by Cambodian standards) and because senior officers were demanding bribes before allowing their troops to participate. A further problem was that more new mines were sown after the peace agreement was concluded and UNTAC arrived than were being removed.[125] There was also resistance to mine-clearing operations in areas where conflict was continuing.[126] In addition, mechanical de-mining equipment proved unsatisfactory in Cambodia's tropical conditions. CMAC eventually imported dogs to help human de-mining teams.

The most significant accomplishments in de-mining, according to Asia Watch, were along major highways, in association with road repair, some of which was done by Thai and Chinese military engineers or by a commercial Thai company funded by US aid.[127] Other de-mining activities were carried out by NGOs.[128]

By the time UNTAC concluded its mission, about 300 000 square metres of countryside had been cleared, 11 000 mines deactivated and nearly 12 000 pieces of unexploded ordnance removed.[129]

[125] *Phnom Penh Post*, vol. 1, no. 3 (7 Aug. 1992), p. 3; and Burslem (note 118), p. 13. Asia Watch reported in Sep. 1992 that in Kompong Thom province the KR and SOC armies continued to lay mines after UNTAC's arrival. See Asia Watch (note 7), p. 48.

[126] Burslem (note 118), p. 13.

[127] Asia Watch (note 7), p. 63.

[128] Such as the HALO Trust, the Mine Awareness Group, Norwegian People's Aid and Handicap International. See UN, Fourth progress report of the Secretary-General, 3 May 1993 (note 5), p. 13.

[129] UN, *The United Nations in Cambodia: A Vote for Peace* (note 14), pp. 38–39.

5. The 1993 election

The election campaign began officially on 7 April 1993 and would last until 19 May, when a four-day cooling-off period would begin.[1] Polling would take place from 23 to 28 May. The start of the official election campaign was postponed by UNTAC from the original tentative date of early March because of the poor security situation and because the election itself was now to be held later than originally envisaged.[2]

Despite the ban on unofficial campaigning provided for in the Electoral Law,[3] such activity, particularly on the part of the CPP, had begun as soon as the election dates were confirmed in October 1992. After complaints from FUNCINPEC, the BLDP and others that the SOC had 'jumped the gun' on electioneering, access to Radio UNTAC and other UNTAC media outlets was granted to all political parties. The SOC/CPP authorities had consistently refused the opposition political parties access to government radio and television networks, and the SOC Customs had seized components destined for FUNCINPEC's own television station. (They were later released under UNTAC pressure.) All print shops were controlled by the SOC and refused to print opposition election material. UNTAC successfully negotiated access to print shops for all parties and established sites for poster display.[4]

Once officially under way, the election campaign was marred by numerous violent incidents, murders, intimidation and undemocratic practices. These mostly took place out of sight or in remote areas beyond UNTAC's reach. Such occurrences, which clearly jeopardized the prospects of the election being free and fair, were mostly perpetrated by SOC government personnel against FUNCINPEC and to a lesser extent against the BLDP. Cambodians were also subjected to

---

[1] In the event, with the CPP dominating access to the state radio, this cooling-off period did not work well: see Roberts, D., 'Democratic Kampuchea', *Pacific Review*, vol. 7, no. 1 (1994), p. 106.

[2] UN, Report on the implementation of Security Council Resolution 792 (1992), UN document S/25289, 13 Feb. 1993, pp. 9–10; *Phnom Penh Post*, 26 Feb.–11 Mar. 1993, p. 1.

[3] *Phnom Penh Post*, 26 Feb.–11 Mar. 1993, p. 1.

[4] McLean, L., 'Civil administration in transition: public information and the neutral political/electoral environment', ed. H. Smith, Australian Defence Force Academy, Australian Defence Studies Centre, *International Peacekeeping: Building on the Cambodian Experience* (ADSC: Canberra, 1994), p. 56.

rumour campaigns about the lack of secrecy of the ballot, about the fingerprinting procedure and, from the Khmer Rouge, about the futility of the whole election process. SOC employees were reportedly warned that they would lose their jobs if they voted against the government, while other voters were reportedly offered large sums by FUNCINPEC (which was financed by US and expatriate Cambodian sources) to vote for them. UNTAC warned that efforts to maintain a neutral political environment had been hampered by 'the surveillance conducted by the authorities of the Cambodian parties at all levels aimed at identifying political opponents and the harassment and intimidation of perceived opponents'.[5]

On the other hand an estimated 1500 political meetings and rallies, involving close to one million people, took place without a single incident.[6] The 20 registered political parties established 2037 offices throughout Cambodia.[7] Cambodians were swamped with electoral and party political information, including radio and television broadcasts, on a scale never before seen in the country. Despite not being fully operational until more than a year after the signing of the Paris Accords, Radio UNTAC was particularly effective in disseminating electoral information, eventually becoming the most popular radio station in the country (confounding those at New York headquarters who had opposed its establishment).[8] By 19 April it was broadcasting 15 hours a day. UNTAC 'Round Table' videos featuring the political parties answering questions about how they would solve the country's problems were widely circulated in towns and villages. The Civil Administration Component organized weekly co-ordination meetings with the political parties, round table meetings and joint rallies to keep the political dialogue open.

The security situation in the countryside, however, remained worrying. The most politically sensitive casualty of the entire UNTAC mission occurred on 8 April, one day into the election campaign, when a Japanese DES and his Khmer interpreter were killed, allegedly by the

---

[5] UN, Fourth progress report of the Secretary-General on the United Nations Transitional Authority in Cambodia, UN document S/25719, 3 May 1993, p. 23.

[6] UN, *UN Chronicle,* Sep. 1993, p. 32; UN, *The United Nations in Cambodia: A Vote for Peace* (United Nations: New York, 1994), p. 31.

[7] UNTAC XII, Information/Education Division, *Brief,* no. 31 (20 May 1993), p. 2.

[8] Akashi, Y., 'The challenges faced by UNTAC', *Japan Review of International Affairs,* summer 1993, p. 195; and Sanderson, J. M. (Lt-Gen.), 'A review of recent peacekeeping operations', Paper presented to the Pacific Armies Management Seminar (PAMS) XVIII Conference, Dacca, Jan. 1994, p. 7.

KR, in Kompong Thom province.[9] Japan had endured an agonizing constitutional debate over the dispatch of its peacekeepers to Cambodia—the first time Japanese troops had been sent abroad since World War II.[10] It was also the largest financial contributor to UNTAC. The Japanese Defence Minister threatened to withdraw all Japanese personnel from Cambodia if any more were harmed.[11] Such a withdrawal, if other military contingents had followed suit, would have led to the complete unravelling of UNTAC. The Japanese volunteer's death, the sixth among UN personnel in two weeks, coincided with a visit by Boutros Boutros-Ghali to Phnom Penh, in which he expressed the UN's determination to stay the course.[12] At what the UN describes as perhaps the most dramatic meeting of the SNC, on 10 April Akashi solemnly warned Khieu Samphan that:

No party or group has the right to stop these elections. The Cambodian people have made it clear that they want an election, and UNTAC is going to give them one. That election will begin on 23 May, and all the preparations for it are going forward as I speak. There is no question of cancellation or postponement . . . [The Khmer Rouge] and its leaders will be held directly responsible for all the attacks it has carried out against UNTAC so far, as well as any further attempts it makes to disrupt the election by killing or injuring UNTAC personnel . . . Let us be clear what this means: nothing less than international and internal isolation. The world will not forgive the Party of Democratic Kampuchea for disrupting the Cambodian elections. There should be no more sanctuaries for that Party, and no more chances.[13]

Concerns about an all-out Khmer Rouge assault on the electoral process were heightened in mid-April by the sudden withdrawal of its representative from Phnom Penh and closure of its office.[14] The group claimed that it no longer felt safe in the capital. It did not, however, withdraw formally from the SNC and continued to claim that it was still abiding by the Paris Accords, although it said that it would not

---

[9] It was later discovered that Mr Nakata had been killed by an officer of the SOC armed forces over the issue of electoral jobs. See UN, Fourth progress report of the Secretary-General, 3 May 1993 (note 5), p. 26; *The Australian*, 29 Apr. 1993, p. 8.

[10] Takahara, T., 'Postwar pacifism in Japan and the new security environment: implications for participation in UN peacekeeping operations', Paper prepared for New York State Political Science Association 47th Annual Meeting, Hunter College, New York, 23–24 Apr. 1993.

[11] *The Age* (Melbourne), 10 Apr. 1993, p. 1.

[12] *Canberra Times*, 9 Apr. 1993, p. 9.

[13] UN, *The United Nations in Cambodia: A Vote for Peace* (note 6), p. 10.

[14] *Bangkok Post*, 15 Apr. 1993.

accept the election result.[15] UNTAC headquarters in Phnom Penh was fortified and 100 French Foreign Legionnaires were deployed to the capital to provide extra security.[16]

Australia became only the second contributing country, after Japan, publicly to equivocate about its determination to stay in Cambodia when Foreign Minister Evans declared that Canberra would consider withdrawing Australian troops if there were a 'major, systematic, full-frontal assault on the UN peacekeepers or on other parties to the peace accords'.[17] Evans later 'clarified' his statement, saying that there was 'no question of Australia taking any unilateral action to withdraw, however much the situation might deteriorate'.[18] Further confusion was created when he announced, prematurely, that Australian communicators, along with other UN personnel, would be withdrawn from Pailin, the Khmer Rouge's designated headquarters. The UN denied that withdrawal was imminent, while Evans rejected allegations that his statement had put Australian forces in danger.[19] On 30 April UNTAC did withdraw from Pailin, on the same day that a Colombian CivPol was killed in Kompong Speu province.[20]

As fear of KR attacks mounted, panic set in among UNTAC personnel in outlying areas, especially among the UNVs, triggering demands for greater military protection.[21] Uneven application by UNTAC military units of the UN's rules of engagement had created uncertainty among UNTAC civilians, some complaining that the military seemed overly passive, even to the point of failing to defend UNTAC storage areas. They also complained of communication difficulties between them and the military, while some, especially those from Western countries, expressed doubts about the validity of the election process given the security situation.[22] Others were concerned at the apparent lack of evacuation plans in the event of the election

[15] *Canberra Times*, 16 Apr. 1993, p. 8; *The Australian*, 19 Apr. 1993, p. 6; *Sydney Morning Herald*, 19 Apr. 1993, p. 8.

[16] *Canberra Times*, 5 Apr. 1993, p. 8.

[17] *The Age* (Melbourne), 12 Apr. 1993, p. 1 and 21 Apr. 1993, p. 1.

[18] *Canberra Times*, 22 Apr. 1993, p. 12.

[19] *The Age* (Melbourne), 22 Apr. 1993, p. 1.

[20] UN, Fourth progress report of the Secretary-General, 3 May 1993 (note 5), p. 10; UN, *The United Nations in Cambodia: A Vote for Peace* (note 6), p. 32.

[21] Magstad, M. K., 'UN workers in Cambodia give ultimatum', *Washington Post,* 16 Apr. 1993.

[22] Akashi, Y., 'The challenges of peace-keeping in Cambodia: lessons to be learned', Paper presented to School of International and Public Affairs, Columbia University, New York, 29 Nov. 1993, p. 5.

going badly wrong. The head of the UN Volunteer Service in Geneva telephoned Akashi to say that she would be compelled to withdraw them from Cambodia if there were another death among them.[23]

These events caused serious divisions within UNTAC, since the military argued that its principal role was to protect the electoral 'process' and that they lacked the resources to protect all UN personnel in the field. The Japanese volunteer, just before his death, had appealed for protection to Indonesian troops, who told him that this was not their role.[24] General Sanderson claims that the standard operating procedures relating to self-defence in fact permitted defence of 'any one going about their legitimate business under the Paris Agreement'.[25] He admits, however, that he had to work hard to convince UNTAC civilians that they would be protected by the UNTAC military, especially since not all the national contingents seemed prepared to ensure their protection.

All UNVs in western and central Cambodia were withdrawn from the countryside and counselled in Phnom Penh while an inter-component security plan was devised involving armed escorts and ready reaction forces.[26] Even this caused difficulties, since the UNVs were instructed not to tell local villagers why they were being withdrawn, making the re-establishment of relationships of trust that much more difficult when they returned two weeks later. Most UNVs did return to their posts, although by the beginning of May some 60 'sceptics' (as Akashi described them) had returned home.[27] This occurred just as 1000 International Polling Station Officers (IPSOs) from 43 countries were arriving from training in Thailand to assist in supervising the polling and counting.[28]

International diplomatic efforts were resumed in April to find ways of saving the peace plan from what looked like impending disaster. On 23 April all the signatory states to the Paris Accords, including China, issued a declaration of support for the election and for UNTAC.[29] In late April China, France and Japan attempted to organ-

[23] Akashi (note 22), p. 6.

[24] *Sydney Morning Herald*, 9 Apr. 1993, p. 5.

[25] Sanderson (note 8), p. 8.

[26] UN, Fourth progress report of the Secretary-General, 3 May 1993 (note 5), p. 8.

[27] Akashi (note 22), p. 5; UN, *The United Nations in Cambodia: A Vote for Peace* (note 6), p. 31.

[28] UN, *The United Nations in Cambodia: A Vote for Peace* (note 6), p. 88.

[29] Australian Minister for Foreign Affairs, Statement on Cambodia, News Release no. M66, 24 Apr. 1993.

ize a crisis meeting of the SNC. This took place without the participation of the KR in Beijing on 6 May. The three Cambodian parties represented agreed to proceed with the election despite pressures within both FUNCINPEC and the BLDP to withdraw.[30]

The military situation in the field, meanwhile, continued to be 'marked by persistent, but low-intensity and small-scale, violations of the cease-fire, particularly in the central and western parts of the country'.[31] On 3 May, 100 KR soldiers mounted a politically significant, although militarily inept, attack on the city of Siem Reap near Angkor Wat. Three days later the KR attacked a civilian train travelling from Phnom Penh to Battambang, killing 30 passengers and wounding about 100.

On 5 May a Japanese policeman was killed and several wounded in an ambush blamed on the KR.[32] Japanese police were reported subsequently to have left their posts and fled to Thailand or Phnom Penh.[33] The head of the 75-man Japanese police contingent reportedly requested withdrawal from Cambodia but was refused by the Japanese Government.[34] At the same time, Akashi reportedly refused Tokyo's requests to have the police at least withdrawn to Phnom Penh.[35] He also asked the Japanese engineering battalion to assist in transporting ballot boxes during the election, under escort by French troops for extra security.[36] Facing extreme political pressure, Japanese Prime Minister Kiichi Miyazawa was eventually forced to declare that he would consider 'suspending operations' by all Japanese personnel in Cambodia if the situation deteriorated.[37] This was widely perceived as a threat to withdraw.

On 21 May the KR killed two Chinese peacekeepers and wounded three in an attack on a government police station in Kompong Cham.[38] Polish and Pakistani peacekeepers also came under attack. China

---

[30] *Sydney Morning Herald*, 29 Apr. 1993, p. 11; *The Independent*, 7 May 1993, p. 10; Tan Lian Choo, 'The Cambodian election: whither the future?', eds T. Carney and Tan Lian Choo, Institute of Southeast Asian Studies, *Whither Cambodia? Beyond the Election* (ISEAS, 1994); Frost, F., Institute of Southeast Asian Studies, 'Cambodia: from UNTAC to Royal Government', *Southeast Asian Affairs 1994* (ISEAS: Singapore, 1994), p. 84.

[31] UN, Fourth progress report of the Secretary-General, 3 May 1993 (note 5), p. 9.

[32] *Financial Times*, 6 May 1993, p. 4.

[33] Thayer, N., 'Cambodia: shot to pieces', *Far Eastern Economic Review*, 20 May 1993, p. 11.

[34] *International Herald Tribune*, 10 May 1993, p. 5.

[35] *International Herald Tribune*, 12 May 1993, p. 1.

[36] *Bangkok Post*, 24 May 1993, p. 5.

[37] *Bangkok Post*, 25 May 1993, p. 6.

[38] *Bangkok Post*, 24 May 1993, p. 4.

requested a meeting of the Security Council, which called on all parties to refrain from violence during the election.[39] A specific reference to KR culpability was, however, removed at Chinese insistence. China expressed its satisfaction with the vote, saying that 'the Chinese position is clear. We will not put up with any faction provoking civil war. All the factions should abide by UN rules so early peace can be achieved'.[40]

Fears remained right up to the election that the KR would mount a major assault, perhaps even on Phnom Penh itself. Information available to the Military Component indicated that polling stations would be attacked with mortar, rocket and small arms fire and that approach roads would be mined.[41] While there was a small KR base about 20 km to the north of Phnom Penh from which it might have been possible to launch sporadic attacks on the capital, these would have been militarily ineffective. Akashi recalls that he was more concerned about 'media-created events and perceptions than the prospects of actual attacks on the elections'.[42] UN headquarters in New York ordered families of UNTAC's international staff to leave the country until after the election—a move which did nothing to boost morale in Cambodia.[43]

On the eve of the election UNTAC issued a report which estimated that since 1 March there had been 200 deaths, 338 injuries and 144 abductions as a result of pre-election violence.[44] Victims included UNTAC personnel, ethnic Vietnamese, other civilians and members of political parties. The Khmer Rouge was alleged to be responsible for most of these, including 131 deaths, 250 injuries and 53 abductions. According to the report, the SOC and its forces were responsible for 15 deaths and nine injuries. Twenty serious attacks on other political parties were attributed to the SOC and its agents. Dennis McNamara explained that the figure did not represent the totality of

---

[39] UN, Security Council Resolution 826, UN document S/RES/826, 20 May 1993.

[40] *Bangkok Post*, 24 May 1993, p. 4. The KR denied responsibility, saying that the Chinese contingent was among an 'overwhelming majority' of peacekeepers from Third World countries who 'want the implementation of the Paris agreements': see *Bangkok Post*, 25 May 1993, p. 8.

[41] UN, *The United Nations in Cambodia: A Vote for Peace* (note 6), p. 3.

[42] Akashi (note 22), pp. 3–4.

[43] *The Independent*, 21 May 1993, p. 13. This was reportedly done without much consultation on the basis of an article in the *New York Times* predicting violence during the polling period. See Ledgerwood, J. L., East–West Center, 'UN peacekeeping missions: the lessons from Cambodia', Asia Pacific Issues no. 11 (East–West Center: Honolulu, Mar. 1994), p. 9.

[44] *Bangkok Post*, 24 May 1993, p. 4.

political violence and human rights abuses, but only those for which UNTAC had been able to identify the culprits. He noted, however, that 'some major political parties have clearly exaggerated the incidents and attributed responsibility to other parties without proper grounds for doing so'. As to whether this affected the ability of UNTAC to conduct an election, McNamara argued that the level of violence 'is only one factor, albeit an important one, to be taken into account in the final assessment of the overall freeness and fairness of the election'.[45]

In the event, the voting period of 23–28 May was the greatest triumph of the entire Cambodia operation. Cambodians turned out in their millions to cast their ballots freely and enthusiastically, despite KR threats to disrupt the poll, intimidation by the SOC Government, early monsoon rain in many parts of the country and poor transport and infrastructure. Confounding allegations by some Western observers that foreign democratic practices were being foisted on an unwilling and puzzled populace, an estimated 89.5 per cent of the 4.6 million enrolled voters cast their vote. Invalid votes were less than 4 per cent of the total number cast.[46] This demonstrated a level of civic commitment that puts many developed democracies to shame.[47] The result is even more remarkable when it is recalled that few Cambodians were old enough to remember Sihanouk's electoral exercises and that the Pol Pot and Hun Sen 'elections' were not multi-party.[48] Moreover, an estimated 52 per cent of Cambodian men and 78 per

---

[45] *Bangkok Post*, 24 May 1993, p. 4.

[46] Akashi (note 22), p. 6. One observer attributes this to the fact that the CPP drew the number one spot on the ballot paper, while FUNCINPEC drew number 11 in the middle of the middle row. Both spots were easy to explain to their supporters. FUNCINPEC showed its supporters how the ballot sheet should be folded in half and then in half again—where the two folds crossed was where the block was to be marked. See de Beer, D.,—Netherlands Institute of International Relations, 'Observing the elections in Angola (Sept. 1992) and in Cambodia (May 1993)', eds D. A. Leurdijk *et al., Case Studies in Second Generation United Nations Peacekeeping*, Clingendael Paper (NIIR: The Hague, Jan. 1994), pp. 48–49.

[47] Cambodia's voter turnout is exceeded by Namibia's in the UN-sponsored election there in 1989: see Fortuna, V. P., 'United Nations Transition Assistance Group', ed. W. J. Durch, *The Evolution of UN Peacekeeping: Case Studies and Comparative Analysis* (St Martin's Press for The Henry L. Stimson Center: Washington, DC, 1993), p. 371. In Australia, where voting is compulsory, the turnout is also usually around 96%. The turnout in the May 1994 South African election was 86%: see *Time*, 30 May 1994, p. 9.

[48] Chopra, J., Mackinlay, J. and Minear, L., Norwegian Institute of International Affairs, *Report on the Cambodian Peace Process*, Research Report no. 165 (NIIA: Oslo, Feb. 1993), p. 12.

cent of women are considered illiterate.[49] UNTAC personnel, hard-headed journalists and old Cambodia watchers alike were surprised and moved by this display of determination and bravery on the part of millions of ordinary Cambodians.

Polling took place in a remarkably free and fair atmosphere.[50] Forty-six per cent of registered voters (2.2 million people) voted on the first day, in an almost carnival atmosphere.[51] At the central polling station in Phnom Penh, located at the Olympic Stadium, long queues formed from the early morning on, as they did elsewhere in the country. The entire period of polling was one of the quietest and least violent in Cambodia for years.[52] While some military incidents did occur in KR-contested areas, the anticipated KR assault on the election process and the rumoured terrorist attacks on the capital did not materialize. Some problems were encountered with seals breaking on ballot boxes, but the polling was generally efficient and well organized. Measures to prevent multiple voting included the UN identity card and the use of a chemical marker on the voter's person visible only under ultra-violet light and impossible to remove for a week.[53]

Some 1400 fixed polling stations operated, as well as 200 mobile ones in remote areas.[54] Fixed polling was concentrated in the first three days, while mobile polling took place over all six days.[55] Although UNTAC had cancelled voting at some 400 polling stations prior to the polls opening because of the security situation, and several more were closed during the poll because of scattered violence, these areas were later covered by mobile polling stations, some of which pushed at the edges of Khmer Rouge zones.[56] Polling stations

[49] UN World Population Fund, *World Population Report* (United Nations: New York, 1993), cited in de Beer (note 46), pp. 47–48.

[50] For the official report on the election see UN, Report of the Secretary-General on the conduct and results of the election in Cambodia, UN document S/25913, 10 June 1993.

[51] UN, *United Nations Focus: Cambodia: Cambodia Election Results*, New York, July 1993, pp. 1–2.

[52] *Bangkok Post,* 26 May 1993, p. 1.

[53] *Bangkok Post,* 27 May 1993, p. 7.

[54] UN, *United Nations Focus: Cambodia* (note 51), pp. 1–2.

[55] UN, Fourth progress report of the Secretary-General, 3 May 1993 (note 5), p. 5.

[56] *Bangkok Post,* 24 May 1993, p. 1 and 26 May 1993, p. 1. Akashi records that UNTAC's Electoral Component, 'stubbornly perfectionist' to the end, resisted the reduction in the number of polling stations from 1900 to 1400: see Akashi (note 22), p. 12. Mobile polling stations consisted of UN trucks which served as polling booths. In some cases they were protected by a cordon of UNTAC military and weaponry. In at least one case an ambulance was on standby: see *Bangkok Post,* 27 May 1993, p. 7. One of the mobile polling stations was

Table 5.1. The May 1993 election results

Party	Number of seats	Percentage of valid votes cast
FUNCINPEC	58	*45.47*
Cambodian People's Party (CPP)	51	*38.23*
Buddhist Liberal Democratic Party (BLDP)	10	*3.81*
Molinaka Party	1	*1.37*
Other parties	–	*11.12*

Source: *Phnom Penh Post*, 18 June–1 July 1993, p. 4; UN, *United Nations Focus: Cambodia: Cambodia Election Results*, July 1993, p. 2.

were also located in New York, Paris and Sydney to allow overseas Cambodians to vote, although only a few hundred votes were cast abroad.

In the final days of polling Cambodia witnessed the amazing spectacle of Khmer Rouge soldiers coming into polling stations to vote.[57] Having failed to disrupt the election campaign or prevent the election taking place and having witnessed a massive turnout, the KR appeared divided over its next move. While its radio station denounced the election as a farce, a KR official in Pailin was reported as saying that the KR would recognize the government if the 'Sihanoukist party' came to power, since Prince Sihanouk had promised that the KR could have a role in any coalition government formed under his leadership.[58] The UN confirmed that the KR had sent hundreds of officials and civilians living in western and north-western guerrilla zones to the nearest polls with instructions to vote for FUNCINPEC.[59]

On 29 May a relieved Yasushi Akashi declared the election 'free and fair',[60] an assessment supported by the Inter-Parliamentary Union

forced out of an area in Siem Reap on 27 May after an attack by the KR wounded a peacekeeper and three others: see *Bangkok Post*, 28 May 1993, p. 6.

[57] A not insignificant number of KR officials and soldiers had registered: see Schear, J. A., 'The case of Cambodia', eds D. Daniel and B. Hayes, *Beyond Traditional Peacekeeping* (Macmillan: London, forthcoming 1995), p. 293.

[58] *Bangkok Post*, 27 May 1993, p. 7.

[59] *Bangkok Post*, 27 May 1993, p. 1.

[60] *Phnom Penh Post*, 6–12 June 1993, p. 3. See also UN, Report of the Secretary-General on the conduct and results of the elections in Cambodia, 10 June 1993 (note 50), Annex II.

and other foreign observers.[61] Raoul Jennar commented that Cambodians 'were able to make a free and fair choice'.[62] Counting was allowed to proceed the same day. It was done only by international personnel and on a provincial basis in order to avoid the identification of voting patterns in particular areas or villages. According to Michael Maley, UNTAC's Senior Deputy Chief Electoral Officer, this latter procedure, which was widely publicized beforehand, was welcomed by voters and 'may well have played a critical role in reassuring [them] of their safety as participants in the electoral process'.[63]

The election results in terms of numbers of seats in the 120-seat Constituent Assembly and percentages of valid votes cast (votes were cast for parties rather than individual candidates) are shown in table 5.1.[64] The extent of the support for parties other than the CPP—61.77 per cent of valid votes cast—was striking.[65] The UN Security Council endorsed the election result on 15 June.[66] Bizarrely, the KR later announced that it also accepted the results.[67]

The reasons for the smooth functioning of the electoral process are many.[68] The efficiency and capability of UNTAC's Electoral Component and the effectiveness of the UNVs were major factors. The presence of the IPSOs contributed both to the effectiveness and to the legitimacy of the election.[69] The UNTAC military and CivPols were also crucial in protecting polling stations and voters and in transporting and guarding ballot boxes. Both Karl Farris and Michael Maley credit the security plan developed by the Military Component with

---

[61] Akashi (note 22), p. 6.

[62] Quoted in Roberts (note 1), p. 106.

[63] Maley, M., 'Reflections on the electoral process in Cambodia', ed. Smith (note 4), p. 97.

[64] For an excellent summary of the main Cambodian political parties, their platforms and personalities, see Thayer, C., 'Who will run Cambodia?', *Business Times*, 10 Feb. 1993. For an analysis of the reasons fror FUNCINPEC's victory, see Roberts (note 1), pp. 106–107. The remainder of this article, which alleges an UNTAC/US conspiracy to deprive the SOC of electoral victory, is tendentious. Julio Jeldres argues, equally implausibly, that 'from the beginning the UN favoured the Hun Sen government' and 'adopted a hostile stance towards the KR . . .': see Jeldres, J. A., 'The UN and the Cambodian transition', *Journal of Democracy*, vol. 4, no. 4 (Oct. 1993), p. 107.

[65] Maley (note 63), p. 97.

[66] UN, Security Council Resolution 840, UN document S/RES/840, 15 June 1993.

[67] UN, Report of the Secretary-General pursuant to paragraph 7 of Resolution 840 (1993), UN document S/26090, 16 July 1993, p. 2.

[68] One of the few hiccups in the process was the slow response of UN members to UNTAC's request for fingerprint and handwriting experts to check tendered ballots. See UN, Fourth progress report of the Secretary-General, 3 May 1993 (note 5), p. 8.

[69] UN, Fourth progress report of the Secretary-General, 3 May 1993 (note 5), p. 8.

much of the success of the balloting.[70] It gave the UNTAC military and police the task of providing security in the immediate vicinity of polling stations, while the military elements of the three co-operating Cambodian factions assumed responsibility for security in the areas under their control. This was not foreseen in the Paris Accords, but it allowed UNTAC to 'use the armed elements of three factions against the fourth in a way that did not jeopardize [the UN's] impartiality'.[71]

The high turnout may be explained, first, by the fact that voters were patently tired of both the Hun Sen Government and the Khmer Rouge. Akashi speculates that the ill-judged KR attacks prior to the election, which killed considerable numbers of civilians and which suggested that the faction did not care about ordinary Cambodians, may have encouraged a higher turnout.[72] Second, it is clear in retrospect that the voter education campaign, in particular that conducted by the UNVs and Radio UNTAC, had worked. As a consequence Cambodians really believed that the vote was secret and that the election could bring peace and/or offer them a genuine voice in choosing their government. According to General Sanderson there was clear evidence that Radio UNTAC, by itself, was instrumental in bringing many of the KR rank and file back into mainstream politics.[73] Third, there was also the novelty and excitement of an event that had been heralded for so long and which, in the context of everyday village life, must have seemed irresistibly alluring. Some Cambodians clearly came to the polling stations out of curiosity and found themselves drawn into the process. Fourth, Prince Sihanouk's arrival home in Phnom Penh from Beijing the day before the election began and his call for a peaceful atmosphere seem also to have calmed tensions and contributed to the large turnout. Also critical was the solid support for the electoral process demonstrated by the international community, although that would have had greater impact in Phnom Penh than in the villages. Finally, a key factor in the success of the election was the courage, dedication and enthusiasm of the Cambodian people, many of whom risked their lives or livelihoods to assist in the registration

---

[70] Farris, K., 'UN peacekeeping in Cambodia: on balance, a success', *Parameters*, vol. 24, no. 1 (1994), p. 46; Maley (note 63), p. 96.

[71] Farris (note 70), p. 47.

[72] Akashi (note 8), pp. 197–98.

[73] Sanderson (note 8), p. 7.

process, participate in the campaign, work at polling booths and cast their ballots.[74]

The election had clearly sidelined the Khmer Rouge. As the US Ambassador, Charles Twining, somewhat too gleefully declared: 'This simply leaves the Khmer Rouge in the forest, and I hope they enjoy the forest'.[75] Why they had not attempted to disrupt the election remained something of a mystery. As Akashi said, 'their minds are unfathomable'.[76]

A first possibility is that they were incapable of causing major disruption. James Schear notes that their field posture was not optimal for doing this.[77] It is clear, however, that the killing of only a handful of election volunteers or observers or a major assault on a couple of polling stations could have sown panic and triggered a chain reaction that might have caused the election process to implode. This suggests that the KR deliberately refrained from disrupting the polls, adopting a 'wait-and-see' attitude. It may have calculated that a FUNCINPEC victory would give it a place in a coalition government as Sihanouk and Ranariddh had long intimated.

Craig Etcheson, Executive Director of the Campaign to Oppose the Return of the Khmer Rouge, offers a second theory: that the KR had already infiltrated FUNCINPEC and was therefore quite willing to encourage a vote for it.[78] This does not explain why the KR took so long to vote and then did so only sporadically rather than *en masse*.

A third suggested explanation is that outside pressure was paramount. China appears to have been the key player. Not only did it refrain from vetoing a Security Council resolution which imposed an oil embargo on the KR,[79] but it also publicly announced in April 1993 that it would not support any Cambodian party that resumed the civil war.[80] China also reportedly warned Khieu Samphan during his visit to Beijing in late May not to disrupt the election.[81] China's support for a strongly worded Security Council resolution on the eve of the elec-

---

[74] Over 50 000 Cambodians were employed during the voting period to assist in the election: see UN, *The United Nations in Cambodia: A Vote for Peace* (note 6), p. 74.

[75] *International Herald Tribune*, 24 May 1993, p. 2.

[76] *Bangkok Post*, 26 May 1993, p. 3.

[77] Schear (note 57), p. 293.

[78] Etcheson, C., 'Pol Pot and the art of war', *Phnom Penh Post*, 13–26 Aug. 1993, p. 7.

[79] Akashi (note 8), p. 198.

[80] *International Herald Tribune*, 23 Apr. 1993, p. 2.

[81] Akashi (note 8), p. 198. China abstained on Security Council Resolution 792, in part because it set a deadline of 31 Jan. for KR participation in the election.

tion was no doubt partly motivated by the fact that the KR had accidentally killed several Chinese peacekeepers in attacks on SOC forces.[82] According to Akashi, China had also been convinced of the KR's bad faith after tortuous but unsuccessful diplomatic efforts were made to meet the KR's legitimate demands and bring it back into the peace process.[83] A Chinese official in Phnom Penh reportedly denied that China had any role in restraining the KR, but said rather that the KR realized that it risked alienating the Cambodian people if it disrupted the election.[84] This may have been because, as Ambassador Twining speculated, 'The KR realized that there was a groundswell among the people for the election'.[85] Akashi intimates that pressure by Japan, the USA and other Western countries on Thailand to sever its remaining links with the KR along the border areas may have had a further dampening effect on KR enthusiasm for disrupting the election.[86]

A fourth possibility is that the Khmer Rouge had no plan but was simply muddling through what was a completely novel situation. This assumes either that Pol Pot's acuity had failed him or that the KR was internally divided and/or lacked central control over its disparate constituency. In this situation, lacking guidance and in some cases accountability, local commanders simply did what they thought would please the hierarchy—in some cases voting, in others attacking polling stations, in most just doing nothing. This, combined with pressure from China on the KR leaders, seems the most likely explanation for the guerrilla group's puzzling behaviour.

Given the level of intimidation and harassment by the KR on the one hand and the SOC Government on the other, questions remain as to how fair the election result was. While it is impossible to determine what made individual voters vote the way they did, it is clear that some would have been influenced by bribes, by rumours that the ballot would not be secret or by threats that they would lose their government jobs if they voted against the government. David Chandler notes of the elections held in the country from the 1940s to the 1960s that 'many peasants voted as they were told to vote by

[82] *Beijing Review*, 17–23 May 1993, p. 7; Akashi (note 8), p. 198; Schear (note 57), pp. 304–305.
[83] Akashi (note 8), p. 191.
[84] Hornik, R., 'Cambodia: the people take charge', *Time* (Australia), 7 June 1993, p. 37.
[85] Hornik (note 84).
[86] Akashi (note 8), p. 198.

people whom they habitually obeyed'.[87] He also remarks that Cambodians 'show a disconcerting ability to organize their followers' to vote in election, which may partly account for the large turnout in the UNTAC-organized poll.

Asia Watch claimed that the 'neutral political environment' which was supposed to be the precondition for holding the election was 'entirely absent' and that the election itself was conducted in a 'virtual state of war'.[88] This contention is exaggerated. While the environment was not entirely neutral, neither was it so far compromised that an election was pointless. Political rallies had been held freely and uninterruptedly with the participation of all parties, electoral information was widely disseminated, and the ballot itself remained secret and secure. Moreover, although UNTAC was not able to ensure a neutral pre-poll environment, it was able to ensure neutrality inside the polling booth and was able to convince the Cambodian people of that.[89] As Akashi was only too well aware, Cambodians' 'authoritarian political tradition' and 'proclivity to using force in settling conflicts' were impossible to change overnight, but this should not have deterred UNTAC from making a start.[90]

UNTAC further stated in its defence that, while the human rights situation was far from satisfactory, it was only one element to be considered in deciding whether a democratic election was possible and should have proceeded. This is almost certainly a reference to the fact that so much momentum had been built up for the election that it would have been difficult to cancel or postpone it, that the expense would have been inordinate and that it would have been a victory for the Khmer Rouge and other anti-democratic forces if the UN had succumbed to their pressure.

The international community has accepted the results of elections in countries like India, Russia, South Africa and Thailand, all of which have questionable human rights records and far from perfect electoral processes. Because of the international scrutiny under which Cambodia has lived for so long there was a danger of insisting on electoral

---

[87] Chandler, D. P., *A History of Cambodia*, 2nd edn (Westview Press: Boulder, Colo., 1993), p. 175.

[88] Asia Watch, 'Cambodia: human rights before and after the elections', *Asia Watch*, vol. 5, no. 10 (May 1993), pp. 1, 8.

[89] Schear (note 57), p. 298.

[90] Akashi (note 8), p. 200.

standards that would not be expected elsewhere. As Boutros-Ghali put it:

given Cambodia's recent tragic history, it would probably be neither realistic nor fair to hold it to prevailing standards in stable democratic countries. Conditions for an election in Cambodia have never been perfect and may not be so for a long time, any more than they are in many other countries. That is no reason to hold back an election which, after all, is not the end of the process of Cambodia's renewal but the beginning.[91]

Certainly the May 1993 election was the freest and fairest in Cambodia's history and the first in Cambodia since 1955 to be openly contested by a range of political parties.[92] For the United Nations, the election provided incontestable proof that it could effectively and efficiently organize an electoral process in the most trying and dangerous of circumstances. The May 1993 election was thus a boost to the confidence of Cambodians and the UN alike.

---

[91] UN, Fourth progress report of the Secretary-General, 3 May 1993 (note 5), p. 29.
[92] Chandler (note 87), p. 189.

6. Formation of a new government and other post-election developments

The stunning success of the election was immediately overshadowed by the ensuing dangerous politicking and manœuvring of various political factions.[1] On 4 June 1993 Prince Sihanouk attempted to stage a 'constitutional coup' by moving to form a 'government' of his own, but abandoned this in the face of opposition from FUNCINPEC and the UN.[2] Sihanouk then moved to construct a government of national unity. Neither of these developments had been foreseen in the Paris Peace Accords and they took foreign governments and UNTAC by surprise. Their main concerns were that a Sihanouk-led interim government would not reflect the outcome of the election, that it would outmanœuvre the Constituent Assembly, and that it would become a permanent fixture, defeating the democratic intentions of the framers of the Paris Accords.[3] UNTAC was reportedly divided about whether or not to encourage a Sihanouk-led coalition.[4]

Further uncertainty was created when Hun Sen alleged that the UN and foreign countries had engineered a conspiracy of massive electoral fraud which had deprived his party of victory.[5] This was followed by an attempted territorial 'secession' by a CPP faction led by Deputy Prime Minister Prince Norodom Chakrapong, one of Prince Sihanouk's sons.[6] Hun Sen added the hint of a military coup to this volatile mix. Nate Thayer described the situation thus: 'Behind the scenes a Byzantine soap opera centred around a feuding royal family came to the surface. It pitted two half-brother princes [Ranariddh and

---

[1] For details of post-election developments, see Carney, T. and Tan Lian Choo, Institute of Southeast Asian Studies, *Whither Cambodia? Beyond the Election* (ISEAS: Singapore, 1994); Frost, F., Institute of Southeast Asian Studies, 'Cambodia: from UNTAC to Royal Government', *Southeast Asian Affairs 1994* (ISEAS: Singapore, 1994); and Vickery, M., Institute of Southeast Asian Studies, 'The Cambodian People's Party: where has it come from, where is it going?', *Southeast Asian Affairs 1994* (ISEAS: Singapore, 1994).

[2] *The Nation* (Bangkok), 5 June 1993. The US Mission circulated a 'non-paper' outlining its objections: see Roberts, D., 'Democratic Kampuchea?', *Pacific Review*, vol. 7, no. 1 (1994), p. 106.

[3] Thayer, N., 'Split emerges in Core Group', *Phnom Penh Post*, 28 June–1 July 1993, p. 3.

[4] Schear, J. A., 'The case of Cambodia', eds D. Daniel and B. Hayes, *Beyond Traditional Peacekeeping* (Macmillan: London, forthcoming 1995), p. 299.

[5] Thayer, N., 'Sihanouk back at the helm', *Phnom Penh Post*, 18 June–1 July 1993, p. 1.

[6] *Phnom Penh Post*, 28 June–1 July 1993, p. 1. Chakrapong and an associate had been fined by UNTAC for holding an election rally in defiance of an UNTAC directive not to do so: see *Bangkok Post*, 26 May 1993, p. 9.

Chakrapong], bitter enemies for years, vying for political power and the allegiance of their father, who himself was obsessed with avenging his disposition from power in a military coup more than twenty years ago'.[7]

Akashi was criticized for remaining silent on these developments for more than 48 hours and for his statement on 15 June that he 'highly appreciated the efforts of Hun Sen'.[8] Akashi was himself, however, working behind the scenes, convincing Prince Ranariddh to issue a message of reconciliation to the CPP and urging the 'sulking' CPP leaders Hun Sen and Chea Sim to avoid reckless action.[9] Meanwhile UNTAC investigated the CPP's allegations, establishing an internal committee of investigation for the purpose, and found them to be baseless.[10]

By mid-June the situation had dramatically improved as a result of delicate statecraft and diplomatic pressure, the latter involving UNTAC and key foreign parties to the Paris Accords. Agreement was reached between Sihanouk, FUNCINPEC and the CPP on the formation of a Provisional National Government of Cambodia (PNGC)—in UN parlance an Interim Joint Administration (IJA)—which would include representatives of all the four parties which had won seats in the Assembly. The Khmer Rouge would not be represented. The UN provided emergency financial assistance of $10 million to the IJA, much of it contributed by Japan,[11] to support the unification and restructuring of the administration, police and military of the three major participating parties.[12]

The UN and the Core Group countries,[13] conscious that the IJA was a departure from the Paris Accords and that Cambodia still lacked a

[7] Thayer (note 5), p. 1.

[8] Thayer (note 5).

[9] Akashi, Y., 'The challenges of peace-keeping in Cambodia: lessons to be learned', Paper presented to School of International and Public Affairs, Columbia University, New York, 29 Nov. 1993, p. 7. This is confirmed by Schear (note 4), p. 296.

[10] Akashi, Y., 'The challenges faced by UNTAC', *Japan Review of International Affairs*, summer 1993, p. 196.

[11] *Canberra Times*, 28 July 1993.

[12] UN, Financing of the United Nations Transitional Authority in Cambodia: report of the Secretary-General, UN document A/48/701, 8 Dec. 1993, p. 7.

[13] The five permanent members of the Security Council, Australia, Canada, Germany, India, Indonesia, Japan and Thailand. It constituted an informal grouping of countries which maintained contact in New York, through diplomatic channels and through their embassies in Phnom Penh, in order to keep up pressure on the Cambodian parties to comply with the Paris Accords and resolve any other implementation difficulties. In Phnom Penh they were known

new democratic constitution, attempted to play down its long-term significance, describing it as simply 'an attempt to fuse three of the existing administrative structures, and as a manifestation of the common desire for peace, stability and national reconciliation'.[14] To emphasize this, the SNC remained in place as the embodiment of Cambodian sovereignty. Akashi notes that, while in terms of democratic principles the formation of the IJA was an unorthodox arrangement, 'We have to admit the practical wisdom of combining the "new wind", represented by the victorious FUNCINPEC, consisting mostly of upper and upper middle class intellectuals aspiring to the restoration of the monarchy, with the experience and power of CPP, which is authoritarian but has 14 years of administrative experience, with much of the army and police under its control'.[15]

Just as important as a symbol of Cambodian hopes for stability was the reinstatement of Prince Sihanouk as Head of State by the Constituent Assembly at its inaugural session on 14 June. In a stage-managed act of acclamation, moved by Prince Ranariddh, the Assembly declared the 1970 *coup d'état* by Lon Nol against Sihanouk null and void. Even more astonishing, the Assembly granted Sihanouk 'full and special powers . . . in order that he may save [the] nation'.[16] Further Sihanoukist revivalism followed. The Assembly restored the pre-coup Cambodian flag and national anthem (with a few changes to the lyrics) and returned Cambodia's national day to 9 November, the day on which the country gained independence from France in 1953.[17]

The Provisional Government was accepted by the Constituent Assembly on 1 July and sworn in the following day. Its composition was bizarre even by Cambodian standards: Prince Ranariddh and Hun Sen became 'Co-Presidents' and Co-Ministers for Defence and the Interior and Public Security.[18] The remaining Cabinet posts were divided between the four parties in the Assembly, with the CPP obtaining slightly more than FUNCINPEC but the latter gaining the

as the Extended Permanent Five, the EP5. See Evans, G., 'Peacekeeping in Cambodia: lessons learned', *NATO Review*, vol. 42, no. 4 (Aug. 1994), pp. 24–27.

[14] UN, Report of the Secretary-General pursuant to paragraph 7 of Resolution 840 (1993), UN document S/26090, 16 July 1993, p. 2.

[15] Akashi (note 9), p. 8.

[16] *Arms Control Today*, July/Aug. 1993, p. 21; *International Herald Tribune*, 15 June 1993, p. 7.

[17] The new Government, no doubt at Sihanouk's behest, soon applied for membership of the association of French-speaking countries, the *Francophonie*. See *Phnom Penh Post*, 13–26 Aug. 1993, p. 8.

[18] *Phnom Penh Post*, 2–15 July 1993, p. 3.

key Ministries of Finance and the Economy and of Foreign Affairs. The CPP, crucially, gained the Ministries of Information and Justice. Each CPP minister had a FUNCINPEC deputy and vice versa.[19] The political balance was roughly the same as that of the new Government installed later following agreement on the Constitution.[20]

These developments had a settling effect on the country. Cambodia's economic indicators began to improve and the value of the riel rose. This helped garner international support and encourage investors and foreign aid donors to begin contributing to Cambodia's rehabilitation. ICORC held its first meeting in Paris to consider disbursement of what remained of the $880 million pledged to Cambodia in Tokyo in 1992.[21] The integration of the former factional military forces into the unified Royal Cambodian Armed Forces (RCAF) also began under the auspices of the MMWG. France signed a controversial agreement with the Provisional Government to provide military training while Australia and Indonesia offered technical assistance.[22]

Perhaps most important, the formation of the coalition government further isolated the Khmer Rouge, which seemed to fall into both strategic and tactical disarray after the election. On the one hand it seized the historic Preah Vihear temple near the Thai border (reportedly with Thai help) and attacked Cambodia's only functioning railway, causing numerous civilian casualties. At the same time Khieu Samphan and other KR officials held inconclusive talks with Sihanouk and UNTAC in an attempt to salvage some role for the guerrilla group in the new Cambodia, even offering to integrate its forces into the new national army if it was given a place in government.[23] Prince Sihanouk, however, soon retreated from his proposal to include the KR, saying that it could only be involved in an 'advisory' capacity. Recognizing that the election had weakened the Khmer Rouge's negotiating hand, Sihanouk declared that the group had

---

[19] See Frost (note 1), p. 86.

[20] See Frost (note 1), p. 113.

[21] Australian Department of Foreign Affairs and Trade, *Insight*, 30 Aug. 1993, p. 7.

[22] *Phnom Penh Post*, 30 July–12 Aug. 1993 and *International Defense Review*, no. 7 (1993), p. 531. France and Australia were reportedly competing over which would lead in assisting in the reorganization of the Cambodian armed forces. See *Jane's Defence Weekly*, 31 July 1993, p. 11.

[23] In the face of accusations that it was interfering in Cambodia's political reconciliation process, the USA backed away from its initial declaration that it would find it difficult to provide aid to a Cambodian government that included the KR.

'suffered a historic defeat, and they will not recover from such a blow'.[24] The KR had originally said that it would be content with an advisory role; now, however, its conciliatory attitude did not last long and the talks were scuttled. Low-level cease-fire violations and military activity continued, mainly initiated by the KR.[25] As Raoul Jennar has pointed out, fighting never completely ceased during UNTAC's tenure.[26]

The task of writing Cambodia's new Constitution, meanwhile, began on 14 June but proceeded slowly. By 30 June the Constituent Assembly had only just elected its President and two Vice-Presidents and adopted its Rules of Procedure.[27] Two permanent committees were then established, the Committee on Drafting the Constitution, under the chairmanship of BLDP leader Son Sann, and the Committee on Rules of Procedure. The Assembly was faced with the seemingly impossible deadline of 15 September, the date when a new government was scheduled to be inaugurated under the Constitution. UNTAC's Human Rights Component provided a model constitution for the Assembly's use, UNTAC initiated constitutional discussions in the SNC and organized seminars, and foreign experts acted as consultants.[28] UNTAC prudently took a hands-off approach to the drafting process, insisting that it was a job for Cambodians, but at the request of the PNGC provided 'technical' comments on the draft constitution, especially in regard to strengthening the human rights provisions.[29] There was early criticism, particularly from human rights and religious groups, that the drafting was being done behind closed doors, without input from the broader Cambodian public; the Paris Accords, however, specified confidentiality until the draft was ready for presentation to the full Assembly. In the meantime a coalition of individuals and NGOs called *Ponleu Khmer* succeeded in popularizing debate on the constitution in Phnom Penh and 11 provinces.[30]

---

[24] Hornik, R., 'Cambodia: the people take charge', *Time* (Australia), 7 June 1993, p. 37.

[25] UN, Report of the Secretary-General, 16 July 1993 (note 14), p. 2.

[26] Jennar, R. M., 'UNTAC: "international triumph" in Cambodia?', *Security Dialogue*, vol. 25, no. 2 (1994), p. 146.

[27] UN, Report of the Secretary-General, 16 July 1993 (note 14), p. 1.

[28] For details see UN, Fourth progress report of the Secretary-General on the United Nations Transitional Authority in Cambodia, UN document S/25719, 3 May 1993, p. 8.

[29] UN, Further report of the Secretary-General pursuant to paragraph 7 of Resolution 840 (1993), UN document S/26360, 26 Aug. 1993, p. 1.

[30] Jennar (note 26), p. 147.

The Paris Accords mandated a liberal democratic constitution based on six principles, derived from a 1982 UN recommendation for Namibia's transition to independence. They stated that the Constitution would: (*a*) be the supreme law of the land; (*b*) include a declaration of human rights; (*c*) declare Cambodia neutral; (*d*) commit the country to 'liberal democracy' based on periodic elections governed by universal suffrage, full participation and secret balloting; (*e*) create an independent judiciary; and (*f*) be adopted by two-thirds of the Constituent Assembly.[31] According to Steve Ratner, the provisions mandating 'liberal democracy, on the basis of pluralism', like those in the Namibian case, transcended existing human rights instruments in establishing a specific political foundation for the future protection of human rights in Cambodia.[32]

The Constituent Assembly managed to complete its draft constitution more or less by the scheduled date. Broadly in line with the requirements of the Paris Accords, it established a 'permanently neutral and non-aligned', democratic, pluralist constitutional monarchy, officially styled the Kingdom of Cambodia, with Prince Sihanouk returning to the throne as King. The King, according to an unamendable provision of the Constitution, would 'reign' but not 'govern'.[33] A late addition to the Constitution effectively barred the Khmer Rouge from joining the new Government, at least at its highest levels, by requiring the Council of Ministers to be chosen from parties represented in the National Assembly.[34] Some of the features of the Constitution are extraordinarily liberal, including the provisions for equal rights for women, in particular the recognition that 'the work by housewives in the home shall have the same value as what [*sic*] they can receive when working outside the home'.[35] The economic system prescribed for Cambodia is the 'market economy'.[36]

---

[31] Ratner, S. R., 'The Cambodia settlement agreements', *American Journal of International Law*, vol. 87, no. 1 (Jan. 1993), p. 27. See also Annex 5 of the Agreement on a Comprehensive Political Settlement in Cambodia, 23 Oct. 1991, published as an annex to UN document A/46/608, S/23177, 30 Oct. 1991; and the text of the Constitution of the Kingdom of Cambodia, official English-language translation provided by the Royal Cambodian Embassy in Paris, both reproduced in the appendix to this volume.

[32] Ratner (note 31), p. 27.

[33] Constitution of the Kingdom of Cambodia (note 31), Articles 7 and 17.

[34] Constitution of the Kingdom of Cambodia (note 31), Article 100; see also *International Herald Tribune*, 22 Sep. 1993.

[35] Constitution of the Kingdom of Cambodia (note 31), Article 36.

[36] Constitution of the Kingdom of Cambodia (note 31), Article 56.

A transitional arrangement was established, no doubt to take into account political realities, whereby 'First' and 'Second' Prime Ministers would be appointed for the duration of the first National Assembly; a single Prime Minister would assume office thereafter. This would make possible a transition from a coalition to a single-party government after the next election, scheduled for 1998.[37] In accepting that he would be obliged to take the post of Second Prime Minister, Hun Sen noted, perspicaciously, that 'some people have said the formula [of two prime ministers] in our country is strange . . . However, it is because we are strange that Cambodia has not become another Angola, another Yugoslavia or another Somalia where fighting is raging'.[38]

The draft Constitution was ratified by the Constituent Assembly on 21 September by 113 votes to five, with two abstentions, well in excess of the two-thirds majority required,[39] and on 24 September Prince Sihanouk as Head of State signed it into law.[40] After being formally elected King by the Royal Council of the Throne,[41] Sihanouk was sworn in as King of Cambodia; at his own request he was not crowned.[42] As envisaged in the Paris Accords, the Constituent Assembly was transformed into the new National Assembly, while the PNGC became the new Royal Government of Cambodia. The SNC formally handed sovereignty to it and immediately dissolved itself.

At this point UNTAC's role in Cambodia's internal affairs formally ended. After a hand-over ceremony, Yasushi Akashi left Phnom Penh on 26 September.[43] UNTAC had already begun to dismantle itself and disengage from Cambodian political life. Electoral monitors and officials had left at an early stage, the CivPols were completely gone

---

[37] Constitution of the Kingdom of Cambodia (note 31), Articles 78, 138.

[38] 'Hun Sen on Copremiership', Phnom Penh National Voice of Cambodia Radio Network, Foreign Broadcast Information Service, FBIS-EAS-73-119, 17 Sep. 1993, p. 36; cited in Frost (note 1), p. 87.

[39] UN, Further report of the Secretary-General on the implementation of Security Council Resolution 745 (1992), UN document S/26529, 5 Oct. 1993, p. 1; Phnom Penh Post, 24 Sep.– 7 Oct. 1993, p. 1.

[40] The Times, 25 Sep. 1993.

[41] Cambodia's monarchs have always been elective, not hereditary. The Royal Council of the Throne comprises the President of the National Assembly, Chea Sim; Prince Ranariddh and Hun Sen as First and Second Prime Ministers; the two Vice-Presidents of the National Assembly; and the two Supreme Monks of the respective Buddhist orders. See Curran, B., 'Whither the Throne?', Phnom Penh Post, 3–16 Dec. 1993, p. 19.

[42] UN, Financing of the United Nations Transitional Authority in Cambodia, 8 Dec. 1993 (note 12), p. 5.

[43] Phnom Penh Post, 8–21 Oct. 1993, p. 4.

by 30 September and the military withdrew completely by 15 November. As a confidence-building measure while the new Government consolidated its position, the Civil Administration Component of UNTAC was withdrawn at a measured pace[44] and the UN Security Council extended the stay of the mine-clearance and training unit of UNTAC until 30 November and that of military police and medical units to 31 December.[45] By the end of 1993 all UNTAC personnel had left.

The Security Council also decided as a separate operation from UNTAC to establish a Military Liaison Team comprising 20 officers for a single six-month period with a mandate to report on matters affecting Cambodia's security, to liaise with the new Government on military issues and to assist it in dealing with residual military matters relating to the Paris Accords.[46] This decision was taken against the better judgement of Boutros-Ghali, who was sceptical that it would have a useful role to play.[47] On his recommendation a separate, integrated UN office was established in Phnom Penh to handle non-military residual matters and overall UN relations with the new Cambodian Government.[48] In addition, the UNHCR established a UN Field Office for Human Rights in Cambodia[49] and appointed an Australian judge, Mr Justice Michael Kirby, as UN Special Representative on Human Rights in Cambodia.[50] He would be required to assist the new Government with human rights issues and to prepare an annual report to the UNHCR and the UN General Assembly on the human rights situation in the country. The Military Liaison Team in Cambodia ceased operations on 15 May 1994, despite a request from the Cambodian Government that its mandate be prolonged. Instead,

[44] UN, Further report of the Secretary-General, 26 Aug. 1993 (note 29), p. 4.

[45] UN Security Council Resolution 880, UN document S/RES/880, 4 Nov. 1993.

[46] UN Security Council Resolution 880 (note 45). Under the command of Col A. N. M. Muniruzzaman of Bangladesh, the Military Liaison Team in Cambodia comprised officers from Austria, Bangladesh, Belgium, China, France, India, Indonesia, Malaysia, New Zealand, Pakistan, Poland, Russia, Singapore, Thailand and Uruguay. See UN, United Nations Transitional Authority in Cambodia, UN document PS/DPI/16/Rev. 3 Oct. 1993. Published as part of UN, *United Nations Peace-keeping Operations Information Notes, 1993,* update no. 2, UN document DPI/1306/Rev. 2, Nov. 1993.

[47] UN, Further report of the Secretary-General pursuant to paragraph 7 of Resolution 840 (1993), UN document S/26546, 7 Oct. 1993, p. 2.

[48] UN, Further report of the Secretary-General pursuant to paragraph 7 of Resolution 840 (1993), 7 Oct. 1993 (note 47), p. 7.

[49] *Phnom Penh Post,* 8–21 Apr. 1994, p. 2. The office opened on 1 Oct. 1993: see *UN Chronicle,* Mar. 1994, p. 71.

[50] Australian Department of Foreign Affairs and Trade, *Insight,* 20 Dec. 1993, p. 17.

three military advisers, from Belgium, France and Malaysia, were appointed to the UN office in Phnom Penh.[51]

CMAC also remained after UNTAC's withdrawal, having been progressively 'Cambodianized'. Controversy followed over the alleged premature abandonment of the de-mining programme by the UN; the withdrawal of UNTAC's mine-clearance and training unit was consequently deferred. The Security Council urged member states to help CMAC after UNTAC's complete withdrawal and called for monies from the UN Trust Fund for Demining Programmes in Cambodia and technical experts to be provided.[52] A total of $15 million was pledged for de-mining at the second meeting of ICORC in Tokyo in March 1994.[53]

The UN's rehabilitation activities also continued after UNTAC's departure, since, as of mid-August 1993, only approximately $200 million of the $880 million pledged in Tokyo in June 1992 had been disbursed. A number of QIPs remained to be completed, as donor money for such projects, withheld prior to the election, suddenly became available. Most of these were labour-intensive, creating jobs at a time of scarce employment opportunities. Special benefits were anticipated for rural communities in northern and eastern Cambodia which, according to the UNTAC Rehabilitation Component, 'have so far been only marginally touched by any form of development assistance'.[54]

Boutros-Ghali reported to the Security Council that 'despite the widespread rebuilding of roads, bridges and other infrastructural installations by UNTAC military engineers over the past 18 months and the major upgrading of Cambodia's airports and communications facilities undertaken as part of the mission, massive reconstruction is still required throughout the country'.[55] The first meeting of ICORC in September 1993 identified a sobering list of Cambodia's future needs, including budget support, administrative reform, mine clearance, resettlement and reintegration of displaced persons, agriculture,

[51] UN, Final report of the Secretary-General on the United Nations Military Liaison Team in Cambodia, UN document S/1994/645, 31 May 1994.

[52] UN Security Council Resolution 880 (note 45).

[53] Cambodia: recent developments, Statement by Peter Tomsen, Deputy Assistant Secretary for East Asian and Pacific Affairs, before the Subcommittee on Asia and the Pacific of the House Foreign Affairs Committee, US Congress, Washington, DC, 11 May 1994. Reproduced in US Department of State Dispatch, vol. 5, no. 21 (23 May 1994), p. 344.

[54] UN, Report of the Secretary-General, 16 July 1993 (note 14), p. 6.

[55] UN, Further report of the Secretary-General, 26 Aug. 1993 (note 29), p. 4.

social services including health care and education, maintenance of public utilities and repair of the transport system and infrastructure. Clearly Cambodia would need international assistance and support for an extended period if its newly won achievements were not to be jeopardized.

7. An assessment of UNTAC's performance

I. Introduction

By their very nature, United Nations peacekeeping and peacemaking operations tend to be Utopian. Driven by the high ideals of the UN Charter and the good intentions of states not directly involved in the conflict at hand and, some would say, by the unworldliness of the UN bureaucracy in New York, such operations tend to assume goodwill where little exists, to take written agreements at face value and to discount the corrosive effects of self-interest and power politics after peace accords have been concluded. Allan Griffith has commented that:

Peace processes, such as that being put to work in Cambodia, are diplomatic marathons, consuming vast reserves of time, money and political capital. Having as their *raison d'être* the dismantling of enmeshed lines of conflict, peace processes are inevitably protracted and wearing of support. In their conception and presentation they are inevitably ambitious, particularly utopian, holding out promises of betterment which are difficult to satisfy in an acceptable time-frame.[1]

The Cambodia operation, the UN's biggest peacekeeping/peace-making/peace-building operation to date, was also its most Utopian. Its intention was to help long-standing warring opponents achieve a cease-fire, canton and disarm their forces, and involve themselves in a democratic process never before experienced in the country, with the aim of establishing a united, stable, pluralistic state based on constitutional law. In addition the UN took on the tasks of repatriating thousands of refugees, instilling in Cambodians civic values and a respect for human rights, and beginning the enormous task of reconstruction and rehabilitation. Never before had the UN organized an election, attempted to supervise and control a functioning government administration or conducted a fully fledged human rights campaign in a member state.

---

[1] Griffith, A., 'World needs benefit of a success in Cambodia', *Canberra Times*, 15 Mar. 1993, p. 9.

The framers of the Paris Accords gave the UN less than two years to achieve all this. Amid the euphoria that surrounded the concept of peacekeeping in the early post-cold war years, the UN was undoubtedly keen to take on the task. In a sense it had no choice. There were no alternative organizations willing, able or altruistic enough to take on the job set out by the Paris negotiators. Yet no extra resources were provided to UN headquarters to manage such a gigantic undertaking: on the contrary, competing demands on the organization's peacekeeping capacity, including the unfolding catastrophe in the former Yugoslavia, were greater than at any point in UN history. The UN Secretariat was also undergoing reform and reorganization.

In this context, the international community had set UNTAC an impossible task. Even with a revitalized UN Secretariat, the co-operation of all the warring factions and a perfectly organized mission, it would not have been possible to transform an impoverished country traumatized by decades of war into a model developing democracy. In retrospect, even Gareth Evans, one of the architects of the Cambodia settlement, acknowledges that UNTAC's mandate was 'overly ambitious and in some respects clearly not achievable'.[2]

Boutros Boutros-Ghali, at the outset of UNTAC's mission, had identified four essential conditions for it to 'discharge its responsibilities effectively and with complete impartiality':[3] (a) the full support of the Security Council; (b) the full co-operation of the Cambodian parties and all other parties concerned; (c) full freedom of movement and communications; and (d) the 'necessary financial resources provided by member states in full and in a timely manner'. Only the first and fourth of these were close to being fully achieved. UNTAC mostly had the full support of the Security Council and of most states in the region, but not the full co-operation of all other external parties involved, especially not that of the Thai military.[4] It was amply funded for its principal activities, although not necessarily in a timely fashion, and voluntary financial contributions were slow in coming

---

[2] Evans, G., 'Peacekeeping in Cambodia: lessons learned', *NATO Review*, vol. 42, no. 4 (Aug. 1994), pp. 24–27.

[3] UN, Report of the Secretary-General on Cambodia, UN document S/23613, 19 Feb. 1992, pp. 40–41.

[4] Viet Nam was in some respects also unhelpful, especially in permitting the illegal migration of Vietnamese into Cambodia, many of them lured by the sudden boom conditions in Phnom Penh. See Jennar, R. M., 'UNTAC: "international triumph" in Cambodia?', *Security Dialogue*, vol. 25, no. 2 (1994), p. 150.

and hedged about with conditions. It had full freedom of communications but not of movement.

The 'essential condition' most notably absent was of course the full co-operation of the Cambodian parties—particularly the Khmer Rouge and the SOC/CPP. The late deployment of UNTAC did not help matters, and its handling of disruptions of the peace process may not always have been optimal, but UNTAC had to work within the constraints of its mandate and cannot be blamed for the non-compliance of the parties. If blame is to lie anywhere but with the parties themselves, it is with the framers of the Paris Accords. It appears in retrospect that the agreement reached between the factions owed more to outside pressure than to genuine reconciliation. This is not unusual in negotiations, and sometimes results in successful outcomes, as confidence is built and the passage of time heals wounds. Moreover, it is difficult to imagine what other choices the international community had in attempting to resolve the Cambodian conflict other than to pressure the parties to make a deal.

All these considerations need to be kept in mind when assessing the performance of UNTAC.

II. Success or failure?

Officially, the Security Council characterized the Cambodia mission at its conclusion as 'a major achievement for the United Nations'.[5] Judged in terms of its mandate, the resources allocated to it and the difficulties under which it operated, UNTAC can at the very least be said to have been a qualified success. Its clear triumphs were the organization and conduct of the May election (which was 'free and fair', although the election campaign was not), its refugee repatriation programme and its promotion (although not its protection) of human rights. UNTAC's Electoral Component and UNHCR deserve special mention as examples of what the UN can do with adequate resources and planning. The Electoral Component should, in particular, be used as a model for future UN electoral missions.

Most other elements of UNTAC's mandate were fulfilled satisfactorily. It verified the Vietnamese withdrawal, thereby satisfying Chinese and US concerns. It cantoned and disarmed those military forces to which it was given access. It began the process of recon-

5 UN, Security Council Resolution 880, UN document S/RES/880, 4 Nov. 1993.

structing Cambodia's infrastructure, administration and economy. It employed 50 000 Cambodians, who gained valuable skills that can be applied to reconstruction and development.[6] At a deeper level, UNTAC set in place the rudiments of a civil society, leaving Cambodia with a more open political process, a freer press and a more politically aware populace than when it arrived. In place of an unelected, authoritarian regime originally imposed on the country by a foreign power, it left a democratically elected legislature and coalition government of the three most favoured political parties in the country. Less tangibly but no less importantly, as Akashi has pointed out:

Cambodia has been exposed to the demands that a civilized state requires of its administration and its law enforcement officers. And for every well-publicized accusation of bad behaviour by UNTAC personnel there were a hundred cases where we demonstrated by quiet professional example that soldiers can build and protect as well as kill and destroy, that police officers can guard citizens against crime instead of oppressing them, and that administrators can be efficient, hard-working and dedicated to the public good.[7]

As regards UNTAC's overall performance, at crucial times elements of the operation displayed creativity and flexibility, the positive side of the improvisation that has characterized UN peacekeeping operations since their inception. UNHCR altered its repatriation programme when problems developed. UNTAC (with Security Council approval) in effect amended the Paris Accords by proceeding with the election without the 70 per cent disarmament and cantonment that had been envisaged. The pattern of military deployments was altered when cantonment and disarmament did not take place, in order to permit the Military Component to protect the electoral process and enhance security throughout the country.[8] Flexibility was shown in the post-election period with the formation of the Provisional Government.

UNTAC also avoided some of the failures of previous and concurrent peacekeeping operations. It avoided being drawn into a shooting war with a recalcitrant party, using force only in self-defence and

---

[6] Sadry, B., 'Introduction', ed. UN, *The United Nations in Cambodia: A Vote for Peace* (United Nations: New York, 1994), p. 7. Cambodia, for example, now has experienced electoral officials, better trained computer operators, traffic police and magistrates.

[7] Akashi, Y., 'Foreword', ed. UN, *The United Nations in Cambodia: A Vote for Peace* (note 6), p. 5.

[8] See chapter 3.

even then with great restraint, largely preserved its impartiality, suffered no catastrophic administrative disasters and came in under budget.

In strategic terms, UNTAC helped achieve what Stephen Solarz identified in 1990 as the 'minimum' and unspoken aim of the Paris Accords—'to place the Khmer Rouge in isolation—which is precisely where it belongs'.[9] Through perseverance and determination it managed to outmanœuvre the KR, surprising them with the size of the turnout and the election outcome. It was suggested at the time the Paris Accords were being concluded that to permit the Khmer Rouge to be involved in the peace process would serve to increase its power and influence. Ultimately this was proved wrong. While the KR was admitted to the SNC, allowed to maintain an office in Phnom Penh and given the chance to participate in the election, none of these provided it with greater power, apparently because it was unwilling to take or incapable of taking advantage of these opportunities. Hence it had little influence on the SNC except for blocking decisions which were subsequently taken by Akashi; it gained no parliamentary representation, despite estimates that it could have taken 10–15 per cent of the vote;[10] it had no influence on the writing of the Constitution; and it formed no part of the new Government, despite post-election opportunities to do so. Furthermore, it lost its principal foreign backer, China, the captive population of the Thai border camps, the cover of the 'united front' with Sihanouk, FUNCINPEC and the KPNLF, its international recognition and its third of a UN seat. It 'lost' the election in the sense that it failed to derail it, saw several hundred of its supporters vote, and was caught unprepared by the election outcome. The guerrilla faction then suffered the humiliation of having promises from Sihanouk and FUNCINPEC to admit it to government broken after the election. Finally, its military reportedly suffered some 2000 defections during UNTAC's tenure.[11] The Khmer Rouge was decidedly worse off after the Paris Accords than before.

This is not to say that it was no longer of consequence by the time of UNTAC's departure: it retained considerable quantities of war *matériel*, was economically sustained through cross-border dealings

[9] Solarz, S., 'Cambodia and the international community', *Foreign Affairs*, spring 1990, p. 113.
[10] Hornik, R., 'Sympathy for the devil', *Time* (Australia), 21 Sep. 1992, p. 43.
[11] Moreau, R., 'Disillusioned, demoralized and defecting', *The Bulletin* (Sydney), 28 Sep. 1993, p. 57.

with the Thai military and invested savings, and had potential political appeal if the new Government foundered. It also reportedly controlled more territory than it did before UNTAC arrived, having seized areas vacated by FUNCINPEC and the KPNLF,[12] and, according to Akashi, had become politically more dedicated, determined and aggressive during UNTAC's tenure.[13] In sum, however, the Paris Accords were not to the KR's overall benefit.

The other unspoken strategic aim of the Paris Accords, the de-internationalization of the Cambodia conflict, was also achieved. In particular, Chinese disengagement was facilitated by UNTAC's refusal to be drawn into armed confrontation with the KR and because it acted sufficiently impartially to retain and even increase Chinese support for the peace process. Cambodia's neighbours, including China, will continue to take a close interest in its internal affairs, and some such as Thailand and Viet Nam will continue to interfere, but UNTAC removed a long-standing international dispute from the UN agenda and peacefully resolved the question of Cambodia's seat at the UN. It helped to install an internationally recognized and recognizable Cambodian Government for the first time since the 1970s and paved the way for Cambodia to resume its rightful place in a range of international organizations, including potentially ASEAN and the newly established ASEAN Regional Forum (ARF).

Unquestionably, however, the Paris Accords failed to bring peace to Cambodia. UNTAC's share of the responsibility for this situation is clear. In the implementation of the Accords, its major failures were: (a) its inability to control and supervise the SOC Administration; (b) its reluctance to deal forcibly with human rights infringements, especially because of its unwillingness to establish a system of justice to deal with the most egregious of these; and (c) its management failures, including poor inter-component co-ordination and co-operation. Aspects of UNTAC's performance which were not entirely within its control but in which it could have done better were: (a) the tardiness of its deployment and installation; (b) its strategic planning; (c) the poor performance of its CivPols; (d) initial neglect of the adverse eco-

---

[12] UN, Report of the Secretary-General pursuant to paragraph 7 of Resolution 840 (1993), UN document S/26090, 16 July 1993, p. 2.

[13] Mallet, V., 'Khmer Rouge keeps the world guessing', *Financial Times*, 27 May 1993, p. 7. Akashi was also reported as saying that their front-line military strength had increased by 50 per cent to about 15 000. Others dispute this, putting KR strength at only 12 000.

nomic effects of its own presence; and (*e*) the slowness of its rehabilitation and de-mining programmes.

It is striking that UNTAC's greatest successes were in those areas where it had the greatest degree of independent control and latitude—those that did not require the full co-operation of all the factions to be effective.[14] Its major failures were in those areas where it was hostage to the whims of its Cambodian partners in the peace process.

III. The factors behind UNTAC's success

The existence of a plan and timetable

The peace plan set out in the Paris Accords remains the most detailed and orderly of any UN peacekeeping operation. It provided a framework and end-point for the mission that other UN operations, notably in Somalia and the former Yugoslavia, have sorely lacked. Having the election as the centre-piece of the plan was also important in helping to provide a tangible, clear-cut goal behind which to rally both UNTAC and the Cambodian people.[15] Even the Khmer Rouge was always careful to assert its desire to comply with the Paris Accords.[16] Credit must be given both to the Australian Government for the initial impetus it gave to the formulation of the plan and to the Permanent Five for following it through. To a great extent the timetable was met as originally envisaged, almost to the day, demonstrating the desirability of future peacekeeping missions having, where possible, a similar detailed plan.

International solidarity

An especially important ingredient in UNTAC's success was the on-going support and involvement of the UN Security Council, which after the end of the cold war and the successful prosecution of the Persian Gulf War had begun to fulfil some of the promises of its

[14] Doyle, M. W., 'UNTAC: sources of success and failure', ed. H. Smith, Australian Defence Force Academy, Australian Defence Studies Centre, *International Peacekeeping: Building on the Cambodian Experience* (ADSC: Canberra, 1994).

[15] Sanderson, J. M. (Lt-Gen.), 'A review of recent peacekeeping operations', Paper presented to the Pacific Armies Management Seminar (PAMS) XVIII Conference, Dacca, Jan. 1994, p. 14.

[16] Schear, J. A., 'The case of Cambodia', eds D. Daniel and B. Hayes, *Beyond Traditional Peacekeeping* (Macmillan: London, forthcoming 1995), p. 300.

founders. Except on one occasion when China abstained, the Security Council acted unanimously on Cambodia.[17] As Khmer Rouge resistance to UNTAC intensified, the Council's attitude towards it hardened.[18] The Permanent Five used their power and influence on the Council to good effect.

Also crucial was the support of key states in the region, particularly Australia, Indonesia, Japan and, more erratically, Thailand, and of ASEAN as an organization. The Core Group of countries played a vital role in shoring up the Paris Accords at moments of potential failure.[19] The Core Group's counterparts in Phnom Penh, the EP5 group of ambassadors,[20] proved instrumental in ensuring that the realities on the ground in Cambodia were relayed accurately to the Security Council, thereby avoiding some of the over-reactions, often media-induced, which have characterized Security Council decisions on Somalia, the former Yugoslavia and Rwanda.[21] Quiet bilateral diplomacy was also almost continuously undertaken in an effort to bring the KR back into the peace process by Australia, Indonesia, Japan and Thailand among others.[22] Anxious to rescue its international image after the Tiananmen Square massacre, China was successfully drawn into a process which sought to afford Cambodians democratic and human rights which it was not prepared to grant its own people.

Broad participation by the international community in UNTAC was also important, both politically and materially, through the contribution of military and civilian contingents. Although, as James Schear notes, such broad multilateral operations are inherently less efficient than narrower coalition-type operations, diversity of participation is the 'key to legitimacy' in peacekeeping operations.[23]

---

[17] Akashi notes that the USA and France alternated in the roles of 'dove' and 'hawk' depending on the issue, with Japan sometimes in between. See Akashi, Y., 'The challenges of peace-keeping in Cambodia: lessons to be learned', Paper presented to School of International and Public Affairs, Columbia University, New York, 29 Nov. 1993, p. 20.

[18] Akashi (note 17), p. 11.

[19] Gen. Sanderson believes that the Core Group was useful in generating unity of purpose of the UN mission both inside and outside Cambodia: see Sanderson (note 15), p. 9. Akashi valued it as 'a good sounding board': see Akashi (note 17), p. 18.

[20] See chapter 6, note 13.

[21] Sanderson, J. M. (Lt-Gen.), 'UNTAC: successes and failures', ed. Smith (note 14), p. 28.

[22] For details see Akashi, Y., 'The challenges faced by UNTAC', *Japan Review of International Affairs*, summer 1993, pp. 190–91.

[23] Schear (note 16), p. 300. An interesting counter-example, where lack of international support caused the failure of a peacekeeping mission, is that of Yemen of 1963. See

On the ground, shortcomings in UNTAC's performance were alleviated by the initiative and generosity of particular participating states. As an Australian, General Sanderson was able to mobilize Australian support in such circumstances.[24] Japan also responded generously when required.

Leadership

Cambodia was fortunate in having what Bill Zartman has termed 'valid spokespersons' for its fractured polity.[25] In particular it had Prince Norodom Sihanouk. Self-interested, manipulative and mercurial, he was at times more of a hindrance than a help to the peace process;[26] but at key moments, particularly after the May election, he exerted leadership and emerged as the single unifying factor in Cambodian political life. He was also someone that UNTAC and the international community could deal with as a genuine symbol, if not always a responsible representative, of the Cambodian people. Other UN peace missions, such as those in Angola and Mozambique, have been hampered by the lack of such a figure. UNTAC was also fortunate in having Prince Ranariddh and Hun Sen as 'valid spokespersons' for the two largest Cambodian political forces (apart from the KR). Part of the problem UNTAC had in dealing with the KR was that its nominal leader, Khieu Samphan, was not perceived as a valid spokesperson but as a front man for Pol Pot. The guerrilla group also often appeared to be internally divided.

UNTAC's leadership was also critical. Akashi and Sanderson, although they did not always see eye to eye, had the political and cultural acuity to steer the operation successfully through multiple

Birgisson, K. Th., 'United Nations Yemen Observation Mission', ed. W. J. Durch, *The Evolution of UN Peacekeeping: Case Studies and Comparative Analysis* (St Martin's Press for The Henry L. Stimson Center: Washington, DC, 1993), pp. 206–18.

[24] According to US Major George Steuber, 'If the Australians had not been in that mission, UNTAC and UNAMIC would have failed in January [1992] at the latest, rather than having plugged along minimally successfully for one year now. The Australians saved our butts'. Quoted in Lewis, W. H. (ed.), National Defense University, Institute for National Strategic Studies, *Military Implications of United Nations Peacekeeping Operations,* McNair Paper no. 17 (INSS: Washington, DC, June 1993), p. 68.

[25] Presentation by I. William Zartman to the 1993 Executive Seminar on Conflict Resolution and Conflict Prevention, Department of Peace and Conflict Research, Uppsala University, Sweden, 26 Sep. 1993.

[26] Pol Pot has reportedly described Sihanouk as 'more than 90 per cent paranoid due to all sorts of hedonism, corruption, financial malfeasance and debauchery and hooliganism': see *Bangkok Post,* 22 May 1993, p. 11.

challenges—ranging from major violations of the Paris Accords to bureaucratic ineptness.

In some respects Akashi was perfectly suited to the role of Special Representative. As a fellow Asian he understood Cambodian cultural norms emphasizing the avoidance of loss of face and of confrontation. He handled the Cambodian parties with tact, wit and considerable finesse. What his detractors saw as chronic indecisiveness his supporters saw as carefully considered tactics. He himself says that he 'tried to combine flexibility with firmness . . . to balance universal values with sensitivity to Asian approaches'.[27] Except on a few occasions when he confronted Khieu Samphan, he tried, he says, to help the parties avoid loss of face.[28] Claiming that he persuaded Hun Sen and Ranariddh to patch up their differences, he emphasizes that he wanted to induce Cambodians to take responsibility for their future.[29] He was also perspicacious enough to realize the vital role that Prince Sihanouk would ultimately play in the electoral dénouement and was prepared to humble himself to retain Sihanouk's support—humility being the first requirement of a peacekeeper.

Akashi clearly did not want to be seen as the General MacArthur of Cambodia, imposing decisions by fiat, since he had witnessed such an approach in Japan as a child. In pursuing consensus so diligently, as would be culturally mandated in Japan, Akashi may have overlooked Cambodians' cultural emphasis on 'hierarchy and ranking, deference and command, hegemony and servitude'.[30] David Chandler points out that until recently Cambodians had no words for 'society' or 'consensus'. It is in any case a matter of fine political judgement how authoritarian the UN can be in attempting to implant democracy and liberal civic values in a country under its tutelage.

Akashi could, however, be tough and stubborn when he felt that it was required. He refused to allow what he regarded as a flawed Electoral Law to be adopted and spent four months negotiating it, in the interests of consensus, until he was satisfied, standing up to both UN headquarters in New York and all the factions represented in the SNC in the process. Eventually he promulgated the Electoral Law without

---

[27] Akashi (note 22), p. 201.
[28] Akashi (note 17), p. 21.
[29] Interview with the author, New York, 22 Nov. 1993.
[30] Chandler, D. P., 'The tragedy of Cambodian history revisited', *SAIS Review*, summer–fall 1994, p. 84.

the agreement of the Khmer Rouge.[31] He also did battle with UN headquarters to have Radio UNTAC established.

The fact that Akashi was Japanese was also undoubtedly a factor in securing for UNTAC both large-scale Japanese financial support and the historic contribution of Japanese ground troops.[32] It was equally crucial when there were strong Japanese domestic pressures for withdrawal from UNTAC after the death of the Japanese volunteer and policeman.

General Sanderson must also be credited with the success of the Cambodia operation:

UNTAC was not a well-oiled military machine to which orders could be issued with reasonable assurance that they would be carried out as intended. Focusing UNTAC's disparate military component—including contingents from 34 nations, each equipped, organized, and trained differently—was a monumental task which only a commander with exceptional abilities could carry out. Peacekeeping operations require a commander possessing strength of mind, calm optimism, confidence, limitless patience, resourcefulness and steady nerve. The leader's vision must be clearly thought-out and consistently applied. He must not waver. He must provide the anchor not only for the military component, but often for the entire UN effort.[33]

Sanderson, says Karl Farris, proved to be such a commander. Some observers argue, for instance, that Sanderson was crucial in steeling UNTAC's nerves in the uncertain days just prior to the election when disaster seemed imminent and there was talk among UNTAC civilians of cancellation.[34]

---

[31] Chopra, J., Mackinlay, J. and Minear, L., Norwegian Institute of International Affairs, *Report on the Cambodian Peace Process*, Research Report no. 165 (NIIA: Oslo, Feb. 1993), p. 26. For details of Akashi's dealings with the four factions over the electoral laws, see Akashi (note 22), p. 194.

[32] In May 1992 Akashi reportedly asked Japan to provide one-third of the $2.4 billion needed to rebuild Cambodia and send Japanese peacekeepers. He also asked Prime Minister Kiichi Miyazawa to open a training centre for UN peacekeepers and a storage depot, preferably on Okinawa. See *Defense News*, 18–24 May 1992, p. 2.

[33] Farris, K., 'UN peacekeeping in Cambodia: on balance, a success', *Parameters*, vol. 24, no. 1 (1994), p. 50.

[34] Branigin, W., 'Curtain falls in Cambodia: a UN success, with flaws', *International Herald Tribune*, 27 Sep. 1993, p. 5.

Popular support

General Sanderson believes that the key to success in Cambodia lay in UNTAC's ability to 'forge an alliance' with the Cambodian people, to 'overcome the intrigues of their faction leaders and deliver an opportunity to them to break free from the prolonged cycle of fear and coercion'.[35] James Schear notes that UNTAC was able to establish its credibility and good intentions with the Cambodian people by organizing an electoral process that 'inspired enormous public enthusiasm'. He argues for peacekeeping operations to keep lines of communication open to all factions, even defiant ones, since this has the potential to undermine support for recalcitrants and avoids giving any faction a pretext for undermining the peace process.[36]

Serendipity

As often in the course of human affairs, the Cambodian operation was blessed with luck. First, it was fortuitous that the famed political nous of the Khmer Rouge failed it at critical junctures. In adopting an unintelligible strategy towards the May election—neither fully participating in it nor making a concerted attempt to disrupt it—the group badly miscalculated Cambodians' strong desire for peace and national reconciliation. It also relieved UNTAC of extraordinarily difficult decisions about how to respond to an all-out armed attack on the electoral process and on its personnel. Hence some of the painful dilemmas of UNOSOM II in Somalia were avoided. Luckily for UNTAC, the KR also alienated China, its erstwhile chief supporter, by violating a peace agreement which China had helped to negotiate and by recklessly killing Chinese peacekeepers. Finally, it was fortunate for UNTAC that at key moments the unpredictable Sihanouk acted in the interests of his people rather than himself.

---

[35] Sanderson (note 15), p. 6.
[36] Schear (note 16), pp. 297, 301.

8. The lessons of Cambodia

While it is axiomatic that each peacekeeping/peacemaking/peace-building operation is unique and yields experiences which may not be replicated elsewhere, the Cambodian operation was so extensive and ambitious that it is likely to prove replete with lessons for a wide variety of future UN and other multilateral operations, ranging from fact-finding to peace enforcement. While it will take sustained research to discern all these lessons, the following are some of the possibilities.

I. The need for prompt deployment

A major lesson of Cambodia is that intense efforts should be made to reduce the delay between a negotiated settlement and deployment of a peacekeeping force and its associated mechanisms and infrastructure. In the words of the US General Accounting Office (GAO), UN peace-keeping operations should 'hit the ground running'. They should 'begin to take control immediately before countervailing forces can solidify and neutralize the impact of the mission'.[1] UNTAC's late deployment was one of the biggest flaws of the Cambodia mission. It tarnished the UN's image even before its work had begun and emboldened the Cambodian factions to violate the Paris Accords, thereby jeopardizing the success of the entire operation. In James Schear's view the delay in deployment did not affect adherence to the overall Paris timetable, but it 'did deny the operation early momen-tum, and it dampened the desired positive psychological impact upon domestic public opinion. It also, most damagingly, contributed to a sense of political drift and disarray allowing the four Khmer factions, in particular the Khmer Rouge and the Hun Sen regime, to hedge positions on full compliance with the Accords'.[2]

---

[1] *UN Peacekeeping: Observations on Mandates and Operational Capability,* Statement of Frank C. Conahan, Assistant Comptroller General, National Security and International Affairs Division, Testimony before the Subcommittee on Terrorism, Narcotics, and Inter-national Operations of the Committee on Foreign Relations, US Senate, 9 June 1993, GAO/T-NSIAD-93-15, p. 3.

[2] Schear, J. A., 'The case of Cambodia', eds D. Daniel and B. Hayes, *Beyond Traditional Peacekeeping* (Macmillan: London, forthcoming 1995), p. 289.

The UN was faced with a dilemma in deploying UNTAC. According to Nick Warner:

In late 1991 there was a real political imperative for the quick deployment of the force. But there was also a realization in parts of the United Nations that early *and* full deployment were logistically and organizationally impossible. In the end early deployment won out, as it should have. But the upshot, as it had been three years earlier for UNTAG in Namibia, was that the force was not deployed in the effective manner anticipated in the operational plan.[3]

There were many reasons for late deployment.

Budgetary problems

The initial cause of delay was Security Council indecision over the UNTAC budget. The Council refused, understandably, to accept the UN Secretariat's somewhat open-ended estimates and demanded more specific calculations based on a detailed operational plan.[4] The need for budgetary discipline was made acute by the fact that other substantial UN operations, in Angola, Croatia, El Salvador and Western Sahara, were under way or in prospect.

Other obstacles to rapid finalization of the budget included the changing situation on the ground, which made it difficult to assess the likely costs.[5] There was also debate over whether the refugee repatriation budget should, for the first time, be included in a peacekeeping budget. In addition, Japan, a major funder of the Cambodia operation, was reportedly concerned about obtaining a commensurate role in budget planning. Boutros-Ghali attempted to cut the cost of the operation by calling for an amendment to the Paris Accords to provide for 100 per cent demobilization and disarmament of the factional armed forces. This would have dramatically cut the number of UN troops needed for security and supervision of cantonments, which could then be closed early;[6] the plan, however, was apparently unacceptable to the factions.

---

[3] Warner, N., 'Cambodia: lessons of UNTAC for future peacekeeping operations', Paper presented to international seminar on UN Peacekeeping at the Crossroads, Canberra, 21–24 Mar. 1993, p. 3.

[4] Awanohara, S., 'Budget blues', *Far Eastern Economic Review*, 27 Feb. 1993, pp. 22–23.

[5] Thayer, N., 'Unsettled land', *Far Eastern Economic Review*, 27 Feb. 1992, p. 22.

[6] *East Asia and Pacific Wireless File* (United States Information Service, Canberra), 20 Feb. 1992, pp. 3, 23. It would also have permitted the early integration of the military into

The General Assembly did, however, approve an unprecedentedly large amount of interim funding for UNTAC—$200 million—until the main budget could be approved.[7]

Lack of organizational capacity at UN headquarters

A second cause of the delay in UNTAC's deployment was that the UN Secretariat lacked the experience, resources and qualified personnel to organize a mission of such complexity, magnitude and novelty at short notice. There were no organizational precedents on which the Secretariat could draw for any of the civilian aspects of UNTAC and even some of the military aspects, such as those related to cantonment, were new to the UN. This was a period in which a dramatic rise in expectations and demands on the UN occurred and a reorganization of the Secretariat was taking place. The negotiators of the Accords and the Security Council apparently gave little thought to how the Secretariat might cope or whether it might need additional resources to organize and maintain UNTAC. The Secretariat itself had, however, been centrally involved in the planning for UNTAC from 1990 onwards, so that it should have been aware of the potential problem.[8] It is unclear whether it requested additional resources to enable it to manage the operation and was refused or whether it was simply caught up unthinkingly in the UN's post-cold war leap into nation building.

Competition with other peacekeeping missions

A third important factor was that five new peacekeeping operations were being organized and serviced by the UN Secretariat at the same time as UNTAC in 1991–92, including the United Nations Protection Force (UNPROFOR) in Yugoslavia.[9] As well as preoccupying the

civilian life and an early start to vocational training. Presumably under Boutros-Ghali's plan a new Cambodian Army would have been established from scratch after the election.

[7] *International Herald Tribune*, 29 Feb.–1 Mar. 1992, p. 1.

[8] Evans, G. and Grant, B., *Australia's Foreign Relations in the World of the 1990s* (Melbourne University Press: Carlton, 1991), pp. 215–16.

[9] These missions were: the UN Iraq–Kuwait Observer Mission (UNIKOM) on the Iraq–Kuwait border; the UN Angola Verification Mission (UNAVEM II); the *Misión de Observadores de las Naciones Unidas en El Salvador* (UN Observer Mission in El Salvador—ONUSAL); the *Mision de las Naciones Unidas para el Referendum del Sahara Occidental* (UN Mission for the Referendum in Western Sahara—MINURSO); and the UN

Secretariat, this led to difficulties in securing military contingents and qualified civilian personnel for UNTAC: the Secretariat, for instance, had great trouble finding civil police, qualified personnel for the Civil Administration and Human Rights Components, and fingerprint and handwriting specialists for the Electoral Component. Some states which had earmarked troops for UNTAC switched them to UNPROFOR.

It will always be difficult to mount major peacekeeping operations at short notice. Often they will be required unexpectedly when the conditions for peace are suddenly realized. The logistics of moving large numbers of personnel, even organized military units trained for rapid deployment, are always complex and subject to unexpected delays. However, the UN needs to equip itself to be able to make better advance preparations and ensure that delays are kept to a minimum. Some of these problems are currently being attended to by the UN and its Department of Peace-keeping Operations (DPKO).

II. The indispensability of advance planning

A major reason for the late deployment of UNTAC was the complete inadequacy of its advance planning which affected UNTAC for the whole of its life cycle. It occurred despite the fact that the UN had a reasonable period of notice—from the 1989 Paris Conference on-wards—of a major UN deployment in Cambodia being a distinct possibility, and despite the existence of a detailed peace plan and timetable long before the Paris Peace Accords were concluded. The UN Secretary-General's delegation at the 1989 Paris Conference, led by Rafeeuddin Ahmed, had in fact played an active role and sub-mitted a number of 'helpful' papers.[10]

An intra-Secretariat Task Force on Cambodia was established as early as February 1990.[11] Seven UN fact-finding missions were dis-

---

Protection Force (UNPROFOR) in the former Yugoslavia. See UN, Department of Public Information, *Background Note: United Nations Peace-keeping Operations* (United Nations: New York, Jan. 1993).

[10] Koh, T., 'The Paris Conference on Cambodia: a multilateral negotiation that "failed"', *Negotiation Journal*, vol. 6, no. 1 (Jan. 1990), p. 83.

[11] *Effects of the Continued Diplomatic Stalemate in Cambodia*, Hearing before the Sub-committee on East Asian and Pacific Affairs of the Committee on Foreign Relations, US Senate, 102nd Congress (US Government Printing Office: Washington, DC, 11 Apr. 1991). Statement of Richard H. Solomon. Reproduced in *East Asia and Pacific Wireless File* (United States Information Service, Canberra), 11 Apr. 1991, p. 4.

patched to Cambodia between 1989 and 1991,[12] in addition to the Australian Technical Mission (whose findings were the basis of the Australian 'Red Book' used in negotiating the Paris Accords). The first UN mission was sent on the agreement of the first session of the Paris Conference. The 15-member team was led by an experienced peacekeeping commander, Norwegian Lieutenant-General Martin Vadset, chief of the UN Truce Supervisory Organization (UNTSO) in the Middle East, who had led a similar mission to Iran and Iraq.[13]

Despite this apparently good start, the UN, according to General Sanderson, appeared to be taken by surprise when the Accords were signed.[14] Advance planning by the UN for the deployment of UNTAC was patchy and unco-ordinated. Instead of a comprehensive UNTAC planning process, each UNTAC component conducted its own survey mission and prepared its own 'plan of sorts'.[15] This resulted in such ludicrous situations as the refugee repatriation programme starting before the Military Component was there to provide security and mark minefields. On the military planning side, a Military Survey Mission, including Sanderson, went to Cambodia in November–December 1991.[16] With this experience Sanderson was able to help shape the structure and composition of the military force for UNTAC before its deployment.[17] He then travelled, uninvited, to New York to speed up the deployment of the Military Component. He discovered that there were no maps of Cambodia, no Khmer-speakers, no operations room, no team of UN military advisers to brief him on the UN's plans, no one able to brief contributing countries on what to expect and what would be expected of them in Cambodia, and, perhaps most worryingly, no concept of how UNTAC's mandate might

[12] Information supplied by Col J. S. Bremner, Director-General, Pol. Ops, Canadian National Defence Headquarters, Ottawa, Canada.

[13] *Canberra Times,* 3 Aug. 1989; *Financial Times,* 7 Aug. 1989.

[14] Sanderson, J. M. (Lt-Gen.), 'UNTAC: successes and failures', ed. H. Smith, Australian Defence Force Academy, Australian Defence Studies Centre, *International Peacekeeping: Building on the Cambodian Experience* (ADSC: Canberra, 1994), p. 18.

[15] Sanderson, J. M. (Lt-Gen.), 'A review of recent peacekeeping operations', Paper presented to the Pacific Armies Management Seminar (PAMS) XVIII Conference, Dacca, Jan. 1994, p. 10.

[16] Sanderson, J. M. (Lt-Gen.), 'Preparation for, deployment and conduct of peacekeeping operations: a Cambodia snapshot', Paper presented at a conference on UN Peacekeeping at the Crossroads, Canberra, 21–24 Mar. 1993, p. 3; *Sydney Morning Herald,* 23 Nov. 1991, p. 15.

[17] Farris, K., 'UN peacekeeping in Cambodia: on balance, a success', *Parameters,* vol. 24, no. 1 (1994), pp. 47–48.

be translated into operational military terms.[18] To alleviate the situation Sanderson recommended, to no avail, the establishment of two planning units, one in New York and one in Phnom Penh.[19]

Apart from the lack of capacity at UN headquarters, advance planning was hindered by a disjunction between the negotiation of the Paris Accords and their implementation—the personnel involved in the former were not involved in the latter. Of the senior UNTAC personnel, only the Director of Repatriation, Sergio Vieira de Mello of UNHCR, had previous experience of Cambodia. Warner estimates that 'maybe half of the difficulties the mission faced in 1992 can be sheeted home to this'.[20] The late appointment and arrival of most of the heads of the components meant that most of them were not involved in the planning for UNTAC at all. UNTAC also suffered from discontinuity between its senior leadership and that of UNAMIC, the advance mission.[21] Nor was continuity of planning helped by the change in the Secretary-Generalship of the UN from Perez de Cuellar to Boutros-Ghali on 1 January 1992. According to M. H. Lao, the former was trusted by all the Cambodian parties, while the latter was new to the issue.[22] Further discontinuities arose with the rapid and 'arbitrarily timed' rotation of senior officers out of UNTAC while it was in the field.[23] One of the reasons for the success of the Electoral Component was continuity of staffing from the 1991 Planning Mission onwards.[24]

One lesson of Cambodia, then, is that all the senior leadership-designate of a peacekeeping mission should be involved, where possible, in the negotiation and planning phases leading up to deploy-

---

[18] Chropa et al. report that at the Nov. 1991 briefing for contingent commanders in New York 'some infantry battalion commanders were disturbed by the lack of operational information and the prospect that all their unit planning would have to be made without the benefit of in-country reconnaissance by their staff'. Chopra, J., Mackinlay, J. and Minear, L., Norwegian Institute of International Affairs, *Report on the Cambodian Peace Process*, Research Report no. 165 (NIIA: Oslo, Feb. 1993), p. 18.

[19] Interview with Lt-Col Damien Healy, Chief Civil Liaison Officer, UNTAC, Phnom Penh, May 1993.

[20] Warner (note 3), p. 7.

[21] Warner (note 3), p. 6.

[22] Lao, M. H., 'Obstacles to peace in Cambodia', *Pacific Review*, vol. 6, no. 4 (1993), p. 391. According to one highly placed military source Boutros-Ghali had little acquaintance with the concept of rules of engagement.

[23] Evans, G., 'Peacekeeping in Cambodia: lessons learned', *NATO Review*, vol. 42, no. 4 (Aug. 1994), pp. 24–27.

[24] Maley, M., 'Reflections on the electoral process in Cambodia', ed. Smith (note 14), p. 88.

ment, allowing for 'a buildup of knowledge, a familiarity with key players, an understanding of bottom lines and the nuances of the mandate or peace agreement'.[25] According to Warner this was a key factor in the success of the United Nations Transition Assistance Group (UNTAG) in Namibia, where the key players had been familiar with each other for 10 years. While this is unlikely to be possible in future missions, the UN needs to ensure that the corporate knowledge of its negotiators is passed on to those who must implement the resulting peacekeeping mission. In future, where possible, leadership of any advance mission should also be carried over into the main mission.

Finally, it would be of help in future if both the civilian and the military heads of UN peacekeeping operations were acceptable to the major parties to the peace accord in question. Although the parties should not be given a veto over UN appointments, the political benefits of consultation should be obvious. In Cambodia neither Akashi's nor Sanderson's appointment was discussed beforehand with the parties.

Information

Part of the difficulty in planning for UNTAC was the understandable dearth of accurate information about a country which had been deliberately isolated by the international community for over a decade and ravaged by war. The various survey missions had been designed to fill this information gap. The GAO concluded, however, that the UN survey missions to Cambodia were often obliged to rely on (presumably suspect) information supplied by the warring parties. In addition, by the time UNTAC was deployed, the information it did have was outdated, incomplete or unreliable.[26] Compounding the problem was UNAMIC's alleged lack of investigative rigour. Warner notes that Cambodia in those days was remote and inaccessible outside Phnom Penh and the resulting field reports 'could not get to the heart of any issue'. Raoul Jennar concurs, noting that the quick surveys done failed to collect information that was precise enough for implementation of UNTAC's mandate.[27]

[25] Warner (note 3), p. 7.
[26] *UN Peacekeeping: Observations on Mandates and Operational Capability* (note 1), p. 5.
[27] Warner (note 3), p. 6; Jennar, R. M., 'UNTAC: "international triumph" in Cambodia?', *Security Dialogue*, vol. 25, no. 2 (1994), p. 153.

Others claim that the problem was not a lack of information but UN headquarters' inability to process and use the information it received. Jennar notes the ignorance of Cambodia among many senior UN officials.[28] In fairness, UNTAC did go to some trouble to recruit leading experts and scholars on Cambodia to fill senior positions in UNTAC and benefited from their insights into Cambodian culture, society and history.[29]

The UN is already making progress in improving its advance planning capabilities for peacekeeping operations, having boosted its planning staff in New York, mostly through secondment of military officers from member states. One clear need is an information technology strategy, given the requirements of modern missions, especially those with electoral components, for timely and speedy data acquisition and processing.[30]

III. The need for measured implementation

While UNTAC's experience points to the need for rapid deployment, it also indicates the need for measured implementation. In the best of circumstances, the Paris Peace Accords had set the UN a seemingly impossible schedule. In the view of Asia Watch, 'Even had the deployment of the UN in Cambodia begun on day one of the Paris accords, such a schedule would have been extremely optimistic for a country with minimal communications and electricity whose dilapidated roads are barely passable for motor vehicles in the dry season, and impassable for the five months of monsoon rains each year.'[31] The Cambodia operation has been called by some critics, including those within the UN system who had to implement it, a 'race against time'.[32] The GAO says that UNTAC's mandate 'stretched the mission both operationally and politically'.[33] Ironically, it was the ambitious-

---

[28] Jennar (note 27), pp. 151, 153.
[29] Akashi, Y., 'The challenges of peace-keeping in Cambodia: lessons to be learned', Paper presented to School of International and Public Affairs, Columbia University, New York, 29 Nov. 1993, p. 22.
[30] Maley (note 24), p. 91.
[31] Asia Watch, *Political Control, Human Rights, and the UN Mission in Cambodia* (Asia Watch: New York, Sep. 1992), p. 8.
[32] Asia Watch (note 31), p. 2.
[33] *UN Peacekeeping: Observations on Mandates and Operational Capability* (note 1), p. 1.

ness of the timetable, not the Khmer Rouge, that most threatened the peace process in its earliest days.

Repatriation, electoral enrolment, the establishment of a neutral, safe political environment and the securing of human rights were subject to almost unbearable time pressures. Akashi and Sanderson were both aware of the UN's lack of preparedness in meeting this timetable, but had little choice but to attempt to fulfil it as envisaged.[34] UNTAC's mandate (unlike that of UNTAG) did not stipulate that the SRSG had to be satisfied at each stage of the process before proceeding to the next. In Namibia this arrangement, according to Jennar, gave the SRSG 'a certain strength'.[35]

The official reason for choosing late April or early May 1993 for the election—a date which drove all other UNTAC deadlines—was that it fell shortly after the Cambodian New Year, when the majority of Cambodians were expected to be gathered at their home locations.[36] However, it also coincided with the start of the rainy season.

Presumably the ambitious timetable was imposed by the Paris negotiators out of fear that delay would lead to a loss of momentum and a breakdown of the fragile consensus on which the agreements were based. There was also an awareness that the international community was tiring of the Cambodian problem, wished to be rid of it as soon as possible and might not be able to sustain political support, domestic or international, for a protracted peace process. There was also a concern to keep costs down.

Future UN undertakings of this magnitude should allow for a more measured timetable if possible. Alternatively, more flexibility could be built into the process without sacrificing compliance incentives. The implementation of missions with tight timetables will be assisted by improvements the UN is currently making to its planning and operational capabilities.

IV. Organizational lessons

Once UNTAC was fully deployed, no organizational disasters jeopardized its mission. When problems did arise, UNTAC often managed,

---

[34] Chopra *et al.* (note 18), p. 20.
[35] Jennar (note 27), p. 152.
[36] UN, Report of the Secretary-General on Cambodia, UN document S/23613, 19 Feb. 1992, p. 9.

with ingenuity and typical UN improvisation, to get by. However, there are major lessons to be learned from the experience.

Management at UN headquarters

Traditionally, once the UN Secretariat had arranged funding and force contributions, UN peacekeeping missions (which used to be principally military operations) were handed over to the force commander to manage thereafter. UN headquarters' organizational role was *ad hoc* and limited: contact between headquarters and the field was spasmodic and arbitrary and UN headquarters did not maintain a round-the-clock operations room to keep in contact with its field commanders.

The Cambodia operation, more than any previous mission, revealed the grave inadequacy of this approach. Compared with the Namibia operation, where there was reportedly 'fearsome' interest on the part of the Secretariat's Senior Task Force for Namibia, 'verging on excessive and ill-advised micro-management', there seems to have been little contact or exchange of views and information between UNTAC and the Secretariat.[37] Sanderson notes that much of what he reported to New York was wasted because there was no one in the Secretariat qualified to interpret it.[38] He reported in March 1993: 'I have not been to New York since my appointment almost 12 months ago, visits by senior officials are few and nobody from the Military Advisor's Office has visited in the life of the mission'.[39] He partly solved such problems by the *ad hoc* appointment of two UNTAC liaison officers to the Secretariat.[40] The secondment of dedicated mission liaison officers to New York on a short-rotation basis should be standard procedure for the duration of complex missions such as UNTAC.[41]

Other organizational deficiencies at UN headquarters included cumbersome procurement procedures. The UN tendering process was complex and time-consuming, involving the soliciting and processing of competitive tenders in New York.[42] One egregious incident

[37] Warner (note 3), p. 4.
[38] Sanderson (note 15), p. 11.
[39] Sanderson (note 16), p. 4.
[40] Farris (note 17), p. 48.
[41] Sanderson (note 14), p. 25.
[42] Akashi, Y., 'The challenges faced by UNTAC', *Japan Review of International Affairs*, summer 1993, p. 188.

occurred when UN headquarters mistakenly ordered an unnecessary 850 minibuses and 500 four-wheel drive vehicles.[43] Installation of the UNTAC communications system, including telephone and fax services, was delayed in New York for three months until after electoral registration had been completed.[44] Two months after UNTAC was deployed the Electoral Component's office automation equipment consisted of one personal computer. The procurement process for photocopiers was described as 'farcical'.[45]

Greater delegation of financial authority, the privatization of some functions and faster and more flexible procurement procedures would all have helped the functioning of UNTAC's administration. The Secretary-General himself understatedly noted that 'the experience of mounting a large and complex United Nations operation such as UNTAC may point to the possible need to re-examine the manner in which existing financial and administrative rules and regulations of the Organization are applied to such operations'.[46] One way to avoid major procurement problems in future missions would be to contract out to single prime contractors on a turn-key basis the provision of critical and complex systems such as office automation, information technology and communications systems. This was done successfully in Cambodia in the case of the Electoral Component's voter registration computer system and voter registration kits.[47] Such an innovation played a large role in the overall success of the Electoral Component.

The performance of future missions would also be enhanced by the provision of timely and high-quality translation and document reproduction facilities, especially in languages which are not among the six official working languages of the UN. In Cambodia there was a critical shortage of Khmer-speakers, translators, typists, computer programmers, and reprographic facilities and no co-ordinated plan for their provision by the UNTAC Administration.[48]

---

[43] UN, Financing of the United Nations Transitional Authority in Cambodia: report of the Secretary-General, UN document A/48/701, 8 Dec. 1993, Annex XXIII.

[44] Ayling, S. (Lt-Col), 'UNTAC: the ambitious mission', ed. H. Smith, Australian Defence Force Academy, Australian Defence Studies Centre, *Peacekeeping: Challenges for the Future* (ADSC: Canberra, 1993), p. 79.

[45] Maley (note 24), p. 91. Warner (note 3, p. 11) cites the case of Radio UNTAC and UNTAC TV, whose inauguration was delayed by 12 months by the need to use cumbersome Secretariat tendering systems in New York.

[46] UN, First progress report of the Secretary-General on the United Nations Transitional Authority in Cambodia, UN document S/23870, 1 May 1992, p. 10.

[47] Maley (note 24), pp. 91, 92 and 94.

[48] Maley (note 24), p. 94.

Criticism of the UN Secretariat alone for its organizational lapses in the Cambodian operation is, however, unfair. It should also be directed at the international community and the Security Council for not equipping the UN with the requisite capacity before entrusting it with such a mission.

The Cambodian operation was one of the three major missions, along with UNPROFOR and UNOSOM II (the United Nations Operation in Somalia II), which have heightened the UN Secretariat's awareness of its organizational shortcomings and stimulated a reform process. While it is beyond the scope of this study to detail these reforms, they include a substantial expansion of the DPKO, its organization into geographical divisions for the first time to make tracking and co-ordination of operations in particular regions easier, the integration of the Field Operations Division into a new Office of Planning and Support in the DPKO and the establishment of a 24-hour 'Situation Centre'.[49]

Management in the field

Warner claims that the administrative structure of UNTAC was inappropriate for the scope and magnitude of its responsibilities: 'it seems that the administrative blueprint of previous—and much smaller and less complex—operations [was] simply dusted off and applied to the Cambodia mission'.[50] In General Sanderson's view, 'the fundamental problem with the UNTAC mission has been our inability to put in place the administrative aspects as quickly as necessary'.[51]

Notwithstanding Akashi's claim that co-operation between UNTAC components was 'mostly very good',[52] a clear lesson of UNTAC is the need for better strategic co-ordination between the components of large multi-purpose UN missions. Sanderson has complained that 'there was never integrated strategic planning within the UNTAC mission', resulting in 'considerable grief and disharmony'.[53] In what has been described as a managerial 'stovepipe', each component

[49] Berdal, M., International Institute for Strategic Studies, *Whither UN Peacekeeping?* Adelphi Paper no. 281 (Brassey's: London, 1993); and Findlay, T., 'Multilateral conflict prevention, management and resolution', SIPRI, *SIPRI Yearbook 1994* (Oxford University Press: Oxford, 1994), pp. 13–52,

[50] Warner (note 3), p. 11.

[51] *Jane's Defence Weekly*, 2 Jan. 1993, p. 32.

[52] Interview with the author, New York, 22 Nov. 1993.

[53] Sanderson (note 15), p. 10.

reported to its own headquarters in Phnom Penh rather than to UNTAC headquarters.[54] Initially, co-ordination was impaired by the separation of these headquarters between 30 separate locations across Phnom Penh.[55] The components did not even have joint co-ordination meetings until March 1993. Akashi, moreover, regarded these meetings as opportunities for the components to 'harmonize' their various priorities[56] rather than to engage in hard-headed strategic co-ordination under his leadership.

UNTAC's loose strategic co-ordination arrangements resulted in waste, duplication of effort and lack of synergy. The GAO reported, for instance, that the absence of a joint military–civilian co-ordination staff at UNTAC headquarters resulted in some projects planned by the civilian Rehabilitation Component, designed in part to provide income and skills to the local populace, being pre-empted and completed by the military as part of its civic action campaign.[57] Other examples include incompatible military and police communications systems and separate public affairs offices for each component.

On the military–civilian relationship, Schear implies that both sides were at fault: 'military personnel had to accept that they were cast in a supporting role, and civilian personnel had to curtail activities in high risk areas, recognizing that the military was not simply there to be an escort and taxi service'.[58] According to Karl Farris, 'The military component of UNTAC, outcome-oriented and accustomed to working systematically, became the *de facto* integrator.'[59] Since it was not mandated to do this, members of other components often resented the military's 'take-charge' attitude.

Only the Military and Electoral Components (the latter described by Akashi as being jealous of its autonomy)[60] eventually forged the necessary co-operative arrangements, but only to see the election through. Akashi describes this as a case of all UNTAC components 'closing ranks' behind the Electoral Component, implying that

[54] Farris (note 17), p. 48.
[55] Ayling (note 44), p. 79.
[56] Interview with the author, New York, 22 Nov. 1993.
[57] *UN Peacekeeping: Observations on Mandates and Operational Capability* (note 1), p. 10.
[58] Schear, J., 'Beyond traditional peacekeeping: the case of Cambodia', Paper presented to the Workshop on Beyond Traditional Peacekeeping, US Naval War College, Newport, R.I., 24 Feb. 1994, p. 25.
[59] Farris (note 17), p. 48.
[60] Akashi (note 29), p. 12.

UNTAC was previously divided.[61] Although a number of 'multi-lateral' meetings between UNTAC's components were held to plan support of the Electoral Component, they were eventually abandoned and no overall plan was ever produced.[62]

Proper co-ordination between the military and civilian personnel of peacekeeping missions is essential. The activities of the military component of future peacekeeping operations should be fully integrated into the mission in terms of supporting and protecting the civilian elements, while the civilian elements should be more readily able to take advantage of the special capabilities of the military. This would be helped by integrated pre-mission planning, training of civilians and military and recruitment of professionally trained civilians for the appropriate mission positions, rather than relying, as in some past cases, on more or less gifted amateurs.

Beyond this the UN must develop a more sophisticated conception of the operation of multifunctional missions like UNTAC. Rather than deploying seven quasi-independent components and trusting them to co-operate in the field once they are deployed, as occurred in Cambodia, the UN needs to determine at the outset how each component's mission dovetails with the strategic goals of the operation. Combined strategic planning should then inform the deployment of the entire mission. Overlaid onto this should be strategic co-ordination with the non-governmental sector and the international monetary and financial institutions which can play such a large role in reconstruction and development. The improvisation that characterized much of UNTAC's performance, noble though it may have been, cannot be the basis for future UN exercises in nation building. Too much in the way of lives, resources and the reputation of the United Nations is at stake.

As to high-level management, experience of international relations and the UN system and the confidence of the Secretary-General are clearly prerequisites for appointment to the position of SRSG. However, a complex organization like UNTAC, which needs to be established with speed and to operate efficiently from the outset, should have among its leadership someone with the requisite high-level managerial training and organizational experience, perhaps with a background in a multinational corporation. UN bureaucrats may not have such skills.

---

[61] Akashi (note 29), p. 21.
[62] Maley (note 24), pp. 92–93.

For future missions the UN should consider a management structure under which the SRSG remains the political head of the operation, carrying out political and representative functions, but with an executive administrator, with the same status as the military commander, to manage the organizational aspects of the mission. In particular he or she should be empowered to force horizontal integration on the mission as well as co-ordinating mission activities with those of other UN agencies, NGOs and the international financial institutions.[63] In any event the UN should establish strict criteria for such positions and conduct a professional search for suitable candidates, rather than simply drawing them from its own ranks. This would help avoid the Secretary-General using such appointments for 'political' purposes, such as rewarding (or penalizing) Secretariat staff.

Financial issues

During the Cambodia operation the UN was in desperate financial straits, struggling to fund the organization and management of its existing peacekeeping operations, even without allowing for the new administrative burdens that a Cambodia-style operation required.

By 30 June 1992 only 27 per cent of the UNTAC budget had been received, from a mere dozen UN member states.[64] On 30 November 1992 outstanding assessments for UNTAC/UNAMIC amounted to over $215 million.[65] This had been partly offset by voluntary contributions in kind and by borrowing from other peacekeeping accounts.[66] By 31 October 1993—one month after UNTAC had formally ended—outstanding contributions to the UNTAC/UNAMIC special accounts were back to approximately $231 million.[67] While these overdue contributions do not seem to have affected the conduct of the Cambodia mission unduly, the financial uncertainty under which UN peacekeeping operations typically function cannot be conducive to sound management practices. The UNTAC exercise reinforced the already loud calls for financial reform of UN peacekeeping operations.

[63] Farris (note 17), p. 48.

[64] *East Asia and Pacific Wireless File* (United States Information Service, Canberra), 30 June 1992, p. 30.

[65] UN, *Yearbook of the United Nations 1992* (United Nations: New York, 1993), p. 259.

[66] Including 3 medium transport aircraft and 6 utility helicopters, 1.5 million meals and an air ambulance service: see UN, *Yearbook of the United Nations 1992* (note 65), p. 259.

[67] UN, *United Nations Peace-keeping Operations Information Notes, 1993*, update no. 2, UN document DPI/1306/Rev. 2, Nov. 1993, p. 68.

The monetary cost of UNTAC was greater than that of any previous peacekeeping mission, even though it came in slightly under budget. The original estimate (including for UNAMIC) had been $1.6 billion, while the final expenditure figure through to 31 March 1994 was approximately $1.5 billion.[68] Savings appear to have been made on premises and accommodation, by the late deployment of the Military Component and of international and local staff and on air and surface freight. These were offset by the extension of the deployment of the Military Component after cantonment and disarmament were abandoned and by the extension of other aspects of the UNTAC operation until the end of 1993.[69] Some observers, both within and outside UNTAC, argue that the cost of the operation was unnecessarily high and that the same result could have been achieved for less money. Examples of where costs could have been cut include the training of Cambodians for tasks such as civil policing which were carried out by expensive international staff.[70]

V. Reaction to non-compliance of the parties

The response of UNTAC to violations of the Paris Accords was quiet diplomacy and negotiation and what has been characterized as a low-key 'administrative approach', rather than enforcement. This was both logical and consistent with the traditional precepts of UN peacekeeping missions.[71] All the Cambodian parties had undertaken to abide fully by the Paris Accords and to accept the presence and prescribed role of UNTAC. Implementation should have simply been a step-by-step process of building confidence and implementing each consecutive phase of the plan. Despite its wide-ranging powers, UNTAC was not intended to be an enforcement mechanism but an implementation mechanism ultimately dependent on the consent, if not the goodwill, of the parties. In the case of the Khmer Rouge, whose violations of the Paris Accords were the most egregious, the UN, with Security

[68] UN, *United Nations Peace-keeping Operations Information Notes* (note 67), p. 68. The original Australian 'mid-range' scenario for UNTAC for an 18-month period was $1.3 billion: see Evans and Grant (note 8), p. 215.

[69] UN, *Yearbook of the United Nations 1992* (note 65), p. 260.

[70] Branigin, W. 'Curtain falls in Cambodia: a UN success, with flaws', *International Herald Tribune*, 27 Sep. 1993, p. 5. For instance, the cost of Radio UNTAC, at $4.4 million, included more sophisticated studios than those at the BBC, requiring expatriates to maintain them.

[71] See the discussion in chapter 2.

Council approval, decided not to attempt to force it to comply (apart from adopting half-hearted and ineffective economic sanctions) but to continue the peace process without them. This resulted in fundamental changes to the way in which the Paris Accords had envisaged peace being brought to Cambodia.

The question of peace enforcement

Akashi notes that his critics, especially the press, interpreted 'UNTAC's caution as . . . timidity and indecisiveness, its flexibility was taken as lack of resolve, its preference for a diplomatic solution was interpreted as spineless abhorrence for forceful measures'.[72] It was argued by some, including some NGOs, that UNTAC should have confronted the KR militarily at an early stage, especially after the 'bamboo pole' incident of early 1992, and that UNTAC's failure to do so 'encouraged the KR to believe that it could get away with any abuse, no matter how blatant; it gave the KR an opportunity to strengthen its forces politically as well as militarily; it gave the other Cambodian parties an incentive to violate provisions of the Accords and in some areas to resume full-scale fighting; and it weakened the credibility of UNTAC as a whole'.[73] Chopra and his colleagues contend that:

Coming from a society ruled by force and not law, it is hard to believe they did not expect the provisions of the Paris Agreement to be policed by an effective military force. This might even be underwritten by a capability for terrible retribution from the sky in the manner of previous B-52 raids. When armed representatives of the world's most powerful nations finally arrived with such lack of impact, the DK were tempted to challenge their authority. And once their expectations of coercive, or at least effective, policing had been removed, they realized they could not be forced to comply with the terms of the Agreements.[74]

To have turned UNTAC into an enforcement mechanism would, however, have required a change of mandate. Neither the participating states nor the Security Council were likely to countenance it, especially given their reluctance to change the mandate in the case of

[72] Akashi (note 42), p. 201.
[73] Asia Watch, 'Cambodia: human rights before and after the elections', *Asia Watch*, vol. 5, no. 10 (May 1993), p. 7.
[74] Chopra *et al.* (note 18), p. 21.

UNPROFOR, where the political pressure and strategic imperatives were so much stronger than in Cambodia. China would certainly have vetoed any such change of mandate. If the mandate had been changed to one of enforcement, the Japanese would have been obliged, constitutionally, to withdraw,[75] and would perhaps have been followed by the Australians, starting a chain reaction that could have decimated the Military Component and possibly the CivPols as well.

Most states involved in the Cambodian problem over the years undoubtedly felt that they had already invested sufficient resources in attempting to bring peace to the country, including the cost of UNTAC, without now going to war against the Khmer Rouge. More rigorous enforcement was moreover not deemed absolutely necessary: the KR had neither renounced the Paris Accords nor demanded UNTAC's removal; UNTAC civilians were quietly gaining access to KR areas from which the military had been barred and were achieving some UNTAC objectives such as electoral enrolment;[76] total breakdown of the peace process, as happened in Angola, was not in prospect. Other international priorities, such as Somalia and Haiti, were also beckoning.

Even if the political problems involved in giving UNTAC an enforcement role had been overcome, daunting military ones would have remained. UNTAC was not equipped or deployed to use force except in self-defence and an aggressive reaction would have risked igniting a widespread military confrontation, jeopardizing the lives of UNTAC personnel and the whole peacekeeping operation. UNTAC's neutrality would have evaporated, as would the consent of the parties—already under severe stress, at least among the Khmer Rouge and the SOC. UNTAC would have become one more combatant in the Cambodian civil war.

UNTAC might have got away with a 'shot across the bows' of the KR without igniting full-scale conflict, especially if consent could have been re-established immediately through negotiations; but comprehensive enforcement of the cease-fire and the peace process by

---

[75] The 1992 Japanese PKO [Peacekeeping Operations] Law restricts Japanese participation in peacekeeping activities to cases where there is agreement on a cease-fire and the neutrality of UN forces is maintained. In addition states surrounding the host nation must all accept Japanese participation; and once these conditions cease to exist Japan must promptly withdraw from the particular operation. See Takahara, T., 'Combatting the specters of the past: the Japanese experience', Paper presented to the Friedrich-Ebert Stiftung/SIPRI conference on Challenges for the New Peacekeepers, Bonn, 21–22 Apr. 1994, p. 9.

[76] Schear (note 2), p. 304.

military means, especially enforcement of cantonment and disarmament, was impossible. A military campaign to force the KR to comply fully with the Paris Accords was out of the question. The experience of the well-equipped and -trained forces of the USA and its allies in neighbouring Viet Nam three decades previously was a potent and ever-present reminder to UNTAC military personnel of what guerrilla fighters could do to conventional armed forces in jungle terrain.[77] Of a cobbled-together multilateral peacekeeping army like UNTAC, John Mackinlay notes: 'It would be almost impossible to conduct a full-scale counter-insurgency campaign with a UN force, because its fractured composition and alien status in the host country are quite different to the successful counter-insurgency forces in history from which the concepts are derived'.[78]

Segal and Berdal cite in particular UNTAC's lack of interoperability of equipment, the absence of close air support, the dearth of adequate tactical communications and tracking equipment and the effective absence of logistical support.[79] UNTAC for instance had only 26 helicopters. They argue that even a 'perimeter defence' or 'bottle-up' campaign directed against the Khmer Rouge in the northwest of the country would have required resources, both political and military, that were beyond the ability of UNTAC ever to command.

A larger military presence and more resolute military posture from the outset, not necessarily including the use of force but combined with political, economic and diplomatic pressure, might have cowed the KR and the Hun Sen Government into greater compliance at an early stage.[80] Initially because it was deployed so late, and then because of an apparent unwillingness to use its powers to the limit, UNTAC failed to take advantage of its greatest assets—the presence of a large international force, led by a personal representative of the UN Secretary-General and backed by the moral and political authority of the Paris Peace Accords, the UN Security Council and influential states in the region. More specifically, UNTAC failed to capitalize on the element of surprise, the unfamiliarity of the combatants with the UN and the deterrent effect of its modern military capabilities

---

[77] Gen. Sanderson had himself served in Viet Nam with the Australian forces.

[78] Mackinlay, J., 'Successful intervention', *Internationale Spectator*, Nov. 1993, p. 661.

[79] Segal, G. and Berdal, M., 'The Cambodian dilemma', *Jane's Intelligence Review*, vol. 5, no. 3 (Mar. 1993), p. 132.

[80] One Western diplomat was quoted as suggesting that a Chinese engineering battalion be sent to KR territory to begin mine clearing. See de Beer, P., 'Khmer Rouge threat to UN peace process', *Guardian Weekly*, 21 June 1992, p. 11.

(especially its mobility and communications). As Warner puts it, there is an element of 'theatre or symbolism' involved in a UN peacekeeping force asserting its visibility and legitimacy.[81] In situations where consent of the parties is fragile or tentative it is even more important that visibility and legitimacy be established as soon as possible.

Akashi claims that the deterioration of the security situation in early 1993 might have been avoided through 'a timely request for a few more infantry battalions and the addition of more armoured personnel carriers and helicopters, which gave mobility, and through a clearer definition of UNTAC's right of self-defense'.[82] It is not clear whether Akashi actually made such a request and it was rejected in New York or whether he was expressing regret that he had not in fact made such a request.[83] In any event, bringing in reinforcements will not necessarily enable peacekeepers to retrieve credibility and legitimacy once they have been lost.

Self-defence

One means by which peacekeeping forces have traditionally asserted their legitimacy is by demonstrating their ability and willingness to defend themselves—with the minimum necessary force, but none the less with force.[84] Akashi admits that at the beginning the UNTAC Military Component adopted 'a somewhat passive attitude *vis-à-vis* the Khmer Rouge' as a result of interpreting the right of self-defence in the strictest sense.[85] UNTAC did not, for instance, resist the detention of its soldiers or even the forced surrender of its weapons and vehicles. Some battalions, for instance the Pakistanis, defended their

---

[81] Warner (note 3), p. 3.

[82] Akashi (note 42), p. 197.

[83] Black Hawk helicopters were in fact provided by Australia at short notice, along with 100 additional troops, for these purposes. See *Phnom Penh Post*, 21 May–3 June 1993, p. 2.

[84] The report of the Secretary-General on the establishment of the United Nations Interim Force in Lebanon (UNIFIL) in 1978 summed up the basic principle of the use of force by peacekeeping operations. It stated, *inter alia*, that 'the Force will be provided with weapons of a defensive character and shall not use force except in self-defence. Self-defence would include resistance to attempts by forceful means to prevent it from discharging its duties under the mandate of the Security Council'. Force can be used only in self-defence against direct attacks on, or threats to, the lives of UN personnel or when UN security in general is under threat. This would include attempts at forceful entry into UN positions and their environs by one party for use as a fire base against the other and attempts by force to disarm UN troops. See United Nations Institute for Training and Research (UNITAR), *A Peacekeeping Training Manual*, 2nd draft (United Nations: New York, 1994), p. 60.

[85] Akashi (note 29), p. 24.

positions determinedly, thereby earning the gratitude of villages in their vicinity.[86] The Indonesian battalion, however, was accused of failing to come to the defence of nearby villagers during an attack by the KR in which 29 people were killed.[87] In early 1993, when a skirmish between KR guerrillas and government troops endangered a French Foreign Legion unit, the legionnaires opened fire on both sides, killing four and putting a stop to the fighting.[88] Both the French and the Netherlands battalions reportedly had a 'more aggressive approach' to establishing control of their sectors than other battalions.[89]

Sanderson appears to lay some of the responsibility at the feet of particular national contingents of his military force which were unwilling even to defend themselves. This, he says, 'emboldened elements opposed to the peace process, and thereby added to the insecurity of other military units and civilian components'.[90] He notes that despite the clearest definitions in standard operating procedures and continuous briefings there was a wide variety of interpretations of 'self-defence' by national units, ranging from 'just handing over your weapons to anyone who points a gun at you, to opening up with everything at the slightest provocation'.[91] Eventually the majority of units were, Sanderson says, 'mentally prepared and equipped' to exercise self-defence.

One contingent treated as a special case with regard to the use of force was the Japanese because of their sensitive political and constitutional situation. The Japanese engineering troops were, according to Japanese parliamentary legislation, permitted to carry only rifles and pistols for self-defence and could not become involved in protecting other UNTAC forces under attack (or even engage in mine clearance).[92] A Japanese major was reported as saying that if fighting broke out his orders were to withdraw to camp. If pinned down, his troops could then act in self-defence.[93]

---

[86] Mahmud, T. (Col), *The Peacekeepers: 2 AK in Cambodia* (2 AK Regiment: Lahore, 1993), p. 85.

[87] *The Guardian*, 27 Apr. 1993, p. 6.

[88] Serrill, M. S., 'Cambodia: back to war', *Time* (Australia), 25 May 1993, p. 32.

[89] Ayling (note 44), p. 81.

[90] Sanderson (note 15), p. 8. This is confirmed by the GAO: see *UN Peacekeeping: Observations on Mandates and Operational Capability* (note 1), p. 11.

[91] Sanderson (note 15), p. 8.

[92] *The Independent*, 11 July 1992, p. 13; *Washington Post*, 26 Sep. 1992, p. 15.

[93] *The Independent*, 15 Oct. 1992, p. 15.

It appears that the UNTAC military became prepared to go beyond the use of force in self-defence and use force to 'defend its mission'—but only the electoral process—after the abandonment of cantonment, disarmament and demobilization. In the event, the use of force to defend the electoral process proved unnecessary.

In Cambodia the Sanderson strategy worked. The General is the first to admit, however, that there was a large element of luck in this. If the Khmer Rouge had pursued an aggressive and organized military or even terrorist campaign against UNTAC and/or the electoral process, especially at a late stage when withdrawal would have been difficult, it is not clear what UNTAC's reaction would have been. An attack on the capital on the first polling day was, for example, a much feared possibility. Competing pressures to withdraw or remain and fight, perhaps with reinforcements, would have been strong. The Japanese would certainly have withdrawn. In practical terms, then, Sanderson had no choice but to hope for a lucky outcome. His force was simply not equipped or trained, nor did it have the political backing, to engage in greater use of force, even a prolonged self-defence operation. Reinforcements were unlikely to be forthcoming.

Proponents of more effective military forces in second generation peace operations argue that the UN cannot afford simply to ignore violations of peace agreements, often painstakingly arrived at, by recalcitrant parties, often small in size and venal in nature.[94] To do so would put the credibility of the UN, the Security Council and the international community at risk and jeopardize major investments of time, resources and personnel. They argue, moreover, that there should be greater flexibility in the use of force and a greater range of options. This does not mean lowering the threshold for the use of force, nor does it mean the UN aggressively 'fighting for peace'.[95] On the contrary, the operational flexibility available to an effective military force may help avoid the use of force rather than increase its likelihood. It should also ensure a much more rigorously policed, monitored and verified peace agreement. Rather than scaring off potential national troop contributors, it should give them greater confidence that their personnel and equipment will not be vulnerable

[94] Mackinlay, J., 'Defining a role beyond peacekeeping', ed. W. H. Lewis, National Defense University, Institute for National Strategic Studies, *Military Implications of United Nations Peacekeeping Operations* (INSS: Washington, DC, June 1993), pp. 32–38.

[95] Mackinlay (note 94), p. 38.

to attack as a result of impromptu and unsustainable UN military action.

The success of the Cambodia operation should not have been left dependent, as it effectively was in the last resort, on luck. While the UNTAC experience reinforces the lessons of traditional peacekeeping values such as impartiality, minimum use of force and the need for retaining the consent of the parties, it does not provide reassurance that peacekeeping forces can defend themselves and their mandate if seriously threatened. It does tell us that any contemplation of such use of force will be impossible if the proper military component is not assembled for the mission at the outset. Even the threat of the use of force and hence the deterrent effect of UN military deployments in similar missions will be weakened if the UN continues to organize military components on the basis of 'best-case' rather than 'worst-case' assumptions.

Liaison and consultation

Some commentators argued that once it became clear that the KR would not participate in cantonment and disarmament UNTAC should have refused to proceed with the peace process and sought further instructions from the Paris negotiators.

Although UNTAC did not refuse to go ahead with the peace process, it did consult widely on how to proceed at every stage at which non-compliance became an issue—with the SNC, the Core Group and the Security Council, in effect all the Paris negotiators. The KR continued to be engaged in discussions in the SNC—of which it remained a member—even though its leadership had retreated from Phnom Penh and it was otherwise failing to comply with the Accords.[96] In addition, France and Indonesia, the two co-chairs of the Paris Conference, held discussions with all the Cambodian parties on three occasions—after the signing of the Accords in Tokyo in June 1992, in

---

[96] Munck, G. L. and Kumar, C., University of Illinois at Urbana-Champaign, Program in Arms Control, Disarmament, and International Security, *Conflict Resolution through International Intervention: A Comparative Study of Cambodia and El Salvador*, Occasional Paper (ACDIS: Urbana, Ill., Apr. 1993), p. 12. The authors claim that the Cambodia operation ran into difficulties because it did not have a body like COPAZ (the National Commission for the Consolidation of Peace) in El Salvador in which the parties could 'regularly interact and express their views on the way in which the accord was being implemented'. This is not the case. The SNC was established partly for that purpose.

Beijing in November 1992 and in Phnom Penh in June 1993.[97] The Beijing meeting was a vain attempt to find a compromise to bring the KR back into the peace process, even though deadlines for registration for the May 1993 election had passed.[98] In making its decisions on Cambodia during the period the Security Council acted only after consultations, either direct or indirect, with all the Paris parties and with the approval of all of them except, ultimately, the Khmer Rouge.

Others argue that Akashi should have had more private negotiation sessions with the KR to try to entice it back into the peace process. This argument assumes that KR concerns over the peace process were genuine and amenable to negotiation. Akashi apparently only sought private negotiation at a late stage in the UNTAC operation. His levers of influence with the KR were not strong, especially as they had begun attacking him personally. His greatest weapon was the links that UNTAC had with China and Thailand, something he emphasized to the KR repeatedly.[99]

General Sanderson records that in addition the MMWG maintained continuous liaison and conducted frequent negotiations on complex issues with the military staff of all factions, was particularly alive during crises and gained the trust of the Khmer Rouge.[100] While none of these constant dealings with the KR succeeded in bringing it back into compliance with the Paris Accords, they may conceivably have blunted any determination on the part of the group to launch an all-out assault on the peace process.

Where compliance is concerned, the overall lesson from UNTAC is that in missions where the UN is charged with implementing a comprehensive peace plan it should, in addition to persisting with constant negotiations and consultations with the parties, make an early display of strength and determination, use its advantages more convincingly and wrest authority from local authorities and factions promptly and confidently.

Subsequently, compliance can be enhanced or induced through carefully targeted and planned non-military incentives. Schear argues that 'given savvy leadership, UN operations do have sources of leverage that can be exploited in poor societies and fragmented political cultures. These tools include rehabilitation aid, humanitarian and elec-

[97] Akashi (note 42), pp. 186–87.
[98] Sanderson (note 15), p. 1.
[99] Interview with the author, New York, 22 Nov. 1993.
[100] Sanderson (note 15), p. 9.

toral work, civic education, and technical training. UNTAC was very skilful in emphasizing these kinds of missions in its operations'.[101] He also notes that financial incentives can be powerful conflict termination tools.[102]

UNTAC's experience does not support the case for the adoption of a peace enforcement strategy in such circumstances as Cambodia's.

VI. Supervision and control of the civil administration

Part of the compliance problems that UNTAC experienced can be attributed to the fact that its intended 'direct supervision and control' over the civil administration of Cambodia were never fully realized. This was the result of (a) a lack of time to plan for the operation of such a concept; (b) the absence of precedents on which to draw;[103] (c) the difficulty of obtaining specialized staff;[104] (d) initial timidity and lack of resolve on the part of UNTAC; (e) the decrepit state of the Cambodian legal system; (f) pervasive language difficulties; and (g) 'the limited and inaccurate assessment of the initial survey missions, which had not detected the many "empty shells" of ministries in Phnom Penh or the problems of effective delegation of power to the provinces'.[105]

If such a supervision and control arrangement is attempted in future, the UN will need to intervene more promptly and determinedly and with better planning and preparation. It should also involve more senior and experienced professional staff and acquire an enhanced language capability.[106]

Yet, even if the Civil Administration Component had been perfectly organized and allocated the appropriate resources, it might be argued that such a concept was never workable in Cambodia. Schear contends that the whole concept of oversight had 'inherently limited

---

[101] Schear (note 2), p. 300.

[102] Schear (note 2), pp. 301–302.

[103] The British and Commonwealth peacekeeping operation in Rhodesia/Zimbabwe in 1979–80 was similar in that a British Governor, Lord Soames, was vested with full executive and legislative powers and took nominal control of the entire machinery of government until Zimbabwe's independence was declared. According to Warner, however, it was a 'fast and dirty' operation, involving more apparent than real control and a short transition. See Warner (note 3), p. 12.

[104] UN, First progress report of the Secretary-General, 1 May 1992 (note 46), p. 7.

[105] 'Executive summary', Institute for Policy Studies and UNITAR International Conference on UNTAC: debriefing and lessons, Singapore, 2–4 Aug. 1994, p. 3.

[106] Warner (note 3), p. 12.

value in the highly personalized decision-making structures that characterize Cambodian public administrations'.[107] The Paris Accords, moreover, had not paid any special attention to control at the subnational level, where 'provincial governors and civil servants proved to be very independent-minded'.[108] Finally, the Paris Accords had assumed co-operation on the part of the SOC. After the KR began violating the Accords, and especially after October 1992 when UNTAC attempted to strengthen its monitoring and supervision capabilities, the SOC also became unco-operative, setting in train an action–reaction pattern of non-compliance that threatened the very foundation of the Paris Accords. Future such operations will need to take into account the possibility of both active and passive opposition to UN supervision and control.

One school of thought holds that UNTAC was unable to supervise and control Cambodia's administration because the idea was itself fundamentally flawed and its execution an impossibility. This is impossible to prove since the UNTAC experiment was not sufficiently well planned or provided for to constitute a valid test. Moreover, the problem may not have been the inherent fallibility of the concept, but a lack of 'political will' on the part of UNTAC. Lyndall McLean sees the Civil Administration Component's greatest failing—its inability to take 'corrective' action—as the result of a combination of legal difficulties and a lack of political will: 'At the senior levels of UNTAC decisions were taken that the risk of non-compliance or the flaunting of a UN directive was likely to be more damaging to UNTAC's image of authority than to just let the case slide.'[109]

The idea that the UN can ever take complete 'control' of a country to implement a peace agreement may be a chimera, but some form of limited, but timely and convincing, supervision may be all that is required in particular circumstances.[110] Whether future UN missions can summon the political will to make even this type of control of the civil administration of an entire country possible is another question. At the very least they should be given the resources to give them a chance of succeeding. In such circumstances capability may help beget political will.

---

[107] Schear (note 2), p. 291.
[108] Schear (note 2), p. 291.
[109] McLean, L., 'Civil administration in transition: public information and the neutral political/electoral environment', ed. Smith (note 14), pp. 55–56.
[110] As in the case of Zimbabwe: see Warner (note 3), p. 12.

VII. The military

The Military Component of UNTAC was generally efficient and effective, despite the changing circumstances of its role. It generally developed good rapport with the Cambodian people, among other things by carrying out a wide range of civic action tasks, such as providing medical care and improving basic village amenities.

There were, naturally, wide disparities in the training, equipment and competence of the various national contingents. The Bulgarians were by far the worst.[111] Lurid press reports related that 30 per cent of the Bulgarian battalion (Bulgabatt) were former prisoners; a dozen of them threatened to kill General Sanderson unless he increased their pay; and on their departure from Cambodia some of the troops attempted to smuggle exotic animals and weapons from the country and harassed flight attendants on the aircraft leased by the UN to take them back to Bulgaria.[112] Without naming them, the GAO records that, by December 1992, 56 members of the battalion, including eight officers, had been sent home for disciplinary reasons.[113]

The Bulgarian Government denied most of these allegations but did admit that exotic animals were smuggled and that there were 'certain shortcomings' in their troops' behaviour.[114] A senior military officer in Cambodia noted that in recruiting their contingent the Bulgarians had accepted anyone who volunteered and some were threatened with gaol if they refused to go to Cambodia. According to General Stoyan Andreyev, National Security and Armed Forces Adviser to the Bulgarian President, the troops were provided with one or two months' basic military training.[115] Sweden also provided some peacekeeping training, but apparently with little effect. Bulgabatt had reportedly only one English-speaker.[116]

Also without naming them, Warner notes that the Bulgarians did 'substantial damage to UNTAC's standing and credibility in the

---

[111] For a defence of the Bulgarians see Smith, C., 'Stop bashing Bulgabatt', letter to the editor, *Phnom Penh Post*, 19 Nov.–2 Dec. 1993, p. 12; Radio Free Europe/Radio Liberty, *RFE/RL Daily Report*, 2 Nov. 1993.

[112] Branigin, W., 'Bulgarians put crimp in UN peacekeeping mission', *Washington Post*, 30 Oct. 1993; McNulty, S., 'Blue helmets, peacekeeping and a few sidelines', Associated Press report from Phnom Penh, 13 Dec. 1993.

[113] *UN Peacekeeping: Observations on Mandates and Operational Capability* (note 1), p. 7.

[114] Bulgarian Defence Ministry statement, Sofia, 13 Dec. 1993.

[115] Interview with the author, Sofia, 12 Oct. 1993.

[116] Ayling (note 44), p. 81.

province in which they were deployed and more broadly'.[117] Farris notes that 'one of the national contingents clearly possessed neither the requisite military skills nor the exemplary discipline necessary for maintaining the standards and image expected of the peacekeeping force'.[118]

Some other military contingents were guilty of misbehaviour at the very least and of cultural insensitivity, mostly during the rest and recreation activities usually associated with armed forces.[119] The press seemed to delight in highlighting the number of white UN vehicles parked outside Phnom Penh bars and brothels. Akashi failed to assuage widespread concern, especially among female members of UNTAC, when he responded by saying that '18-year old hot-blooded soldiers enduring the rigours of Cambodia had the right to enjoy themselves, drink a few beers and chase beautiful young beings of the opposite sex'.[120] Mild behaviour such as Akashi described would not generally have been unacceptable; but his remarks seemed to disregard the importance of UN forces being seen to occupy a higher moral ground than other military forces and the danger to the whole mission if UNTAC's Military Component were to lose the confidence of the Cambodian people.

Sanderson emphasizes, however, that a UN force commander has no legal authority over the national contingents under his command and must rely on the contributing countries themselves to respond rapidly to poor behaviour on the part of their troops. He notes that in Cambodia some did and some did not.[121] His inability to choose the composition of his forces in the first place he described as 'distressing'.[122]

Other military problems arose from national contingents pursuing national rather than UNTAC goals. The French, for instance, tended to run the province in which they were stationed, Kompong Som, as a

---

[117] See Warner (note 3), p. 10.

[118] Farris (note 17), p. 49.

[119] The Thai battalions were alleged to have opened a Thai restaurant in Battambang, reaping substantial profits: see Prasso, S., 'Cambodia: a heritage of violence', *World Policy Journal*, vol. 11, no. 3 (fall 1994), p. 75.

[120] Branigin, W., 'UN Cambodian force is malfunctioning', *International Herald Tribune*, 5 Oct. 1992, p. 5.

[121] Sanderson (note 15), p. 9.

[122] Sanderson (note 14), p. 24.

French fiefdom rather than as part of a multinational operation.[123] One senior UNTAC officer described the behaviour of the French military as 'treasonous'.[124] Akashi himself had some criticism of the UNTAC Military Component, in particular the 'somewhat superficial military information' he received.[125]

The morale of the military component is clearly a key ingredient in the success of a peacekeeping mission. In Cambodia morale was adversely affected by disparities in pay and conditions between the military and the civilian components and among national contingents within the Military Component.[126] Some troops were paid less than they had expected before they left home, while others were not paid at all for several months. The Bulgarian conscripts were not paid at all, while the Australians received generous pay with allowances.[127] According to Sanderson, these anomalies led to 'two near mutinies and some very serious morale problems'.[128] The Irish staff at UNTAC military headquarters withdrew over the issue of pay disparities.[129] In future missions the UN should ensure that its civilian employees do not enjoy living standards significantly higher than those of the military and that common standards of pay and conditions are set for all troops in the Military Component.

General Sanderson believes that the success of the military aspect of peacekeeping depends on 'unity of purpose, unity of command, unity of understanding' and neutrality.[130] The KR attempted to fracture the UNTAC military by playing off 'good' and 'bad' units against each other, for instance by singling out for attack battalions with poor reputations for personal conduct, such as the Bulgarians.[131]

---

[123] Private communication from a highly placed military source in Cambodia. Some UN officials reportedly called it the 'autonomous region of France'. See Murdoch, L., 'The spoils of peace', *Good Weekend* (Sydney), Apr. 1993, p. 48.

[124] Private communication, Phnom Penh, May 1993.

[125] Akashi (note 29), p. 22.

[126] Barrington, K., 'Pay dispute undermines UNTAC morale', *Phnom Penh Post*, 12–25 Mar. 1993, p. 13.

[127] Ayling (note 44), p. 82.

[128] Sanderson (note 15), p. 12.

[129] Ayling (note 44), p. 82.

[130] Sanderson (note 15), p. 8.

[131] Schear (note 2), p. 301. A more convincing explanation for KR attacks on the Bulgarians was the guerrilla group's perception that the Bulgarians and 'all other East Europeans were traitors and supporters of Soviet reformers . . . that had been collaborating with the Vietnamese invaders for decades'. See Behar, N., 'Bulgarian peacekeeping prospects: new experiences and new dilemmas', Paper presented to the Friedrich-Ebert Stiftung/SIPRI conference on Challenges for the New Peacekeepers, Bonn, 21–22 Apr. 1994, p. 6.

Sanderson says that he 'has reason to believe' that some units went along with such attempts or even encouraged them for national political reasons.[132] Fortunately, he says, these difficulties were overcome by involving all units in the planning process, by continuous briefings and by issuing clear directives and orders.

The Cambodia experience reinforces the proposition that sound military training is the key to the success of the military component of a peacekeeping operation. The use of reservists or untrained recruits in such operations is clearly counter-productive. Support units such as engineering battalions must also have the capacity to secure and defend themselves lest they place excessive burdens on the rest of the force. General Sanderson notes that, while some countries might prefer, for domestic political reasons, to offer a 'passive' logistics unit in order to emphasize the humanitarian nature of their contribution, this places an unfair burden on the rest of the mission.[133] In UNTAC's case this was true of at least the Japanese contingent, which gained a reputation for refusing to take any risks, withdrawing to their base well before sunset, for example, in order to avoid possible contact with the Khmer Rouge.

Ironically, Sanderson contends that some of the less well equipped and -trained troops were able to establish better rapport with the local Cambodian population and thereby a better peacekeeping environment than some of the better equipped and more sophisticated military contingents. General Lars-Eric Wahlgren, former commander of the United Nations Interim Force in Lebanon (UNIFIL), has said that, in circumstances where renegade groups threaten an otherwise popular UN operation, the people become the protectors of the peacekeeping mission.[134] Linguistic skills and cultural sensitivity are obvious requirements in these situations.

Both the KR and the SOC attempted to undermine UNTAC's credibility in order to pose as saviours of the Cambodian people. In such circumstances the UN needs actively to seek to win the 'hearts and minds' of the populace through such measures as civic action programmes. Sanderson complains that the UN saw no value in giving the Military Component a budget for such activities on the grounds

[132] This may be a reference to the behaviour of the French contingent.

[133] Sanderson (note 15), p. 13.

[134] Remarks made at the Executive Seminar on Conflict Prevention and Conflict Resolution, Department of Peace and Conflict Research, Uppsala University, Sweden, 23–29 Sep. 1993.

that other UN agencies were carrying out the job. He argues that the military had a much more substantial presence in the countryside than other UN agencies and that 'hearts and minds' activities are a vital part of the military's method of operation in peacekeeping missions. In the event, the military was able to conduct a 'reasonable programme' as a result of voluntary donations from individual countries, close co-operation with other UN agencies and effective use of the individual skills of members of the Military Component. In March 1993 Sanderson established a Civil Action Cell to co-ordinate the military's civic action programme, the first time this had been done in a UN peacekeeping mission.[135] Each battalion thereafter appointed its own civic action co-ordinator.[136] These are useful precedents for future peacekeeping missions.

A final military lesson of Cambodia concerns the extent of 'multilateralization'. In the past the number of countries involved in a peacekeeping force was used as a measure of success. Certainly, a crucial lesson of Cambodia, as Schear says, is: 'Work hard at being multilateral'.[137] However, in the more demanding circumstances of 'second generation' missions there needs to be a more appropriate trade-off between multilateralism and efficiency. It has been suggested for instance that military forces be structured on a functional basis, whereby only one or two countries contribute troops for each particular function, such as the air wing or the military observers. While this was done to some extent successfully in Cambodia—for instance, the Australians provided the communications system and a small number of countries provided the engineers—the concept could be taken further to reduce the number of participating countries involved in any particular function. The concept is especially relevant to the civil police function.

---

[135] Adolph, R. B. Jr (Lt-Col), 'UN military civil action in Cambodia', *Special Warfare*, vol. 7, no. 3 (July 1994), pp. 12–13.

[136] Adolph (note 135), p. 15.

[137] Schear (note 2), p. 300. An interesting counter-example, where lack of international support caused the failure of a peacekeeping mission, is that in Yemen in 1963: see Birgisson, K. Th., 'United Nations Yemen Observation Mission', ed. W. J. Durch, *The Evolution of UN Peacekeeping: Case Studies and Comparative Analysis* (St Martin's Press for The Henry L. Stimson Center: Washington, DC, 1993), pp. 206–18.

VIII. The civil police

The use of civil police in a peacekeeping mission was a relatively new experience for the UN—only the United Nations Peace-keeping Force in Cyprus (UNFICYP), the United Nations Angola Verification Mission (UNAVEM II) and UNTAG in Namibia had previously involved civil police or police monitors. The CivPol element of UNTAC was the largest in UN peacekeeping history. It was, moreover, the first time that civil police had come under the direct control of a mission head rather than a military command.

The UNTAC Civilian Police Component was, however, widely perceived as disastrous. Drawn from 32 UN member states, it comprised a large number of small units of police from a wide range of countries with different methods and ethics and indifferently trained individuals. Deployment was slow: they were still not fully in the field in November 1992.[138] Unlike the military, the police units lacked their own command structures, disciplinary procedures and the equivalent of military police. Also in contrast to the military, police units tend not to be self-sufficient in harsh and dangerous environments and may even require military assistance and/or protection. In Cambodia they were initially not given the necessary support. Some police spoke neither of the two languages specified—English or French—still less Khmer, while others lacked the six years of community policing experience and driver's licence that the UN had stipulated as minimum requirements. Many were not police at all, but paramilitary border guards or military police. One country contributed a medical doctor.[139] Thirteen of the 14 states which contributed more than 100 CivPols were developing countries, whose police forces are often associated with indiscipline, human rights abuses and widespread corruption.[140] Although they were meant to be unarmed, some CivPols bought weapons from the SOC police.

There was also confusion about their role. Although the CivPols had been intended to oversee law and order and monitor the Cambodian police forces, their role was not precisely explained in the Paris Accords, and UNTAC appeared to have a very narrow interpretation

[138] As of 13 Nov. 1992, 3392 police officers from 31 countries, representing 95% of the planned force of 3600, had been deployed: see Chopra *et al.* (note 18), p. 24.
[139] *UN Peacekeeping: Observations on Mandates and Operational Capability* (note 1), p. 7.
[140] Akashi (note 42), p. 189.

of it, based on the Namibia precedent, and no operational plan for fulfilling it. According to Australian Federal Police Commissioner Peter McAulay, while the police were briefed generally on what their role would be, they were not given specific objectives or targets'.[141] Many CivPols became increasingly involved in security escorting, a job they disliked and for which they were not trained.[142] Moreover, according to Chris Eaton of the Australian Federal Police:

Its members were in the field working directly with the indigenous citizenry, facing a daily and unremitting task of bringing confidence and trust back to fragmented and factionalised Cambodian communities and villages. In essence they were sent into an anarchic nation without law and even the most rudimentary of justice systems, let alone a general public appreciation of the need for it. It was a task that was not only poorly articulated but also one set in a structural vacuum. UN police in Cambodia had none of the tools that underpin their role in their domestic country: no laws, no justice administration, no courts and no jails.[143]

Another problem was the lack of advance planning and preparation. Warner notes that 'Planning and execution came at the same time'.[144] The UNTAC Police Commissioner was not appointed until March 1992 and arrived three weeks later, leaving insufficient time for serious planning, including the drafting of standard operating procedures, before the force was deployed. There was no UN doctrine for police operations, the police role being relatively new, nor was any significant training conducted in cultural awareness and other matters. Some of the police, for instance, had no conception of the tragedy of the 'killing fields' and its place in the Cambodian psyche. A community relations programme was eventually initiated but too late to rescue the CivPols' reputation.

The civil police element in any comprehensive peacekeeping mission is critical to good relations with the local populace and must be the subject of more careful UN attention. According to Eaton, 'The role of UN civilian police should therefore be greater than simply observing and should involve a combination of supervision, management, policy guidance, training, development, equipping, remunerat-

---

[141] McAulay, P., 'Civilian police and peacekeeping: challenges in the 1990s', ed. Smith, (note 44), p. 37.
[142] Schear (note 2), p. 301.
[143] Eaton, C., 'The role of police in institution building', ed. Smith (note 14), p. 61.
[144] Warner (note 3), p. 5.

ing and, most importantly, sensitizing and empowering indigenous police'.[145] Since the termination of UNTAC the UN has begun drafting a code of conduct and other guidance for CivPols.

In addition, consideration should be given in future missions to assigning the policing task to fewer countries. This is problematic given that most countries have only enough police for their own domestic needs, as compared with the military, which usually has spare capacity and is trained and on standby for overseas experience. One solution would be to establish a UN police force or to expand and provide better training to the UN guard force which currently secures UN headquarters and was deployed in Iraqi Kurdish territory after the Persian Gulf War. This would be less controversial than the UN acquiring a military force of its own and could be just as beneficial to future peacekeeping missions. Julio Jeldres suggests that it would have been cheaper to train a new Cambodian police force than to pay for the deployment of the CivPols.[146] Training was in fact conducted for the police forces of all Cambodian factions, but it is difficult to see how an apolitical, impartial and unified Cambodian police force could have been created in the short period available to UNTAC.

While in the past the capabilities of national contingents, both military and police, were not so significant because of the more passive role they took in most peacekeeping missions, in the 'second generation' missions currently being undertaken a greater capability is desirable. Greater pre-deployment training, for both military and police components, is essential and is now being undertaken.[147]

The UN must also be more selective in making up its peacekeeping forces. The Secretary-General has always had the right to refuse particular national contributions if he suspects that they are unsuitable. This has usually been done on political grounds rather than on the basis of their failure to meet UN standards: quiet diplomacy or bureaucratic obfuscation has been used gently to dissuade some potential contributors. In future, UN standards should be made more explicit and member states given to understand that only the most

[145] Eaton (note 143), p. 61.

[146] Jeldres, J. A., 'The UN and the Cambodian transition', *Journal of Democracy*, vol. 4, no. 4 (Oct. 1993), p. 108.

[147] The UN has begun work on a Peace-keeping Training Manual and has compiled a list of peacekeeping training efforts being undertaken nationally with the aim of enabling national efforts to be better co-ordinated. The UN Institute for Training and Research (UNITAR) has established a peacekeeping training unit under Lt-Col Christian Hårleman, former Commanding Officer of the Swedish Training Centre for UN Peace-keeping.

capable and appropriate forces will be accepted for difficult UN missions. Akashi himself has enjoined the UN to 'tighten criteria for recruitment of civilian police . . . We should be more strict in our standards and pay more attention to [other cultures'] sensitivities'.[148]

The UN Secretariat and Secretary-General moreover should not have sole responsibility for the composition of UN peacekeeping forces. The military and civil police heads should be appointed early and consulted extensively on such issues.

IX. Other civilian personnel

The quality of UNTAC's other civilian personnel varied enormously, from efficient and effective to incompetent. Akashi has drily noted that 'the quality of personnel was not uniformly outstanding'.[149] Three types of civilian staff were involved in UNTAC: (*a*) UN Secretariat staff seconded to the mission; (*b*) non-UN civilian staff recruited by the UN; and (*c*) staff seconded by national governments.

In the case of UN staff there have traditionally been major financial and career disincentives to service in a peacekeeping mission. These should be remedied. A second problem, which the UN is currently paying attention to, is the recruitment and training of UN staff, which to date has been unprofessional and unsystematic.

Observers have noted that some of the most successful aspects of UNTAC's operations were carried out by units staffed primarily from outside the UN bureaucracy.[150] A major difficulty with using non-UN personnel, however, is the lengthy, inflexible recruitment process, which can mean months of delay in the arrival of key personnel. Furthermore, such staff are likely to be unfamiliar with UN ethos, practices and procedures. Pre-mission training, or at the very least briefing, is essential. Training in conflict resolution and self-protection techniques would be useful for all UN civilians dealing with localized conflict situations in peacekeeping missions.

The problem with personnel seconded from UN member states is that they often lack the necessary qualifications or experience for the position in question but are foisted on an unwilling UN Secretariat by enthusiastic governments. Warner records that in Cambodia the UN

---

[148] Branigin (note 112).
[149] Michaels, M., 'Blue-helmet blues', *Time,* 15 Nov. 1993, p. 56.
[150] Branigin (note 70), p. 5.

sought 150 qualified military police (MPs) who would undertake UN investigations.[151] Of the 150 sent to Cambodia about one-third could speak no English or French. UNTAC eventually requested more MPs to make up the backlog of work caused by these deficiencies, and of the first 20 sent 16 could speak neither of the designated languages. It is clearly incumbent on national governments to ensure that their contributions are timely and appropriate.

The UN should also be more cognizant of inequities in its treatment of locally engaged staff as compared with its international staff. UNTAC paid its foreign staff much more promptly than Cambodians, some of the latter waiting up to three months for payment. Foreign electoral officials were issued with flak jackets and helmets when the security situation deteriorated, while Cambodian employees were not. These discriminatory practices can undermine the goodwill that the UN garners from employing local staff in the first place.

X. Human rights and law and order

A major lesson to be learned from Cambodia is that human rights should be a paramount concern in cases where government authority has collapsed or when a neutral political environment is required for electoral purposes. Asia Watch and Human Rights Watch, while acknowledging UNTAC's achievements, argue that 'the UN's timid promotion of human rights will have bequeathed the Cambodian people a troubling precedent of impunity for political violence'.[152] Comparing the Cambodian operation with the UN role in El Salvador, Asia Watch claims that UNTAC subordinated most of the human rights agenda 'in a rush to the ballot box'. In its view, 'accountability is no luxury, to be deferred to a more stable, peaceful moment. It is the very cornerstone of a society ruled by laws, including international laws that require that those who violate human rights be held answerable for their actions'.[153]

A major issue that arose in Cambodia was how far the UN should intervene to establish a legal system in a country for which it has assumed responsibility. One sensitive question is whether foreign

---

[151] Warner (note 3), p. 9.

[152] *The Australian*, 4 June 1993.

[153] Asia Watch, 'An exchange on human rights and peace-keeping in Cambodia', *Asia Watch*, vol. 5, no. 14 (23 Sep. 1993), p. 1.

judges should be imported as an interim measure while the local judiciary is re-established or retrained. There are precedents: British judges continued to sit in courts in Kenya, Uganda and Zimbabwe after independence, as did Australian judges in Papua New Guinea. There are complex legal issues to be considered, including the question which legal system should be employed. In Cambodia, both the Pol Pot and the Hun Sen systems were clearly flawed, while the French system, on which Cambodia's original post-colonial legal system was based, was regarded as less than satisfactory by those trained in the Anglo-American legal tradition. The 'colonialist' implications of importing foreign judges must also be carefully weighed.

A possible solution to such difficulties, which have also plagued the UN in Somalia, is for the UN to develop 'justice packages' comprising all the elements of a model legal system which can be employed when the UN is required to take over the administration of so-called failed states or those otherwise needing temporary international tutelage. To the extent possible, the legal precepts for such 'packages' should be drawn from relevant international treaty law such as the Universal Declaration of Human Rights and the International Convention on Civil and Political Rights. Such packages would 'put a criminal justice system in place, establish an independent judiciary, appoint public prosecutors and defenders, create a functioning police force and establish detention centres'.[154] The UN should have a pre-arranged list of judges, lawyers and other elements of a judicial system which can be brought in to such situations. Preferably these should work closely with any existing elements of a legal system. The UN should also, at an early stage in such operations, begin training programmes for local personnel to permit the reform or re-establishment of local judicial systems.

The UN also needs to make a firm policy decision at the outset of peacekeeping missions as to whether it will establish its own gaols, preferably under the auspices of the International Committee of the Red Cross and the World Health Organization, and under what circumstances it will arrest, detain and try suspects. Decisions should be communicated to all parties concerned before a mission begins to gain maximum deterrent value. They must then be followed up in practice if the credibility of the mission is not to be damaged.

---

[154] Plunkett, M., 'The establishment of the rule of law in post-conflict peacekeeping', ed. Smith (note 14), p. 77.

XI. Handling the economic impact

Much of the economic impact on Phnom Penh was probably unavoidable because of the sheer size and sophistication of the UN operation compared with the primitiveness of the Cambodian economy. It was also inevitable that the Khmer Rouge would use the creation of boom conditions in Phnom Penh as evidence of the corruption of the SOC Government and the evil intentions of the UN. Combined with the increase in prostitution, the spread of HIV infection,[155] an influx of Thai investment and the conspicuous consumption patterns of Cambodia's *nouveaux riches*, the economic impact of UNTAC gave credibility to KR propaganda which has traditionally pitted urban decadence against rural purity.[156]

Some remedial or preventative steps by the UN were still possible. UNTAC should have consulted NGOs long established in Phnom Penh about the going rate for rents and salaries before paying exorbitant prices. In future the UN should also consider paying a smaller per diem to its own staff based on local conditions, rather than New York or Geneva rates, or not paying such allowances in full in the country of operation. The possibility of taxing all UN employees in the field, with the revenues to be contributed to the rehabilitation of the country, should be considered. UNTAC should also have promulgated appropriate foreign investment laws to ensure that Cambodians were trained and employed in newly established foreign businesses.[157]

In general many unintended economic and social consequences could be avoided if the UN were more cognizant of the economic impact of its operations on local economies and societies. Some of the unavoidable consequences can be offset by using the economic weight of the UN, relative to the economy in question, in creative ways—such as UNTAC's importing of rice to keep local prices low and through its Quick Impact Projects.

---

[155] The World Health Organization reported in Oct. 1992 that voluntary blood donations at Phnom Penh's blood bank showed a rate of HIV infection 10 times higher in the first 6 months of 1992 than in 1991: see *International Herald Tribune*, 5 Oct. 1992, p. 5.

[156] Chandler, D. P., *Brother Number One: A Political Biography of Pol Pot* (Westview Press: Boulder, Colo., 1992), p. 108.

[157] Chopra *et al.* (note 18), p. 23.

XII. Press and information strategies

Both Akashi and Sanderson complained of the attitude of the press in covering the Cambodia operation.[158] The media's emphasis on negative aspects can affect the morale and international perceptions of a UN mission. This is a perennial problem for peacekeeping missions, where the need for compromise, subtlety and patient negotiations conflicts with the media's need for attention-grabbing headlines. There is often, moreover, a basic misunderstanding of the function of UN peacekeeping missions, particularly about the enforcement role and capabilities of the military component.

In UNTAC's case this was compounded, according to Sanderson, by the UN civilian spokesperson's ignorance of military matters and tendency to 'poor timing and judgement' on the release of military information.[159] Sanderson was obliged to recruit an experienced military public relations officer to rectify the UN spokesperson's tendency to 'poor timing and judgement' on the release of military information.

Initially UNTAC suffered from not having a single, integrated public relations office: each component ran its own public relations campaign, leading to duplication, inconsistency and lost opportunities. Eventually UNTAC did acquire such a capability, but only after prompting from without. In October 1992 the Deputy SRSG announced the creation of a Community Relations Office, headed by Ms Hiroko Miyamura. It was established primarily in response to an open letter to Akashi published in the *Phnom Penh Post* of 11 October,[160] signed by 100 men and women from UNTAC, NGOs and the Cambodian community. It detailed serious concerns about the 'inappropriate behaviour' of some male UNTAC personnel towards women and listed sexual harassment, stereotyping, an increase in prostitution and sexually transmitted diseases, and the lack of women in high-level positions in UNTAC among the signatories' major grievances. Apart from the appointment of an ombudsperson for women, it suggested the establishment of an UNTAC office that would liaise with the Cambodian community and educate UNTAC personnel on issues of cultural sensitivity and gender awareness. Ms Miyamura's office was intended to perform these functions and

[158] Akashi (note 42), p. 201.
[159] Sanderson (note 15), p. 10.
[160] UNTAC Electoral Component, Phnom Penh, *Free Choice: Electoral Component Newsletter*, no. 10 (18 Dec. 1992), p. 4.

receive complaints from the Cambodian community about misbehaviour on the part of UNTAC personnel. In mid-November 1992 an UNTAC Information Centre was also opened 'to foster understanding among Cambodians about UNTAC's mission, mandate and activities'.[161] Future UN missions should establish community relations and information centres or an office combining both functions from the outset and appoint an ombudsperson for the duration of the mission.

A final lesson that may be drawn from the Cambodian experience is that an early, proactive public relations campaign by the UN to explain its presence, capabilities (and, in order to avoid creating unnecessary expectations, its limitations) is essential. A campaign of this kind, particularly one using the UN's own media, can be extraordinarily effective in legitimizing and solidifying the UN presence and mission. In Cambodia, the setting up of a nationwide radio station under UNTAC control, although advocated by the 1991 Military Survey Mission, was initially opposed by UN headquarters and came about late. Once installed it proved to be a powerful tool in familiarizing Cambodians with UN intentions and plans, weaning support away from those opposed to the UN, counteracting anti-UNTAC propaganda and educating the populace in electoral and human rights matters. According to the Bangkok correspondent for the *Straits Times*, Radio UNTAC

assured would-be voters over and over again that their vote would be secret, and that they could go ahead and lie to whoever was intimidating them . . . they could exercise their free choice once they were in the polling booth alone . . . Cambodians responded to this. They felt UNTAC actually understood their predicament *vis-à-vis* their so-called leaders . . . People started to whisper around the assurances that UNTAC had given, such as there was no such thing as a secret electronic eye to detect who they were voting for.[162]

UNTAC proved that a secret ballot—its 'secret weapon' against those who would attempt to obstruct a free and fair election[163]—is something that the UN can successfully deliver. It also proved that the UN can convince an uneducated and fearful populace of that fact.

[161] UNTAC Electoral Component, Phnom Penh, *Free Choice: Electoral Component Newsletter*, no. 11 (15 Jan. 1993), p. 8.

[162] Tan Lian Choo, 'The Cambodian election: whither the future?', eds T. Carney and Tan Lian Choo, Institute of Southeast Asian Studies, *Whither Cambodia? Beyond the Election* (ISEAS: Singapore, 1994), p. 23.

[163] UN, *The United Nations in Cambodia: A Vote for Peace* (United Nations: New York, 1994), p. 75.

Future UN missions should attempt to emulate UNTAC's success in employing the power of the media in the cause of peace.

XIII. Lessons for negotiators

Most of the lessons identified in the foregoing have related to the planning and administration of peace operations by the United Nations, whether at UN headquarters or in the field. However, the UNTAC experience reaffirms the obvious point that UN operations are shaped by the peace accords that precede them and that improvements in the way such accords are written and organized can have an enormous bearing on the success or failure of UN implementation efforts. Naturally, peace accords are political documents representing finely-honed compromise rather than masterpieces of logic and precision. They may be unfathomable or simplistic or contain elements that are politically essential but in practical terms impossible to implement. None the less, negotiators do look for successful precedents and may derive lessons from previous failures.

From the Cambodian experience one might extract the following lessons for negotiators of future accords:

1. An orderly implementation plan is essential; but implementation should be more measured and based on realistic feasibility studies carried out by in-country inspection teams.

2. Peace accords should embody incentives to induce all the parties concerned to continue to comply with agreements after they have been concluded (including financial incentives, such as paying the salaries of armed forces in order to head off discontent that may follow changes in their status after a cease-fire, and reconstruction and development assistance to all parties).[164]

3. As much independent scope for action by the UN as possible should be built in, to enable it to fulfil substantial elements of a peace agreement with minimal or tacit co-operation of the local parties.[165] There will be limits to how far this process can be taken, but it does permit the UN to bypass existing political structures and work in league with the general population who may desire peace more than their political élite.

---

[164] Doyle, M., 'UNTAC: sources of success and failure', ed. Smith (note 14), p. 97.
[165] Doyle (note 164), p. 98.

4. Practical objectives should be set for all aspects of implementation rather than vague goals that may be subject to interpretation or confusion. The Cambodia experience demonstrated the need for this in the areas of human rights, the civil administration and police.

5. Consideration should be given to mandating an early start to retraining and restructuring of local military and police forces to enable them to assume as much of the UN's burden as soon as possible.

6. Detailed arrangements should be agreed for the transitional period between the election of a new government and its assumption of the reins of power.

7. A 'justice' package should be included where local legal and judicial systems are weak or non-existent.

8. The UN Secretariat should be involved in the negotiation process at an early stage to ensure that it is capable of carrying through the tasks envisaged for it and afforded the necessary resources.

9. Conclusion

Although it was unable to oversee the extinguishing of the Cambodian civil war as intended by the Paris Peace Accords, the UN mission in Cambodia helped to de-internationalize the conflict, isolate the Khmer Rouge, begin the tortuous process of national reconciliation and permit the Cambodian people for the first time in almost 40 years to choose their government in a comparatively free, fair and democratic manner. Following the surprisingly successful May 1993 election, a new constitution was written, a new government formed, King Sihanouk was restored to the throne as Cambodia's constitutional monarch and a national army was established. In addition the UN repatriated all Cambodian refugees from the Thai border and closed the camps there, freed the press, alleviated conditions in Cambodia's prisons, started the gargantuan task of mine clearance, imparted new skills to thousands of Cambodians, fostered the rapid growth of human rights consciousness and other civic values and began restoring Cambodia's shattered infrastructure. Perhaps most important, UNTAC gave hope to the people of Cambodia that the cycle of war and dissolution that had plagued their country for decades had been broken.

The mission was troubled from the outset by the non-compliance of the Khmer Rouge and the Hun Sen Government, which threatened to unravel the Paris Peace Accords altogether. While this was obviously not the fault of UNTAC, the way the authority handled these threats, unanticipated in the Paris Accords, was a key determinant of the outcome of the Cambodia operation. UNTAC skilfully managed to prevail over these challenges, but its own organizational flaws, especially its late deployment, poor advance planning, lacklustre civil police, cursory co-ordination between UNTAC's components, and a lack of consultation with Cambodians and NGOs at times also jeopardized the peace process. These flaws were compounded by timidity in some areas, including in law and order matters, especially in safeguarding human rights, and in confronting at a tactical level the Khmer Rouge and Hun Sen administration and security machines. The Cambodia operation exposed significant defects in the management of peacekeeping missions by UN headquarters in New York and in the field, some of which are now being attended to.

The monetary cost of UNTAC was high—approximately $1.5 billion. The human cost was also great. Among UNTAC personnel there were, as of 31 August 1993, 142 casualties, including 84 killed and 58 seriously injured.[1] None the less it stayed the course while retaining the unanimous support of the international community. Overall, the UN can legitimately claim the Cambodia exercise as its first major success of the post-cold war era and one that establishes benchmarks for future similar UN operations. As Boutros-Ghali told UNTAC personnel in Phnom Penh in April 1993: 'a new system of international co-operation for peace-building has been launched here. It is not only the future of Cambodia which hangs in the balance. This operation will influence the nature and scope of future UN mandates and operations all over the world'.[2]

It is difficult to place UNTAC in the evolution of United Nations peacekeeping and on the spectrum of peacekeeping, peacemaking and peace building. At first glance the range and complexity of the tasks it performed make it the quintessential post-cold war 'second generation' UN peace operation.[3] More than any other UN mission before or since, UNTAC sought to combine a mix of peacemaking, peacekeeping and peace building as foreshadowed in Boutros-Ghali's *Agenda for Peace* in 1992.[4] That is, UNTAC continued negotiating peace (peacemaking) despite the signing of the Paris Peace Accords (to the extent that Akashi was required to act more like a negotiator than an administrator); it played traditional and new peacekeeping roles; and

---

[1] UN, Financing of the United Nations Transitional Authority in Cambodia: report of the Secretary-General, UN document A/48/701, 8 Dec. 1993, Annex III, p. 3. Three civilian staff, 14 civil police, 23 local staff, 39 military personnel, 3 military observers and 2 UNVs were killed, 20 by hostile action, the rest from other causes. Apart from Cambodians, those killed in hostile action were from Bangladesh, Bulgaria, China, Columbia, Japan, the Philippines and Uruguay. Fatalities resulting from other than hostile action involved, besides Cambodians, personnel from Algeria, Bangladesh, Bulgaria, Canada, China, France, Ghana, India, Indonesia, Malaysia, Morocco, Nepal, Pakistan, the Philippines, Poland, Spain, Tunisia, the UK and Uruguay: UN, *The United Nations in Cambodia: A Vote for Peace* (United Nations: New York, 1994), p. 104.

[2] UN, *The United Nations in Cambodia: A Vote for Peace* (note 1), p. 110.

[3] Also called expanded, broadened, wider, muscular, protected or enforced peacekeeping.

[4] UN, An Agenda for Peace, Report of the Secretary-General pursuant to the statement adopted by the Summit Meeting of the Security Council, 31 Jan. 1992, UN document A/47/277, S/24111, United Nations, New York, 1992. For a discussion of the differences between these concepts, from the UN and other perspectives, see Findlay, T., 'Multilateral conflict prevention, management and resolution', SIPRI, *SIPRI Yearbook 1994* (Oxford University Press: Oxford, 1994), pp. 14–19 and *passim*.

it began the process of reconstructing Cambodia politically and economically (peace building).[5]

As with other second-generation operations in Angola, Central
America, Somalia, the former Yugoslavia and Mozambique, the
deployment of UNTAC took place in a situation of civil war rather
than inter-state conflict, moreover in a situation where the civil war
never entirely ceased.

In other respects UNTAC was not a second-generation operation
but a traditional one in that it abided strictly by the traditional peacekeeping ethos emphasizing first the maintenance of consent, second
impartiality, and third the use of force only in self-defence. Some
observers of second-generation missions have argued that one of their
characteristics is an ill-defined 'grey area' between peacekeeping and
peace enforcement in which consent may be strained or even lost
altogether or impartiality sacrificed for the sake of broader political
goals and where the use of force may need to be more 'robust' or
'muscular'.[6] UNTAC did not stray on to this grey area.

While consent became increasingly strained during its tenure, the
mission worked assiduously to maintain it and it was never entirely
lost. Even the Khmer Rouge never renounced the Paris Peace Accords
(although it did denounce particular aspects of them) or called for
UNTAC's withdrawal (although it did call for Akashi's resignation).

UNTAC's political and military leadership also attempted valiantly
to adhere to the traditional peacekeeping doctrine of impartiality,
despite many provocations from all the parties. This was particularly
difficult in a situation where one party—the Khmer Rouge—was
responsible for the most blatant violations of the accord and when an
embargo was placed on that party despite the fact that UNTAC
needed its continued co-operation in the peace process. General
Sanderson stresses the importance of neutrality and impartiality:

A lesson learned by the UNTAC Military Component was that neutrality
and unity were the strength of the Force. Impartiality in its actions would not

---

[5] For theoretical musings on these issues see Fetherston, A. B., University of Bradford,
Department of Peace Studies, *Toward A Theory of United Nations Peacekeeping*, Peace
Research Report no. 31 (University of Bradford: Bradford, Feb. 1993), pp. 36-40.

[6] See Wurmser, D., *et al.*, *The Professionalization of Peacekeeping* (US Institute of Peace:
Washington, DC, Aug. 1993) and Daniel, D., US Naval War College, Centre for Naval War
Studies, *Issues and Considerations in UN Gray Area and Enforcement Operations*, Strategic
Research Department Research Memorandum 4-94 (US Naval War College: Newport, R.I.,
1994).

have been perceived if any component member had wavered in this regard. Attempts to undermine this strength were made. The international community was resolute in defence of these principles, thereby ensuring their sanctity.[7]

Finally, UNTAC adhered strictly to traditional UN peacekeeping doctrine of the minimum use of force and its use only in self-defence. Sanderson argues vigorously that to have engaged the KR militarily would have been to court disaster.[8] There is, in his view, no place for peace enforcement in peacekeeping missions and hence no 'grey area': 'Any reasoned debate about the transition from peacekeeping to enforcement operations will very quickly lead to the conclusion that it is beyond the practical scope of a neutral peacekeeping force and would be to its political detriment. Enforcement action is war!'[9] Unlike UNPROFOR in the former Yugoslavia and UNOSOM II in Somalia, UNTAC did not attempt to use military force to induce the recalcitrant parties to adhere to the peace process or to punish their leaders. Even in self-defence its use of force was mostly extremely restrained. While it was avowedly prepared to use force to defend its carrying out of its mission, particularly to protect the electoral process, in practice it did not need to do so.

In its genesis the Cambodia operation was not typically a second-generation one in that it was deployed in a situation which did not represent a current threat to international peace and security. Even the threat to regional security which the Cambodian situation posed was not particularly pressing. The civil war was sputtering on, its ebbs and flows conforming more to the pattern of the seasons than to political or strategic imperatives. The actual loss of life and scale of the fighting at the outset of UNTAC's mission were comparatively small, compared to those in Afghanistan, Angola, Sudan or Tajikistan. Both India and the Philippines, which contributed troops to UNTAC,

---

[7] Sanderson, J., Lt. Gen., 'Preliminary study of lessons learnt by the UNTAC Military Component', report submitted to Akashi on 31 Aug. 1993, cited in Dobbie, C., 'A concept for post-cold war peacekeeping', *Survival*, vol. 36, no. 3 (autumn 1994), p. 134.

[8] Sanderson's views appear to be supported by General Michael Rose, commander of UNPROFOR in Bosnia, who insists that 'Patience, persistence and pressure is how you conduct a peacekeeping mission. Bombing is a last resort because then you cross the Mogadishu line . . . Hitting a tank is peacekeeping. Hitting infrastructure, command and control, logistics, that is war, and I'm not going to fight a war in white-painted tanks'. See *International Herald Tribune*, 30 Sep. 1994, p. 2.

[9] Sanderson, J. M. (Lt-Gen.), 'Australia, the United Nations and the emerging world order', the 28th Alfred Deakin Lecture, Melbourne, 5 Sep. 1994, p. 10.

arguably had more destructive conflicts on their own territories than did Cambodia.[10] There was no great humanitarian crisis as in Somalia, no fratricidal orgy of bloodletting as in Rwanda, no savage ethnic warfare as in the former Yugoslavia.[11]

The main aim of the Cambodia peace settlement was to resolve a long-standing regional quandary which was preventing the normalization of interstate relationships throughout the region and more broadly. That the international community agreed so readily to fund and participate in the most expensive and comprehensive multilateral operation ever mounted—in a situation which did not feature the emergency conditions that had propelled other peacekeeping operations into existence—is remarkable.

It is not true of UNTAC, as one observer remarked, that 'Needs were being met, but few of them were Cambodian'.[12] The response of the majority of Cambodians to the May elections disproved that. Whether the Paris Accords and UNTAC were the correct response to Cambodia's ills is difficult to judge—although the alternatives at the time all seemed worse than the prospect that an internationally supervised and supported peacekeeping effort might conceivably break the log-jam of history and allow Cambodia to move forward.

The mission was at the very least daring considering Cambodia's renowned physical, cultural and psychological impenetrability to outsiders. 'Understanding Cambodia has always seemed like trying to put together a three-dimensional jigsaw of morality, politics and geography.'[13] It should not be too surprising, therefore, if an organization as far from perfect as the UN got some of its mission wrong.

[10] The Department of Peace and Conflict Research at Uppsala University in 1992 classified Cambodia as having an 'intermediate armed conflict', but Afghanistan, Angola, Ethiopia, Liberia, the Philippines, Sri Lanka, Sudan, Tajikistan and the former Yugoslavia as being involved in 'war'. See Axell, K. (ed.), Uppsala University, Department of Peace and Conflict Research, *States in Armed Conflict 1992*, Report no. 36 (Uppsala, 1993).

[11] See Wurst, J., 'Mozambique: peace and more', *World Policy Journal*, vol. 11, no. 3 (fall 1994), pp. 78–82. The only comparable cases to the Cambodia operation seem to be those of Namibia and Mozambique. In Namibia, however, while there was also no pressing crisis, the UN had a major responsibility of its own towards the country since it was still in theory a dependent, non-sovereign territory under a trusteeship arrangement with South Africa. ONUMOZ (the *Operación de las Naciones Unidas en Mozambique*—UN Operation in Mozambique) was mounted after the parties had fought themselves to a standstill. The civil war in El Salvador and Nicaragua was much more intense at the time the relevant agreements were signed than the fighting in Cambodia at the time of the Paris Accords.

[12] Moser-Phoungsuwan, Y., Asia Pacific Research Association, 'Cambodia article', *APRA Newsletter*, no. 5 (Sep./Oct. 1994), p. 12.

[13] Shawcross, W, 'Cambodia: the UN's biggest gamble', *Time* (Australia), 28 Dec. 1992, p. 16.

The most impressive aspect of UNTAC was that it got crucial aspects right: it correctly estimated the depth of Cambodians' desire for peace; it confounded those who argued that any attempt to introduce a democratic mechanism like voting was absurd in a culture like Cambodia's; it believed in the ability of ordinary Cambodians to understand the concept of a secret ballot; and it persisted, despite tribulations, in supporting the one Cambodian who could help deliver a national renaissance and unity, Prince Sihanouk.

The international community can continue to assist Cambodians in nurturing their fragile democracy and in rehabilitating and reconstructing their country, but the future now essentially lies with the Cambodians themselves. Their ability to take advantage of a new beginning—rarely afforded to any nation, much less through such concerted, costly international effort—will be a true test of UNTAC's legacy.

Postscript

In the year since UNTAC departed, Cambodia has led a roller-coaster existence, experiencing the highs of newly won international recognition and support along with the lows of continuing political instability and violence. The country's wildly fluctuating fortunes have jeopardized some of the gains of the Paris Accords and called into question some of the fundamental assumptions behind the deployment of UNTAC. More broadly they lend credence to the growing body of evidence which suggests that the United Nations needs to rethink its strategy towards rescuing and rehabilitating member states that have in some senses 'failed', especially in view of the massive injections of international political and monetary capital that such international tutelage requires.

Contrary to the claims of some observers few of the negative developments that have occurred in Cambodia since late 1993 can be attributed to the failings of UNTAC. On the contrary, they tend to support the thesis that UNTAC's achievements were little short of miraculous in a country whose current political leadership was and remains so apparently devoid of integrity, political maturity and vision.[1]

The most widely publicized and politically potent threat to the new order in Cambodia—although not the most immediately menacing—is the continued existence of the Khmer Rouge. The other major threats are the persistent weaknesses and disarray of the new Government, partly resulting from splits within the CPP and FUNCINPEC; persisting lawlessness; and the poor performance of the new Royal Cambodian Armed Forces.

In the aftermath of the election in May 1993 it seemed as if the KR had been politically outmanoeuvred and left to wither in its jungle bastions without Chinese succour, the international recognition it had enjoyed previously through its membership of the anti-Hun Sen coalition, or its captive population base in the border refugee camps. Militarily, the RCAF appeared to gain the upper hand against the KR

---

[1] For a revealing portrait of post-UNTAC Cambodia by the former Australian Ambassador to the country, John Holloway, see his 3500-word secret cable leaked to the press in Oct. 1994, an edited version of which was published in the *Sydney Morning Herald*, 5 Oct. 1994, pp. 1, 8 and 9.

early, capturing Anlong Veng in February 1994[2] and Pailin in March.[3] Between August and December 1993 more than 1000 KR fighters defected to the Government.[4]

Politically the Khmer Rouge fared no better. There was evidence of a bitter internal split within the party over the outcome of the Paris Peace Accords, resulting in Ieng Sary, a long-standing member of the party's standing committee and Foreign Minister during the Pol Pot era, being stripped of his offices.[5] Attempts by King Sihanouk to negotiate KR participation in government in Phnom Penh in return for disarming and integrating its forces into the RCAF led nowhere. To the CPP's consistent opposition to power-sharing with the KR was now added that of FUNCINPEC, flush from electoral victory. There were now also constitutional barriers: the new Constitution would require amendment to enable the KR to be admitted to government.

The Government's confidence in dealing with the KR appeared to stem partly from the extent of the international support it was receiving and from its economic performance. Cambodia became eligible for World Bank and International Monetary Fund (IMF) loans, including balance-of-payments support, after Australia, Japan and the USA paid off its outstanding IMF debt, while the Asian Development Bank scheduled a series of medium-term loans to the new Government.[6] In March 1994 a meeting of ICORC in Tokyo resulted in new pledges of $500 million in aid.[7] The Government's 79-page National Programme to Rehabilitate and Develop Cambodia and the performance of the then FUNCINPEC Minister for Finance, Sam Rainsy, clearly impressed the international donor community.[8] The budget had been passed unanimously by the National Assembly in December,[9] the annual inflation rate had dropped from a peak of 340 per cent per

---

[2] *Phnom Penh Post*, 11–24 Feb. 1994, p. 1.

[3] *International Herald Tribune*, 22 Mar. 1994, p. 5.

[4] Thayer, N., 'No way home for KR defectors', *Phnom Penh Post*, 17–31 Dec. 1993, p. 1.

[5] Thayer, N., 'Shake-up in KR hierarchy', *Phnom Penh Post*, 28 Jan.–10 Feb. 1994, p. 1.

[6] Cambodia: recent developments, Statement by Peter Tomsen, Deputy Assistant Secretary for East Asian and Pacific Affairs, before the Subcommittee on Asia and the Pacific of the House Foreign Affairs Committee, US Congress, Washington DC, 11 May 1994. Reproduced in *US Department of State Dispatch*, vol. 5, no. 21 (23 May 1994), pp. 343–44.

[7] Cambodia: recent developments (note 6), p. 344. While the *Phnom Penh Post* reported the figure to be $777 million, some of this had been pledged earlier: *Phnom Penh Post*, 25 Mar.–7 Apr. 1994, pp. 8–9.

[8] Rainsy was forced to resign in Oct. 1994: see *Phnom Penh Post*, 4–17 Nov. 1994, p. 1.

[9] Thayer, N., 'Budget law passed unanimously', *Phnom Penh Post*, 31 Dec. 1993–13 Jan. 1994, p. 1.

year in March 1993 to around 10 per cent in 1993[10] and annual growth in gross domestic product (GDP) was expected to be 7–8 per cent in 1994, up from 6 per cent in 1993.[11] Most economic analysts believed that Cambodia's economic planners—European-educated technocrats who had returned since the Paris Accords—had done a remarkable job in stabilizing the economy and instituting structural changes.[12] These included reform of the customs system and budgetary procedures which increased government revenue eightfold.

These favourable economic trends and early successes against the Khmer Rouge failed, however, to mask troubling weaknesses within the new Government or the host of inherited problems which threatened at times to overwhelm it. The very structure of the coalition Government, a forced union of two erstwhile enemy parties of vastly different structure, experience and motivation, was itself a threat to political stability. The greatest difficulties appeared to come more from the fractured nature of the CPP and FUNCINPEC than from rivalry between their top leaders. Hun Sen and Prince Ranariddh appeared to have established an acceptable working relationship. As Ranariddh told a *Time* journalist, 'to be frank with you I have more trouble with my own ministers than I do with the ministers of Mr Hun Sen'.[13] Within the CPP, a long-term generational struggle appears to have climaxed after the election, pitting supporters of an old hardliner, Chea Sim, against those of the younger Hun Sen. In July 1994 a farcical coup attempt was made by CPP hard-liners, purportedly led by Prince Norodom Chakrapong (who had attempted an abortive secession just after the May 1993 election) and Sin Song, a former SOC Minister of the Interior. More powerful CPP figures were also reportedly involved.[14]

FUNCINPEC, meanwhile, although it had won the 1993 election, seemed unable to retain sufficient internal unity and sense of purpose to capitalize on its victory.[15] Most of the compromises within the

[10] Friedland, J., 'Someone to trust: Cambodia's free-market plan wins over donors', *Far Eastern Economic Review*, 24 Mar. 1994, p. 47.

[11] Friedland (note 10), p. 47; *The Independent*, 27 May 1994, p. 16.

[12] Thayer, N., 'IMF to press over logs', *Phnom Penh Post*, 29 July–11 Aug. 1994, p. 1.

[13] *Time*, 2 May 1994, p. 47.

[14] Thayer, N. and Tasker, R., 'The plot thickens', *Far Eastern Economic Review*, 21 July 1994, p. 20.

[15] Vickery, M., Institute of Southeast Asian Studies, 'The Cambodian People's Party: where has it come from, where is it going?', *Southeast Asian Affairs 1994* (ISEAS: Singapore, 1994), pp. 111–14.

coalition seemed to be made by Ranariddh. Julio Jeldres remarked that the party had:

operated since its inception more as a royal court than as a political party, a trait that heretofore has worked to its advantage in Cambodian society, which retains an enduringly feudal character that not even the horrendous political experiments of the past 20 years have been able to eradicate. The courtier's style, however, is not likely to be of much help in a power struggle against the hard-bitten cadres of the CPP.[16]

There were also structural barriers to FUNCINPEC translating its electoral and international support into political power.[17] The CPP had secured a majority of ministries in the power-sharing arrangement; it controlled the bureaucracy, most of the military and the state security apparatus, and it retained entrenched power in the provinces. It was revealed in August, for instance, that senior CPP military intelligence officers were continuing to conduct a reign of terror in western Cambodia a year after UNTAC's departure, murdering political opponents and systematically extorting wealth from merchants and villagers.[18] A secret detention centre in Battambang exposed by UNTAC in August 1992 had continued to be used for torture and summary executions. After an internal investigation the Government denied the allegations, causing concern among human rights organizations that the election had had little affect on the traditional lack of accountability, arbitrariness and secretiveness of Cambodian governance.

There had been a formal 50/50 division of provincial governorships between FUNCINPEC and the CPP in December 1993.[19] Each governor provided by the one party was given two deputies of the other, with the Buddhist Liberal Democratic Party (BLDP) providing third deputy governorships in two provinces. However, without an established political base in these provinces, and with corruption and nepotism rife, FUNCINPEC appointees faced difficulties in asserting

---

[16] Jeldres, J., 'The UN and the Cambodian transition', *Journal of Democracy*, vol. 4, no. 4 (Oct. 1993), p. 113.

[17] Brown, J., 'FUNCINPEC's evaporating mandate', *Phnom Penh Post*, 25 Mar.–7 Apr. 1994, p. 6.

[18] Thayer, N., 'Murder with impunity', *Far Eastern Economic Review*, 18 Aug. 1994, p. 22.

[19] *Phnom Penh Post*, 31 Dec. 1993–13 Jan. 1994, p. 3.

their authority. The CPP, moreover, retained numerous posts at a local level, from those of powerful district chiefs to police and teachers.[20]

Lawlessness throughout Cambodia also threatened the stability of the country. Disaffected returnees, former and serving military personnel, bandits and extortionists increasingly operated with impunity as the old order continued to decay. The widespread availability of weapons added to the problem. The UN Military Liaison Team reported in February 1994 that 'internal security in Cambodia has become more precarious following the withdrawal of the military component of UNTAC'.[21] In particular, illegal checkpoints had been set up throughout the countryside by RCAF soldiers and others, who extorted money from travellers. Kidnapping of foreigners threatened to become a new cottage industry. The kidnapping by KR and criminal elements of an Australian, a Briton and a Frenchman in July 1994 and their murder in September aroused international concern for the stability of the country and the competence of the Cambodian Government, as well as straining relations with the three countries involved.[22] The KR demanded that these countries promise not to provide military assistance to the Government.

The Government meanwhile suffered humiliating military defeats at the hands of the KR, which easily retook Anlong Veng and Pailin in May and threatened Battambang, accentuating the dire need for restructuring and reforming the RCAF. The government forces appeared to have treated their earlier victories as opportunities for looting, compounding this by failing to plan for the defence of their newly-won territory and exhibiting disorganization and cowardice in the face of the KR counter-offensive. Corruption appeared rife at all levels of the force, with military supplies even being sold to the KR. The amnesty programme for KR defectors was failing because of corruption and mishandling by the Government. While many expressed fear at the possibility of a revival of the KR, most observers believed the battlefield reverses revealed RCAF weakness rather than Khmer Rouge strength.

---

[20] Ross, J., 'Cambodia hasn't been rescued', *International Herald Tribune*, 24 May 1994, p. 6.

[21] UN, Mid-term report of the Secretary-General on the United Nations Military Liaison Team in Cambodia, UN document S/1994/169, 14 Feb. 1994, p. 2.

[22] Thayer, N., 'Theatre of the absurd', *Far Eastern Economic Review*, 1 Sep. 1994, pp. 14–15.

Countries which had expressed interest in assisting the RCAF were adamant that the primary need was not for weapons and military *matériel* but for restructuring and retraining.[23] Australia, France, Malaysia and the USA all refused requests for lethal aid and pressured Phnom Penh to reform its military.[24] It was revealed that the RCAF had 2000 generals and 10 000 colonels for a total force of 90 000.[25] The figure of 130 000 military personnel claimed by the Government turned out to include phantom forces 'created' by individual commanders to boost their 'take' when the UN decided after the May 1993 election to pay military salaries.[26]

Peace talks between the KR and the Government continued to fare badly. After refusing the King's initial proposal for a 'round table' in Phnom Penh, the KR eventually agreed in May 1994 to talks in Pyongyang. These failed to produce any result except an agreement to continue 'working committee talks',[27] which also collapsed. Moreover, KR demands seemed designed to scuttle any agreement. One of them was for an international force to monitor a cease-fire, drawn from five countries to be chosen from a list of 10, among them Fiji and Papua New Guinea. As the Government noted, if the KR had declined to co-operate with UNTAC there seemed little prospect of its treating a smaller, less capable group of observers without UN backing any more respectfully.

When the round table talks in Phnom Penh on 15 and 16 June failed, the KR office in the capital was closed. In July the National Assembly passed a bill outlawing the KR. It was widely criticized as likely to be ineffective.[28] In response the KR announced the formation of a 'provisional government of national union and national salvation' based in Preah Vihear province and led by Khieu Samphan.[29] Relations between Thailand and the Government also deteriorated following accusations from Phnom Penh that Thailand was still supporting

[23] *International Herald Tribune,* 28 July 1994, p. 5. North Korea also offered military assistance: see *Jane's Defence Weekly,* 2 July 1994.

[24] *International Herald Tribune,* 28 July 1994, p. 5.

[25] *Sydney Morning Herald,* 5 Oct. 1994, p. 9.

[26] *Military and Arms Transfers News,* 26 Aug. 1994, p. 6; *The Australian,* 27 July 1994, p. 1.

[27] Harris, B., 'Gloomy PM warns of more fighting', *Phnom Penh Post,* 3–16 June 1994, p. 1.

[28] Cummings-Bruce, N., '"Futile" bill to ban Khmer Rouge', *The Guardian,* 6 July 1994, p. 5.

[29] *Financial Times,* 12 July 1994, p. 7.

the Khmer Rouge—as evidenced by the discovery of a huge KR arms cache on Thai territory in December 1993.[30]

Dismayed at the disarray that appeared to be overtaking the country and avowedly anxious once more to appear as the saviour of his beloved people, King Sihanouk suggested in June that he be invited by parliament and the Government to assume the reins of power—presumably as Prime Minister, not as King, since the provision of the Constitution that the monarch shall reign but not rule is unamendable.[31] He proposed the formation of a government of national unity which would give some senior positions to the KR. Sihanouk apologized for the mess that Cambodia's politicians seemed to be making of the post-UNTAC situation: 'I present my apologies to the United Nations. We did not deserve $3 billion [in peacekeeping costs]—our behaviour is so bad, so bad'.[32] Yet his own political manœuvres continued to be aimed at overturning the May 1993 election result, the new Constitution and the hard-won democratic gains of the Cambodian people. His offer to 'save the nation' was rejected out of hand by Hun Sen and Ranariddh. Even without this political rebuff, the future role of the monarchy is increasingly in doubt because of Sihanouk's poor health. There is no automatic succession in Cambodia and no one of royal extraction who has Sihanouk's popular aura and experience. His wife, Queen Monique, comes closest.

Several questions are raised by Cambodia's experience in the year since UNTAC left. The first is whether UNTAC, within the limits of its mandate and resources, could have done more itself to help avoid some of the problems now being faced. The answer is probably not. UNTAC could have moved faster to remove more mines, rehabilitate more parts of Cambodia's infrastructure and retrain police and soldiers. However, these would have been marginal improvements in the broader context of Cambodia's current difficulties. No one, least of all the UN, which had experienced Cambodia's problems at first hand, had any expectation that all of them would be solved by the Paris Accords and the fleeting presence of UNTAC. As Behrooz Sadry, Deputy Special Representative of the Secretary-General for Cambodia, put it:

---

[30] Prasso, S., 'Cambodia: a heritage of violence', *World Policy Journal,* vol. 11, no. 3 (fall 1994), p. 75.

[31] Thayer, N., 'King talks of taking power', *Phnom Penh Post,* 17–30 June 1994, pp. 1, 3.

[32] *Phnom Penh Post,* 20 May–2 June 1994, p. 5.

No one has any illusions that the transition to a new government will be an easy process. The Cambodian people are reminded on a daily basis that the tradition of mistrust is still pervasive among the factions. The quest for political power often translates both into ideological struggles for land and public assets which are coveted by all sides. The people forced to live in this climate of insecurity are caught in the middle. Their fears are combined with other threats to their well-being, such as the hundreds of thousands of mines on Cambodia's roads, which continue to be planted, and the easy availability of weapons to settle disputes and to commit acts of banditry. These problems will not vanish just because the international community has focused so many of its resources on Cambodia.[33]

A more fundamental question is whether the Paris Accords should have allowed for more extensive 'post-operative care' of Cambodia after the departure of UNTAC. The Paris Accords did in fact provide for an unprecedented degree of UN 'peace building' after UNTAC's mandate expired, ranging from rehabilitation and mine clearance to human rights monitoring. However, without an extended mandate for post-UNTAC activities of a political and/or military nature, and in the light of pressing demands from other conflict situations and the resources already expended on Cambodia, Boutros-Ghali was reluctant to commit the UN to a large-scale continuing presence and clearly felt that Cambodia needed to stand on its own feet. He opposed a substantial UN military presence to monitor the military situation and the civilian UN office in Phnom Penh was restricted to liaising with the Government over outstanding matters relating to UNTAC.

On the one hand this was logical and politically sound. The UN had intervened in Cambodia in an unprecedentedly intrusive fashion and it was now politic to let the Cambodians resume responsibility for their own political affairs. It was especially important to allow a clean break for UNTAC and to avoid charges that UN tutelage represented a form of neocolonialism, a particularly sensitive issue for developing states after the UN experience in Somalia. It also suited the Permanent Five and the regional states. All of them had seen the realization of their major foreign policy and/or domestic goals in relation to Cambodia and felt collective relief at being off the Cambodia 'hook'.

---

[33] UN, *The United Nations in Cambodia: A Vote for Peace* (United Nations: New York, 1994), pp. 6–7.

On the other hand, there remained some danger that if the situation in Cambodia went terribly wrong there would be renewed domestic and international pressures for further international involvement. Furthermore, when so much had been invested in Cambodia's political rehabilitation, to abandon the country suddenly to its fate seems like false economy. This is a not only an immediate policy question but a broader one for those who negotiate peace agreements: when it is decided to engage the UN in comprehensive peacemaking, peace-keeping and peace building endeavours, to what extent should plans be made for extended post-settlement commitments? In Cambodia (and in Somalia), Mats Berdal argues, 'insufficient attention was given to autonomous sources of conflict and to the consequent need for long-term post-election strategies'.[34] The Paris Accords were even silent on the question of a transitional post-election government and on hand-over arrangements from the existing regime to the newly elected one.

Various types of arrangement might be envisaged, including a series of confidence-building measures that would operate in a post-election situation, such as regular meetings between winners and losers at all levels of government to ensure a smooth transition. These could be enhanced by the presence of international observers or facili-tators or even be chaired by UN representatives. UN personnel charged with the supervision and control of key government agencies could be left in place until they were satisfied that a fair and smooth transition had taken place. Mechanisms could also be envisaged to help reassure losing parties that they will not be discriminated against unfairly or even persecuted. Legal mechanisms could be instituted prior to the ending of a major UN presence to ensure that the prose-cution and trial of those who have committed human rights violations or criminal acts against the UN are followed through by the new government. None of these measures would be expensive or compli-cated, although they would need the prior approval of the parties to a peace agreement.

Ultimately, however, the UN and the contributor states are obliged to weigh competing priorities in deciding where to invest their limited resources. This will involve essentially abandoning some states to their own devices when, despite best endeavours, the international

[34] Berdal, M., Institutt for forsvarsstudier, *United Nations Peacekeeping at a Crossroads*, IFS Info. no. 7 (IFS: Oslo, 1993), p. 5.

community appears unable appreciably to affect political outcomes. Somalia has come to epitomize this dawning realization. While Cambodia is a shining success story compared to Somalia, the inability of its political élite to strike appropriate national political bargains and adopt acceptable standards of governance will eventually erode the patience of the international community—at least at government level, if not at that of the less judgemental NGOs. According to UNTAC's former Director of Information and Education:

The tragedies of the more than 40 years since Norodom Sihanouk's [initial] coronation engender the fear among some foreign and many Cambodian intellectuals and analysts that political maturity may never develop. This is despite the sophistication the electorate showed making their political choices in May 1993. Poor political institutionalization and limited opportunity for a civil society to develop remain key to the medium- and long-term future of Cambodia.[35]

While it is too early to conclude that Cambodia has, proverbially, got the government it deserves, none the less the state of the country a year after UNTAC departed is a salutary reminder of the limitations of multilateral attempts in effect to fast-track the socio-political re-engineering of a nation-state. Although UNTAC did much more than hold an election and leave, fundamental political transformation must come not from the UN but from Cambodians themselves.

---

[35] Carney, T., 'Compromise and confrontation: the Cambodian future', eds T. Carney and Tan Lian Choo, Institute of Southeast Asian Studies, *Whither Cambodia? Beyond the Election* (ISEAS: Singapore, 1994), p. 3. See also Prasso (note 30), pp. 71–77.

Appendix. Documents on Cambodia, 1991–93

FINAL ACT OF THE PARIS CONFERENCE ON CAMBODIA

Paris, 23 October 1991

1. Concerned by the tragic conflict and continuing bloodshed in Cambodia, the Paris Conference on Cambodia was convened, at the invitation of the Government of the French Republic, in order to achieve an internationally guaranteed comprehensive settlement which would restore peace to that country. The Conference was held in two sessions, the first from 30 July to 30 August 1989, and the second from 21 to 23 October 1991.

2. The Co-Presidents of the Conference were H. E. Mr Roland Dumas, Minister for Foreign Affairs of the French Republic, and H. E. Mr Ali Alatas, Minister for Foreign Affairs of the Republic of Indonesia.

3. The following States participated in the Conference: Australia, Brunei Darussalam, Cambodia, Canada, the People's Republic of China, the French Republic, the Republic of India, the Republic of Indonesia, Japan, the Lao People's Democratic Republic, Malaysia, the Republic of the Philippines, the Republic of Singapore, the Kingdom of Thailand, the Union of Soviet Socialist Republics, the United Kingdom of Great Britain and Northern Ireland, the United States of America and the Socialist Republic of Vietnam.

In addition, the Non-Aligned Movement was represented at the Conference by its current Chairman at each session, namely Zimbabwe at the first session and Yugoslavia at the second session.

4. At the first session of the Conference, Cambodia was represented by the four Cambodian Parties. The Supreme National Council of Cambodia, under the leadership of its President, H. R. H. Prince Norodom Sihanouk, represented Cambodia at the second session of the Conference.

5. The Secretary-General of the United Nations, H. E. M. Javier Perez de Cuellar, and his Special Representative, M. Rafeeuddin Ahmed, also participated in the Conference.

6. The Conference organized itself into three working committees of the whole, which met throughout the first session of the Conference. The First Committee dealt with military matters, the Second Committee dealt with the question of international guarantees, and the Third Committee with the repatriation of refugees and displaced persons and the eventual reconstruction of Cambodia.

The officers of each committee were as follows:

First Committee

Co-Chairmen: Mr C. R. Gharekhan (India); Mr Allan Sullivan (Canada)
Rapporteur: Ms Victoria Sisante-Bataclan (Philippines)

Second Committee

Co-Chairmen: Mr Soulivong Phrasithideth (Laos); Dato' Zainal Abidin Ibrahim (Malaysia)
Rapporteur: Mr Hervé Dejean de la Batie (France)

Third Committee

Co-Chairmen: Mr Yukio Imagawa (Japan); Mr Robert Merrillees (Australia)
Rapporteur: Colonel Ronachuck Swasdikiat (Thailand).

The Conference also established an *Ad Hoc* Committee, composed of the representatives of the four Cambodian Parties and chaired by the representatives of the two Co-Presidents of the Conference, whose mandate involved matters related to national reconciliation among the Cambodian Parties. The *Ad Hoc* Committee held several meetings during the first session of the Conference.

The Coordination Committee of the Conference, chaired by the representatives of the two Co-Presidents, was established and given responsibility for general coordination of the work of the other four committees. The Coordination Committee met at both the first and second sessions of the Conference. An informal meeting of the Coordination Committee was also held in New York on 21 September 1991.

7. At the conclusion of the first session, the Conference had achieved progress in elaborating a wide variety of elements necessary for the achievement of a comprehensive settlement of the conflict in Cambodia. The Conference noted, however, that it was not yet possible to achieve a comprehensive settlement. It was therefore decided to suspend the Conference on 30 August 1989. However, in doing so, the Conference urged all parties concerned to intensify their efforts to achieve a comprehensive settlement, and asked the Co-Presidents to lend their good offices to facilitate these efforts.

8. Following the suspension of the first session of the Conference, the Co-Presidents and the Secretary-General of the United Nations undertook extensive consultations, in particular with the five permanent members of the United Nations Security Council, with the Supreme National Council of Cambodia, and with other participants in the Paris Conference. The object of these consultations was to forge agreement on all aspects of a settlement, to ensure that all initiatives to this end were compatible and to enhance the prospects of ending

the bloodshed in Cambodia at the earliest possible date. The efforts of the Co-Presidents and the Secretary-General paved the way for the reconvening of the Paris Conference on Cambodia.

9. At the inaugural portion of the final meeting of the Paris Conference, on 23 October 1991, the Conference was addressed by H. E. Mr François Mitterrand, President of the French Republic, H. R. H. Prince Norodom Sihanouk, President of the Supreme National Council of Cambodia, and H.E. Mr Javier Perez de Cuellar, Secretary-General of the United Nations.

10. At the second session, the Conference adopted the following instruments:

1. Agreement on a Comprehensive Political Settlement of the Cambodia Conflict, with annexes on the mandate for UNTAC, military matters, elections, repatriation of Cambodian refugees and displaced persons, and the principles for a new Cambodian constitution;

2. Agreement concerning the Sovereignty, Independence, Territorial Integrity and Inviolability, Neutrality and National Unity of Cambodia; and

3. Declaration on the Rehabilitation and Reconstruction of Cambodia.

These instruments represent an elaboration of the 'Framework for a Comprehensive Political Settlement of the Cambodia Conflict' adopted by the five permanent members of the United Nations Security Council on 28 August 1990, and of elements of the work accomplished at the first session of the Conference. They entail a continuing process of national reconciliation and an enhanced role for the United Nations, thus enabling the Cambodian people to determine their own political future through free and fair elections organized and conducted by the United Nations in a neutral political environment with full respect for the national sovereignty of Cambodia.

11. These instruments, which together form the comprehensive settlement the achievement of which was the objective of the Paris Conference, are being presented for signature to the States participating in the Paris Conference. On behalf of Cambodia, the instruments will be signed by the twelve members of the Supreme National Council of Cambodia, which is the unique legitimate body and source of authority enshrining the sovereignty, independence and unity of Cambodia.

12. The States participating in the Conference call upon the Co-Presidents of the Conference to transmit an authentic copy of the comprehensive political settlement instruments to the Secretary-General of the United Nations. The States participating in the Conference request the Secretary-General to take the appropriate steps in order to enable consideration of the comprehensive settlement by the United Nations Security Council at the earliest opportunity. They pledge their full co-operation in the fulfilment of this comprehensive settlement and their assistance in its implementation.

Above all, in view of the recent tragic history of Cambodia, the States participating in the Conference commit themselves to promote and encourage respect for and observance of human rights and fundamental freedoms in Cambodia, as embodied in the relevant international instruments to which they are party.

13. The States participating in the Conference request the International Committee of the Red Cross to facilitate, in accordance with its principles, the release of prisoners of war and civilian internees. They express their readiness to assist the ICRC in this task.

14. The States participating in the Conference invite other States to accede to the Agreement on a Comprehensive Political Settlement of the Cambodia Conflict and to the Agreement concerning the Sovereignty, Independence,

Territorial Integrity and Inviolability, Neutrality and National Unity of Cambodia.

15. Further recognizing the need for a concerted international effort to assist Cambodia in the tasks of rehabilitation and reconstruction, the States participating in the Conference urge the international community to provide generous economic and financial support for the measures set forth in the Declaration on the Rehabilitation and Reconstruction of Cambodia.

. . .

DONE AT PARIS this twenty-third day of October one thousand nine hundred and ninety one, in two copies in the Chinese, English, French, Khmer and Russian languages, each text being equally authentic. The originals of this Final Act shall be deposited with the Governments of the French Republic and of the Republic of Indonesia.

Source: UN document A/46/608, S/23177, 30 Oct. 1991, pp. 2–7.

AGREEMENT ON A COMPREHENSIVE POLITICAL SETTLEMENT OF THE CAMBODIA CONFLICT

Paris, 23 October 1991

The States participating in the Paris Conference on Cambodia, namely Australia, Brunei Darussalam, Cambodia, Canada, the People's Republic of China, the French Republic, the Republic of India, the Republic of Indonesia, Japan, the Lao People's Democratic Republic, Malaysia, the Republic of the Philippines, the Republic of Singapore, the Kingdom of Thailand, the Union of Soviet Socialist Republics, the United Kingdom of Great Britain and Northern Ireland, the United States of America, the Socialist Republic of Vietnam and the Socialist Federal Republic of Yugoslavia,

In the presence of the Secretary-General of the United Nations,

In order to maintain, preserve and defend the sovereignty, independence, territorial integrity and inviolability, neutrality and national unity of Cambodia,

Desiring to restore and maintain peace in Cambodia, to promote national reconciliation and to ensure the exercise of the right to self-determination of the Cambodian people through free and fair elections,

Convinced that only a comprehensive political settlement to the Cambodia conflict will be just and durable and will contribute to regional and international peace and security,

Welcoming the Framework document of 28 August 1990, which was accepted by the Cambodian Parties in its entirety as the basis for settling the Cambodia conflict, and which was subsequently unanimously endorsed by Security Council resolution 668 (1990) of 20 September 1990 and General Assembly resolution 45/3 of 15 October 1990,

Noting the formation in Jakarta on 10 September 1990 of the Supreme National Council of Cambodia as the unique legitimate body and source of authority in Cambodia in which, throughout the transitional period, national sovereignty and unity are enshrined, and which represents Cambodia externally,

Welcoming the unanimous election, in Beijing on 17 July 1991, of H. R. H. Prince Norodom Sihanouk as the President of the Supreme National Council,

Recognizing that an enhanced United Nations role requires the establishment of a United Nations Transitional Authority in Cambodia (UNTAC) with civilian and military components, which will act with full respect for the national sovereignty of Cambodia,

Noting the statements made at the conclusion of the meetings held in Jakarta on 9–10 September 1990, in Paris on 21–23 December 1990, in Pattaya on 24–26 June 1991, in Beijing on 16–17 July 1991, in Pattaya on 26–29 August 1991, and also the meetings held in Jakarta on 4–6 June 1991 and in New York on 19 September 1991,

Welcoming United Nations Security Council resolution 717 (1991) of 16 October 1991 on Cambodia,

Recognizing that Cambodia's tragic recent history requires special measures to assure protection of human rights, and the non-return to the policies and practices of the past,

Have agreed as follows:

PART I. ARRANGEMENTS DURING THE TRANSITIONAL PERIOD

Section I. Transitional period

Article 1

For the purposes of this Agreement, the transitional period shall commence with the entry into force of this Agreement and terminate when the constituent assembly elected through free and fair elections, organized and certified by the United Nations, has approved the constitution and transformed itself into a legislative assembly, and thereafter a new government has been created.

Section II. United Nations Transitional Authority in Cambodia

Article 2

(1) The Signatories invite the United Nations Security Council to establish a United Nations Transitional Authority in Cambodia (hereinafter referred to as 'UNTAC') with civilian and military components under the direct responsibility of the Secretary-General of the United Nations. For this purpose the Secretary-General will designate a Special Representative to act on his behalf.

(2) The Signatories further invite the United Nations Security Council to provide UNTAC with the mandate set forth in this Agreement and to keep its implementation under continuing review through periodic reports submitted by the Secretary-General.

Section III. Supreme National Council

Article 3

The Supreme National Council (hereinafter referred to as 'the SNC') is the unique legitimate body and source of authority in which, throughout the transitional period, the sovereignty, independence and unity of Cambodia are enshrined.

Article 4

The members of the SNC shall be committed to the holding of free and fair elections organized and conducted by the United Nations as the basis for forming a new and legitimate Government.

Article 5

The SNC shall, throughout the transitional period, represent Cambodia externally and occupy the seat of Cambodia at the United Nations, in the United Nations specialized agencies, and in other international institutions and international conferences.

Article 6

The SNC hereby delegates to the United Nations all powers necessary to ensure the implementation of this Agreement, as described in annex 1.

In order to ensure a neutral political environment conducive to free and fair general elections, administrative agencies, bodies and offices which could directly influence the outcome of elections will be placed under direct United Nations supervision or control. In that context, special attention will be given to foreign affairs, national defence, finance, public security and information. To reflect the importance of these subjects, UNTAC needs to exercise such control as is necessary to ensure the strict neutrality of the bodies responsible for them. The United Nations, in consultation with the SNC, will identify which agencies, bodies and offices could continue to operate in order to ensure normal day-to-day life in the country.

Article 7

The relationship between the SNC, UNTAC and existing administrative structures is set forth in annex 1.

Section IV. Withdrawal of foreign forces and its verification

Article 8

Immediately upon entry into force of this Agreement, any foreign forces, advisers, and military personnel remaining in Cambodia, together with their weapons, ammunition, and equipment, shall be withdrawn from Cambodia and not be returned. Such withdrawal and non-return will be subject to UNTAC verification in accordance with annex 2.

Section V. Cease-fire and cessation of outside military assistance

Article 9

The cease-fire shall take effect at the time this Agreement enters into force. All forces shall immediately disengage and refrain from all hostilities and from any deployment, movement or action which would extend the territory they control or which might lead to renewed fighting.

The Signatories hereby invite the Security Council of the United Nations to request the Secretary-General to provide good offices to assist in this process until such time as the military component of UNTAC is in position to supervise, monitor and verify it.

Article 10

Upon entry into force of this Agreement,

there shall be an immediate cessation of all outside military assistance to all Cambodian Parties.

Article 11

The objectives of military arrangements during the transitional period shall be to stabilize the security situation and build confidence among the parties to the conflict, so as to reinforce the purposes of this Agreement and to prevent the risks of a return to warfare.

Detailed provisions regarding UNTAC's supervision, monitoring, and verification of the cease-fire and related measures, including verification of the withdrawal of foreign forces and the regrouping, cantonment and ultimate disposition of all Cambodian forces and their weapons during the transitional period are set forth in annex 1, section C, and annex 2.

PART II. ELECTIONS

Article 12

The Cambodian people shall have the right to determine their own political future through the free and fair election of a constituent assembly, which will draft and approve a new Cambodian Constitution in accordance with Article 23 and transform itself into a legislative assembly, which will create the new Cambodian Government. This election will be held under United Nations auspices in a neutral political environment with full respect for the national sovereignty of Cambodia.

Article 13

UNTAC shall be responsible for the organization and conduct of these elections based on the provisions of annex 1, section D, and annex 3.

Article 14

All Signatories commit themselves to respect the results of these elections once certified as free and fair by the United Nations.

PART III. HUMAN RIGHTS

Article 15

1. All persons in Cambodia and all Cambodian refugees and displaced persons shall enjoy the rights and freedoms embodied in the Universal Declaration of Human Rights and other relevant international human rights instruments.

2. To this end,

(a) Cambodia undertakes:

– to ensure respect for and observance of human rights and fundamental freedoms in Cambodia;

– to support the right of all Cambodian citizens to undertake activities which would promote and protect human rights and fundamental freedoms;

– to take effective measures to ensure that the policies and practices of the past shall never be allowed to return;

– to adhere to relevant international human rights instruments;

(b) the other Signatories to this Agreement undertake to promote and encourage respect for and observance of human rights and fundamental freedoms in Cambodia as embodied in the relevant international instruments and the relevant resolutions of the United Nations General Assembly, in order, in particular, to prevent the recurrence of human rights abuses.

Article 16

UNTAC shall be responsible during the transitional period for fostering an environment in which respect for human rights shall be ensured, based on the provisions of annex 1, section E.

Article 17

After the end of the transitional period, the United Nations Commission on Human Rights should continue to monitor closely the human rights situation in Cambodia, including, if necessary, by the appointment of a Special Rapporteur who would report his findings annually to the Commission and to the General Assembly.

PART IV. INTERNATIONAL GUARANTEES

Article 18

Cambodia undertakes to maintain, preserve and defend, and the other Signatories undertake to recognize and respect, the sovereignty, independence, territorial integrity and inviolability, neutrality and national unity of Cambodia, as set forth in a separate Agreement.

PART V. REFUGEES AND DISPLACED PERSONS

Article 19

Upon entry into force of this Agreement, every effort will be made to create in Cambodia political, economic and social conditions conducive to the voluntary return and harmonious integration of Cambodian refugees and displaced persons.

Article 20

(1) Cambodian refugees and displaced persons, located outside Cambodia, shall have the right to return to Cambodia and to live in safety, security and dignity, free from intimidation or coercion of any kind.

(2) The Signatories request the Secretary-General of the United Nations to facilitate the repatriation in safety and dignity of Cambodian refugees and displaced persons, as an integral part of the comprehensive political settlement and under the overall authority of the Special Representative of the Secretary-General, in accordance with the guidelines and principles on the repatriation of refugees and displaced persons as set forth in annex 4.

PART VI. RELEASE OF PRISONERS OF WAR AND CIVILIAN INTERNEES

Article 21

The release of all prisoners of war and civilian internees shall be accomplished at the earliest possible date under the direction of the International Committee of the Red Cross (ICRC) in co-ordination with the Special Representative of the Secretary-General, with the assistance, as necessary, of other appropriate international humanitarian organizations and the Signatories.

Article 22

The expression 'civilian internees' refers to all persons who are not prisoners of war and who, having contributed in any way whatsoever to the armed or political struggle, have been arrested or detained by any of the parties by virtue of their contribution thereto.

PART VII. PRINCIPLES FOR A NEW CONSTITUTION FOR CAMBODIA

Article 23

Basic principles, including those regarding human rights and fundamental freedoms as well as regarding Cambodia's status of neutrality, which the new Cambodian Constitution will incorporate, are set forth in annex 5.

PART VIII. REHABILITATION AND RECONSTRUCTION

Article 24

The Signatories urge the international community to provide economic and financial support for the rehabilitation and reconstruction of Cambodia, as provided in a separate declaration.

PART IX. FINAL PROVISIONS

Article 25

The Signatories shall, in good faith and in a spirit of co-operation, resolve through peaceful means any disputes with respect to the implementation of this Agreement.

Article 26

The Signatories request other States, international organizations and other bodies to co-operate and assist in the implementation of this Agreement and in the fulfilment by UNTAC of its mandate.

Article 27

The Signatories shall provide their full co-operation to the United Nations to ensure the implementation of its mandate, including by the provision of privileges and immunities, and by facilitating freedom of movement and communication within and through their respective territories.

In carrying out its mandate, UNTAC shall exercise due respect for the sovereignty of all States neighbouring Cambodia.

Article 28

(1) The Signatories shall comply in good faith with all obligations undertaken in this Agreement and shall extend full co-operation to the United Nations, including the provision of the information which UNTAC requires in the fulfilment of its mandate.

(2) The signature on behalf of Cambodia by the members of the SNC shall commit all Cambodian parties and armed forces to the provisions of this Agreement.

Article 29

Without prejudice to the prerogatives of the Security Council of the United Nations, and upon the request of the Secretary-General, the two Co-Chairmen of the Paris Conference on Cambodia, in the event of a violation or threat of violation of this Agreement, will immediately undertake appropriate consultations, including with members of the Paris Conference on Cambodia, with a view to taking appropriate steps to ensure respect for these commitments.

Article 30

This Agreement shall enter into force upon signature.

Article 31

This Agreement shall remain open for accession by all States. The instruments of accession shall be deposited with the Governments of the French Republic and the Republic of Indonesia. For each State acceding to the Agreement it shall enter into force on the date of deposit of its instruments of accession. Acceding States shall be bound by the same obligations as the Signatories.

Article 32

The originals of this Agreement, of which the Chinese, English, French, Khmer and Russian texts are equally authentic, shall be deposited with the Governments of the French Republic and the Republic of Indonesia, which shall transmit certified true copies to the Governments of the other States participating in the Paris Conference on Cambodia, as well as the Secretary-General of the United Nations.

. . .

Annex 1

UNTAC Mandate

Section A. General procedures

1. In accordance with article 6 of the Agreement, UNTAC will exercise the powers necessary to ensure the implementation of this Agreement, including those relating to the organization and conduct of free and fair elections and the relevant aspects of the administration of Cambodia.

2. The following mechanism will be used to resolve all issues relating to the implementation of this Agreement which may arise between the Secretary-General's Special Representative and the Supreme National Council (SNC):

(*a*) The SNC offers advice to UNTAC, which will comply with this advice provided there is a consensus among the members of the SNC and provided this advice is consistent with the objectives of the present Agreement;

(*b*) If there is no consensus among the members of the SNC despite every endeavour of its President, H. R. H. Samdech Norodom Sihanouk, the President will be entitled to make the decision on what advice to offer to UNTAC, taking fully into account the views expressed in the SNC. UNTAC will comply with the advice provided it is consistent with the objectives of the present Agreement;

(c) If H. R. H. Samdech Norodom Sihanouk, President of the SNC, the legitimate representative of Cambodian sovereignty, is not, for whatever reason, in a position to make such a decision, his power of decision will transfer to the Secretary-General's Special Representative. The Special Representative will make the final decision, taking fully into account the views expressed in the SNC;

(d) Any power to act regarding the implementation of this Agreement conferred upon the SNC by the Agreement will be exercised by consensus or, failing such consensus, by its President in accordance with the procedure set out above. In the event that H. R. H. Samdech Norodom Sihanouk, President of the SNC, the legitimate representative of Cambodian sovereignty, is not, for whatever reason, in a position to act, his power to act will transfer to the Secretary-General's Special Representative who may take the necessary action;

(e) In all cases, the Secretary-General's Special Representative will determine whether advice or action of the SNC is consistent with the present Agreement.

3. The Secretary-General's Special Representative or his delegate will attend the meetings of the SNC and of any subsidiary body which might be established by it and give its members all necessary information on the decisions taken by UNTAC.

Section B. Civil administration

1. In accordance with Article 6 of the Agreement, all administrative agencies, bodies and offices acting in the field of foreign affairs, national defence, finance, public security and information will be placed under the direct control of UNTAC, which will exercise it as necessary to ensure strict neutrality. In this respect, the Secretary-General's Special Representative will determine what is necessary and may issue directives to the above-mentioned administrative agencies, bodies and offices. Such directives may be issued to and will bind all Cambodian Parties.

2. In accordance with article 6 of the Agreement, the Secretary-General's Special Representative, in consultation with the SNC, will determine which other administrative agencies, bodies and offices could directly influence the outcome of elections. These administrative agencies, bodies and offices will be placed under direct supervision or control of UNTAC and will comply with any guidance provided by it.

3. In accordance with Article 6 of the Agreement, the Secretary-General's Special Representative, in consultation with the SNC, will identify which administrative agencies, bodies, and offices could continue to operate in order to ensure normal day-to-day life in Cambodia, if necessary, under such supervision by UNTAC as it considers necessary.

4. In accordance with article 6 of the Agreement, the authority of the Secretary-General's Special Representative will include the power to:

(a) Install in administrative agencies, bodies and offices of all the Cambodian Parties, United Nations personnel who will have unrestricted access to all administrative operations and information;

(b) Require the reassignment or removal of any personnel of such administrative agencies, bodies and offices.

5. (a) On the basis of the information provided in Article I, paragraph 3, of annex 2, the Special Representative of the Secretary-General will determine, after consultation with the Cambodian Parties, those civil police necessary to perform law enforcement in Cambodia.

All Cambodian Parties hereby undertake to comply with the determination made by the Special Representative in this regard;

(*b*) All civil police will operate under UNTAC supervision or control, in order to ensure that law and order are maintained effectively and impartially, and that human rights and fundamental freedoms are fully protected. In consultation with the SNC, UNTAC will supervise other law enforcement and judicial processes throughout Cambodia to the extent necessary to ensure the attainment of these objectives.

6. If the Secretary-General's Special Representative deems it necessary, UNTAC, in consultation with the SNC, will undertake investigations of complaints and allegations regarding actions by the existing administrative structures in Cambodia that are inconsistent with or work against the objectives of this comprehensive political settlement. UNTAC will also be empowered to undertake such investigation on its own initiative. UNTAC will take, when necessary, appropriate corrective steps.

Section C. Military functions

1. UNTAC will supervise, monitor and verify the withdrawal of foreign forces, the cease-fire and related measures in accordance with annex 2, including:

(*a*) Verification of the withdrawal from Cambodia of all categories of foreign forces, advisers and military personnel and their weapons, ammunition and equipment, and their non-return to Cambodia;

(*b*) Liaison with neighbouring Governments over any developments in or near their territory that could endanger the implementation of this Agreement ;

(*c*) Monitoring the cessation of outside military assistance to all Cambodian Parties;

(*d*) Locating and confiscating caches of weapons and military supplies throughout the country;

(*e*) Assisting with clearing mines and undertaking training programmes in mine clearance and a mine awareness programme among the Cambodian people.

2. UNTAC will supervise the regrouping and relocating of all forces to specifically designated cantonment areas on the basis of an operational time-table to be agreed upon, in accordance with annex 2.

3. As the forces enter the cantonments, UNTAC will initiate the process of arms control and reduction specified in annex 2.

4. UNTAC will take necessary steps regarding the phased process of demobilization of the military forces of the parties, in accordance with annex 2.

5. UNTAC will assist, as necessary, the International Committee of the Red Cross in the release of all prisoners of war and civilian internees.

Section D. Elections

1. UNTAC will organize and conduct the election referred to in Part II of this Agreement in accordance with this section and annex 3.

2. UNTAC may consult with the SNC regarding the organization and conduct of the electoral process.

3. In the exercise of its responsibilities in relation to the electoral process, the specific authority of UNTAC will include the following:

(*a*) The establishment, in consultation with the SNC, of a system of laws, procedures and administrative measures necessary for the holding of a free and fair election in Cambodia, including the adoption of an electoral law and of a code of conduct regulating participation in the election in a manner consistent with respect for human rights and prohibiting coercion or financial inducement in order to influence voter preference;

(*b*) The suspension or abrogation, in consultation with the SNC, of provisions of existing laws which could defeat the objects and purposes of this Agreement;

(c) The design and implementation of a voter education programme, covering all aspects of the election, to support the election process;

(d) The design and implementation of a system of voter registration, as a first phase of the electoral process, to ensure that eligible voters have the opportunity to register, and the subsequent preparation of verified voter registration lists;

(e) The design and implementation of a system of registration of political parties and lists of candidates;

(f) Ensuring fair access to the media, including press, television and radio, for all political parties contesting in the election;

(g) The adoption and implementation of measures to monitor and facilitate the participation of Cambodians in the elections, the political campaign, and the balloting procedures;

(h) The design and implementation of a system of balloting and polling, to ensure that registered voters have the opportunity to vote;

(i) The establishment, in consultation with the SNC, of co-ordinated arrangements to facilitate the presence of foreign observers wishing to observe the campaign and voting;

(j) Overall direction of polling and the vote count;

(k) The identification and investigation of complaints of electoral irregularities, and the taking of appropriate corrective action;

(l) Determining whether or not the election was free and fair and, if so, certification of the list of persons duly elected.

4. In carrying out its responsibilities under the present section, UNTAC will establish a system of safeguards to assist it in ensuring the absence of fraud during the electoral process, including arrangements for Cambodian representatives to observe the registration and polling procedures and the provision of an UNTAC mechanism for hearing and deciding complaints.

5. The timetable for the various phases of the electoral process will be determined by UNTAC, in consultation with the SNC as provided in paragraph 2 of this section. The duration of the electoral process will not exceed nine months from the commencement of voter registration.

6. In organizing and conducting the electoral process, UNTAC will make every effort to ensure that the system and procedures adopted are absolutely impartial, while the operational arrangements are as administratively simple and efficient as possible.

Section E. Human rights

In accordance with article 16, UNTAC will make provisions for:

(a) The development and implementation of a programme of human rights education to promote respect for and understanding of human rights;

(b) General human rights oversight during the transitional period;

(c) The investigation of human rights complaints, and, where appropriate, corrective action.

Annex 2

Withdrawal, Cease-fire and Related Measures

Article I. Cease-fire

1. All Cambodian Parties (hereinafter referred to as 'the Parties') agree to observe a comprehensive cease-fire on land and water and in the air. This cease-fire will be implemented in two phases. During the first phase, the cease-fire will be observed with the assistance of the Secretary-General of the United Nations through his good offices. During the second phase, which should commence as soon as possible, the cease-fire will be supervised, monitored and verified by UNTAC. The Commander of the military component of UNTAC, in consulta-

tion with the Parties, shall determine the exact time and date at which the second phase will commence. This date will be set at least four weeks in advance of its coming into effect.

2. The Parties undertake that, upon the signing of this Agreement, they will observe a cease-fire and will order their armed forces immediately to disengage and refrain from all hostilities and any deployment, movement or action that would extend the territory they control or that might lead to a resumption of fighting, pending the commencement of the second phase. 'Forces' are agreed to include all regular, provincial, district, paramilitary, and other auxiliary forces. During the first phase, the Secretary-General of the United Nations will provide his good offices to the Parties to assist them in its observance. The Parties undertake to co-operate with the Secretary-General or his representatives in the exercise of his good offices in this regard.

3. The Parties agree that, immediately upon the signing of this Agreement, the following information will be provided to the United Nations:

(a) Total strength of their forces, organization, precise number and location of deployments inside and outside Cambodia. The deployment will be depicted on a map marked with locations of all troop positions, occupied or unoccupied, including staging camps, supply bases and supply routes;

(b) Comprehensive lists of arms, ammunition and equipment held by their forces, and the exact locations at which those arms, ammunition and equipment are deployed;

(c) Detailed record of their mine-fields, including types and characteristics of mines laid and information of booby traps used by them together with any information available to them about mine-fields laid or booby traps used by the other Parties;

(d) Total strength of their police forces, organization, precise numbers and locations of deployments, as well as comprehensive lists of their arms, ammunition and equipment, and the exact locations at which those arms, ammunition and equipment are deployed.

4. Immediately upon his arrival in Cambodia, and not later than four weeks before the beginning of the second phase, the Commander of the military component of UNTAC will, in consultation with the Parties, finalize UNTAC's plan for the regroupment and cantonment of the forces of the Parties and for the storage of their arms, ammunition and equipment, in accordance with Article III of this annex. This plan will include the designation of regroupment and cantonment areas, as well as an agreed timetable. The cantonment areas will be established at battalion size or larger.

5. The Parties agree to take steps to inform their forces at least two weeks before the beginning of the second phase, using all possible means of communication, about the agreed date and time of the beginning of the second phase, about the agreed plan for the regroupment and cantonment of their forces and for the storage of their arms, ammunition and equipment and, in particular, about the exact locations of the regroupment areas to which their forces are to report. Such information will continue to be disseminated for a period of four weeks after the beginning of the second phase.

6. The Parties shall scrupulously observe the cease-fire and will not resume any hostilities by land, water or air. The commanders of their armed forces will ensure that all troops under their command remain on their respective positions, pending their movement to the designated regroupment areas, and refrain from all hostilities and from any deployment or movement or action which would extend the territory they

control or which might lead to a resumption of fighting.

Article II. Liaison system and Mixed Military Working Group

A Mixed Military Working Group (MMWG) will be established with a view to resolving any problems that may arise in the observance of the cease-fire. It will be chaired by the most senior United Nations military officer in Cambodia or his representative. Each Party agrees to designate an officer of the rank of brigadier or equivalent to serve on the MMWG. Its composition, method of operation and meeting places will be determined by the most senior United Nations military officer in consultation with the Parties. Similar liaison arrangements will be made at lower military command levels to resolve practical problems on the ground.

Article III. Regroupment and cantonment of the forces of the Parties and storage of their arms, ammunition and equipment

1. In accordance with the operational timetable referred to in paragraph 4 of article I of the present annex, all forces of the Parties that are not already in designated cantonment areas will report to designated regroupment areas, which will be established and operated by the military component of UNTAC. These regroupment areas will be established and operational not later than one week prior to the date of the beginning of the second phase. The Parties agree to arrange for all their forces, with all their arms, ammunition and equipment, to report to regroupment areas within two weeks after the beginning of the second phase. All personnel who have reported to the regroupment areas will thereafter be escorted by personnel of the military component of UNTAC, with their arms, ammunition and equipment, to designated cantonment areas. All Parties agree to ensure that personnel reporting

to the regroupment areas will be able to do so in full safety and without any hindrance.

2. On the basis of the information provided in accordance with paragraph 3 of article I of the present annex, UNTAC will confirm that the regroupment and cantonment processes have been completed in accordance with the plan referred to in paragraph 4 of article I of this annex. UNTAC will endeavour to complete these processes within four weeks from the date of the beginning of the second phase. On the completion of regroupment of all forces and of their movement to cantonment areas, respectively, the Commander of the military component of UNTAC will so inform each of the four Parties.

3. The Parties agree that, as their forces enter the designated cantonment areas, their personnel will be instructed by their commanders to immediately hand over all their arms, ammunition and equipment to UNTAC for storage in the custody of UNTAC.

4. UNTAC will check the arms, ammunition and equipment handed over to it against the lists referred to in paragraph 3 (b) of article I of this annex, in order to verify that all the arms, ammunition and equipment in the possession of the Parties have been placed under its custody.

Article IV. Resupply of forces during cantonment

The military component of UNTAC will supervise the resupply of all forces of the Parties during the regroupment and cantonment processes. Such resupply will be confined to items of a non-lethal nature such as food, water, clothing and medical supplies as well as provision of medical care.

Article V. Ultimate disposition of the forces of the Parties and of their arms, ammunition and equipment

1. In order to reinforce the objectives

of a comprehensive political settlement, minimize the risks of a return to warfare, stabilize the security situation and build confidence among the Parties to the conflict, all Parties agree to undertake a phased and balanced process of demobilization of at least 70 per cent of their military forces. This process shall be undertaken in accordance with a detailed plan to be drawn up by UNTAC on the basis of the information provided under Article I of this annex and in consultation with the Parties. It should be completed prior to the end of the process of registration for the elections and on a date to be determined by the Special Representative of the Secretary-General.

2. The Cambodian Parties hereby commit themselves to demobilize all their remaining forces before or shortly after the elections and, to the extent that full demobilization is unattainable, to respect and abide by whatever decision the newly elected government that emerges in accordance with Article 12 of this Agreement takes with regard to the incorporation of parts or all of those forces into a new national army. Upon completion of the demobilization referred to in paragraph 1, the Cambodian Parties and the Special Representative of the Secretary-General shall undertake a review regarding the final disposition of the forces remaining in the cantonments, with a view to determining which of the following shall apply:

(a) If the Parties agree to proceed with the demobilization of all or some of the forces remaining in the cantonments, preferably prior to or otherwise shortly after the elections, the Special Representative shall prepare a timetable for so doing, in consultation with them.

(b) Should total demobilization of all of the residual forces before or shortly after the elections not be possible, the Parties hereby undertake to make available all of their forces remaining in

cantonments to the newly elected government that emerges in accordance with Article 12 of this Agreement, for consideration for incorporation into a new national army. They further agree that any such forces which are not incorporated into the new national army will be demobilized forthwith according to a plan to be prepared by the Special Representative. With regard to the ultimate disposition of the remaining forces and all the arms, ammunition and equipment, UNTAC, as it withdraws from Cambodia, shall retain such authority as is necessary to ensure an orderly transfer to the newly elected government of those responsibilities it has exercised during the transitional period.

3. UNTAC will assist, as required, with the reintegration into civilian life of the forces demobilized prior to the elections.

4. (a) UNTAC will control and guard all the arms, ammunition and equipment of the Parties throughout the transitional period;

(b) As the cantoned forces are demobilized in accordance with paragraph 1 above, there will be a parallel reduction by UNTAC of the arms, ammunition and equipment stored on site in the cantonment areas. For the forces remaining in the cantonment areas, access to their arms, ammunition and equipment shall only be on the basis of the explicit authorization of the Special Representative of the Secretary-General;

(c) If there is a further demobilization of the military forces in accordance with paragraph 2 (a) above, there will be a commensurate reduction by UNTAC of the arms, ammunition and equipment stored on site in the cantonment areas;

(d) The ultimate disposition of all arms, ammunition and equipment will be determined by the government that emerges through the free and fair elections in accordance with article 12 of this Agreement.

Article VI. Verification of withdrawal from Cambodia and non-return of all categories of foreign forces

1. UNTAC shall be provided, no later than two weeks before the commencement of the second phase of the cease-fire, with detailed information in writing regarding the withdrawal of foreign forces. This information shall include the following elements:

(*a*) Total strength of these forces and their organization and deployment;

(*b*) Comprehensive lists of arms, ammunition and equipment held by these forces, and their exact locations;

(*c*) Withdrawal plan (already implemented or to be implemented), including withdrawal routes, border crossing points and time of departure from Cambodia.

2. On the basis of the information provided in accordance with paragraph 1 above, UNTAC will undertake an investigation in the manner it deems appropriate. The Party providing the information will be required to make personnel available to accompany UNTAC investigators.

3. Upon confirmation of the presence of any foreign forces, UNTAC will immediately deploy military personnel with the foreign forces and accompany them until they have withdrawn from Cambodian territory. UNTAC will also establish checkpoints on withdrawal routes, border crossing points and airfields to verify the withdrawal and ensure the non-return of all categories of foreign forces.

4. The Mixed Military Working Group (MMWG) provided for in article II of this annex will assist UNTAC in fulfilling the above-mentioned tasks.

Article VII. Cessation of outside military assistance to all Cambodian Parties

1. All Parties undertake, from the time of the signing of this Agreement, not to obtain or seek any outside military assistance, including weapons, ammunition

and military equipment from outside sources.

2. The Signatories whose territory is adjacent to Cambodia, namely, the Governments of the Lao People's Democratic Republic, the Kingdom of Thailand and the Socialist Republic of Vietnam, undertake to:

(*a*) Prevent the territories of their respective States, including land territory, territorial sea and air space, from being used for the purpose of providing any form of military assistance to any of the Cambodian Parties. Resupply of such items as food, water, clothing and medical supplies through their territories will be allowed, but shall, without prejudice to the provisions of sub-paragraph (*c*) below, be subject to UNTAC supervision upon arrival in Cambodia;

(*b*) Provide written confirmation to the Commander of the military component of UNTAC, not later than four weeks after the second phase of the cease-fire begins, that no forces, arms, ammunition or military equipment of any of the Cambodian Parties are present on their territories;

(*c*) Receive an UNTAC liaison officer in each of their capitals and designate an officer of the rank of colonel or equivalent, not later than four weeks after the beginning of the second phase of the cease-fire, in order to assist UNTAC in investigating, with due respect for their sovereignty, any complaints that activities are taking place on their territories that are contrary to the provisions of the comprehensive political settlement.

3. To enable UNTAC to monitor the cessation of outside assistance to all Cambodian Parties, the Parties agree that, upon signature of this Agreement, they will provide to UNTAC any information available to them about the routes and means by which military assistance, including weapons, ammunition and military equipment, have [*sic*] been supplied to any of the Parties. Immediately after the second phase of the

cease-fire begins, UNTAC will take the following practical measures:

(a) Establish check-points along the routes and at selected locations along the Cambodian side of the border and at airfields inside Cambodia;

(b) Patrol the coastal and inland waterways of Cambodia;

(c) Maintain mobile teams at strategic locations within Cambodia to patrol and investigate allegations of supply of arms to any of the Parties.

Article VIII. Caches of weapons and military supplies

1. In order to stabilize the security situation, build confidence and reduce arms and military supplies throughout Cambodia, each Party agrees to provide to the Commander of the military component of UNTAC, before a date to be determined by him, all information at its disposal, including marked maps, about known or suspected caches of weapons and military supplies throughout Cambodia.

2. On the basis of information received, the military component of UNTAC shall, after the date referred to in paragraph 1, deploy verification teams to investigate each report and destroy each cache found.

Article IX. Unexploded ordnance devices

1. Soon after arrival in Cambodia, the military component of UNTAC shall ensure, as a first step, that all known mine-fields are clearly marked.

2. The Parties agree that, after completion of the regroupment and cantonment processes in accordance with Article III of the present annex, they will make available mine-clearing teams which, under the supervision and control of UNTAC military personnel, will leave the cantonment areas in order to assist in removing, disarming or deactivating remaining unexploded ordnance devices. Those mines or objects which

cannot be removed, disarmed or deactivated will be clearly marked in accordance with a system to be devised by the military component of UNTAC.

3. UNTAC shall:

(a) Conduct a mass public education programme in the recognition and avoidance of explosive devices;

(b) Train Cambodian volunteers to dispose of unexploded ordnance devices;

(c) Provide emergency first-aid training to Cambodian volunteers.

Article X. Investigation of violations

1. After the beginning of the second phase, upon receipt of any information or complaint from one of the Parties relating to a possible case of non-compliance with any of the provisions of the present annex or related provisions, UNTAC will undertake an investigation in the manner which it deems appropriate. Where the investigation takes place in response to a complaint by one of the Parties, that Party will be required to make personnel available to accompany the UNTAC investigators. The results of such investigation will be conveyed by UNTAC to the complaining Party and the Party complained against, and if necessary to the SNC.

2. UNTAC will also carry out investigations on its own initiative in other cases when it has reason to believe or suspect that a violation of this annex or related provisions may be taking place.

Article XI. Release of prisoners of war

The military component of UNTAC will provide assistance as required to the International Committee of the Red Cross in the latter's discharge of its functions relating to the release of prisoners of war.

Article XII. Repatriation and resettlement of displaced Cambodians

The military component of UNTAC will provide assistance as necessary in the repatriation of Cambodian refugees and displaced persons carried out in accordance with articles 19 and 20 of this Agreement, in particular in the clearing of mines from repatriation routes, reception centres and resettlement areas, as well as in the protection of the reception centres.

Annex 3

Elections

1. The constituent assembly referred to in article 12 of the Agreement shall consist of 120 members. Within three months from the date of the election, it shall complete its tasks of drafting and adopting a new Cambodian Constitution and transform itself into a legislative assembly which will form a new Cambodian Government.

2. The election referred to in Article 12 of the Agreement will be held throughout Cambodia on a provincial basis in accordance with a system of proportional representation on the basis of lists of candidates put forward by political parties.

3. All Cambodians, including those who at the time of signature of this Agreement are Cambodian refugees and displaced persons, will have the same rights, freedoms and opportunities to take part in the electoral process.

4. Every person who has reached the age of eighteen at the time of application to register, or who turns eighteen during the registration period, and who either was born in Cambodia or is the child of a person born in Cambodia, will be eligible to vote in the election.

5. Political parties may be formed by any group of five thousand registered voters. Party platforms shall be consistent with the principles and objectives of the Agreement on a comprehensive political settlement.

6. Party affiliation will be required in order to stand for election to the constituent assembly. Political parties will present lists of candidates standing for election on their behalf, who will be registered voters.

7. Political parties and candidates will be registered in order to stand for election. UNTAC will confirm that political parties and candidates meet the established criteria in order to qualify for participation in the election. Adherence to a Code of Conduct established by UNTAC in consultation with the SNC will be a condition for such participation.

8. Voting will be by secret ballot, with provision made to assist those who are disabled or who cannot read or write.

9. The freedoms of speech, assembly and movement will be fully respected. All registered political parties will enjoy fair access to the media, including the press, television and radio.

Annex 4

Repatriation of Cambodian Refugees and Displaced Persons

Part I. Introduction

1. As part of the comprehensive political settlement, every assistance will need to be given to Cambodian refugees and displaced persons as well as to countries of temporary refuge and the country of origin in order to facilitate the voluntary return of all Cambodian refugees and displaced persons in a peaceful and orderly manner. It must also be ensured that there would be no residual problems for the countries of temporary refuge. The country of origin with responsibility towards its own people will accept their return as conditions become conducive.

Part II. Conditions conducive to the return of refugees and displaced persons

2. The task of rebuilding the Cambodian nation will require the harnessing of all its human and natural resources. To this end, the return to the place of their choice of Cambodians from their temporary refuge and elsewhere outside

their country of origin will make a major contribution.

3. Every effort should be made to ensure that the conditions which have led to a large number of Cambodian refugees and displaced persons seeking refuge in other countries should not recur. Nevertheless, some Cambodian refugees and displaced persons will wish and be able to return spontaneously to their homeland.

4. There must be full respect for the human rights and fundamental freedoms of all Cambodians, including those of the repatriated refugees and displaced persons, in recognition of their entitlement to live in peace and security, free from intimidation and coercion of any kind. These rights would include, *inter alia*, freedom of movement within Cambodia, the choice of domicile and employment, and the right to property.

5. In accordance with the comprehensive political settlement, every effort should be made to create concurrently in Cambodia political, economic and social conditions conducive to the return and harmonious integration of the Cambodian refugees and displaced persons.

6. With a view to ensuring that refugees and displaced persons participate in the elections, mass repatriation should commence and be completed as soon as possible, taking into account all the political, humanitarian, logistical, technical and socio-economic factors involved, and with the co-operation of the SNC.

7. Repatriation of Cambodian refugees and displaced persons should be voluntary and their decision should be taken in full possession of the facts. Choice of destination within Cambodia should be that of the individual. The unity of the family must be preserved.

Part III. Operational factors

8. Consistent with respect for principles of national sovereignty in the countries of temporary refuge and origin, and in close co-operation with the countries of temporary refuge and origin, full access by the Office of the United Nations High Commissioner for Refugees (UNHCR), ICRC and other relevant international agencies should be guaranteed to all Cambodian refugees and displaced persons, with a view to the agencies undertaking the census, tracing, medical assistance, food distribution and other activities vital to the discharge of their mandate and operational responsibilities; such access should also be provided in Cambodia to enable the relevant international organizations to carry out their traditional monitoring as well as operational responsibilities.

9. In the context of the comprehensive political settlement, the signatories note with satisfaction that the Secretary-General of the United Nations has entrusted UNHCR with the role of leadership and co-ordination among intergovernmental agencies assisting with the repatriation and relief of Cambodian refugees and displaced persons. The Signatories look to all non-governmental organizations to co-ordinate as much as possible their work for the Cambodian refugees and displaced persons with that of UNHCR.

10. The SNC, the Governments of the countries in which the Cambodian refugees and displaced persons have sought temporary refuge, and the countries which contribute to the repatriation and integration effort, will wish to monitor closely and facilitate the repatriation of the returnees. An *ad hoc* consultative body should be established for a limited term for these purposes. The UNHCR, the ICRC, and other international agencies as appropriate, as well as UNTAC, would be invited to join as full participants.

11. Adequately monitored short-term repatriation assistance should be provided on an impartial basis to enable the families and individuals returning to Cambodia to establish their lives and livelihoods harmoniously in their society. These interim measures would be

phased out and replaced in the longer term by the reconstruction programme.

12. Those responsible for organizing and supervising the repatriation operation will need to ensure that conditions of security are created for the movement of the refugees and displaced persons. In this respect, it is imperative that appropriate border crossing points and routes be designated and cleared of mines and other hazards.

13. The international community should contribute generously to the financial requirements of the repatriation operation.

Annex 5

Principles for a New Constitution for Cambodia

1. The constitution will be the supreme law of the land. It may be amended only by a designated process involving legislative approval, popular referendum, or both.

2. Cambodia's tragic recent history requires special measures to assure protection of human rights. Therefore, the constitution will contain a declaration of fundamental rights, including the rights to life, personal liberty, security, freedom of movement, freedom of religion, assembly and association including political parties and trade unions, due process and equality before the law, protection from arbitrary deprivation of property or deprivation of private property without just compensation, and freedom from racial, ethnic, religious or sexual discrimination. It will prohibit the retroactive application of criminal law. The declaration will be consistent with the provisions of the Universal Declaration of Human Rights and other relevant international instruments. Aggrieved individuals will be entitled to have the courts adjudicate and enforce these rights.

3. The constitution will declare Cambodia's status as a sovereign, independent and neutral State, and the national unity of the Cambodian people.

4. The constitution will state that Cambodia will follow a system of liberal democracy, on the basis of pluralism. It will provide for periodic and genuine elections. It will provide for the right to vote and to be elected by universal and equal suffrage. It will provide for voting by secret ballot, with a requirement that electoral procedures provide a full and fair opportunity to organize and participate in the electoral process.

5. An independent judiciary will be established, empowered to enforce the rights provided under the constitution.

6. The constitution will be adopted by a two-thirds majority of the members of the constituent assembly.

Source: UN document A/46/608, S/23177, 30 Oct. 1991, pp. 8–47.

AGREEMENT CONCERNING THE SOVEREIGNTY, INDEPENDENCE, TERRITORIAL INTEGRITY AND INVIOLABILITY, NEUTRALITY AND NATIONAL UNITY OF CAMBODIA

Paris, 31 October 1991

Australia, Brunei Darussalam, Cambodia, Canada, the People's Republic of China, the French Republic, the Republic of India, the Republic of Indonesia, Japan, the Lao People's Democratic Republic, Malaysia, the Republic of the Philippines, the Republic of Singapore, the Kingdom of Thailand, the Union of Soviet Socialist Republics, the United Kingdom of Great Britain and Northern Ireland, the United States of America, the Socialist Republic of Vietnam and the Socialist Federal Republic of Yugoslavia,

In the presence of the Secretary-General of the United Nations,

Convinced that a comprehensive political settlement for Cambodia is essential for the long-term objective of maintaining peace and security in South-East Asia,

Recalling their obligations under the Charter of the United Nations and other rules of international law,

Considering that full observance of the principles of non-interference and non-intervention in the internal and external affairs of States is of the greatest importance for the maintenance of international peace and security,

Reaffirming the inalienable right of States freely to determine their own political, economic, cultural and social systems in accordance with the will of their peoples, without outside interference, subversion, coercion or threat in any form whatsoever,

Desiring to promote respect for and observance of human rights and fundamental freedoms in conformity with the Charter of the United Nations and other relevant international instruments,

Have agreed as follows:

Article 1

1. Cambodia hereby solemnly undertakes to maintain, preserve and defend its sovereignty, independence, territorial integrity and inviolability, neutrality, and national unity; the perpetual neutrality of Cambodia shall be proclaimed and enshrined in the Cambodian constitution to be adopted after free and fair elections.

2. To this end, Cambodia undertakes:

(*a*) To refrain from any action that might impair the sovereignty, independence and territorial integrity and inviolability of other States;

(*b*) To refrain from entering into any military alliances or other military agreements with other States that would be inconsistent with its neutrality, without prejudice to Cambodia's right to acquire the necessary military equipment, arms, munitions and assistance to enable it to

exercise its inherent right of self-defence and to maintain law and order;

(*c*) To refrain from interference in any form whatsoever, whether direct or indirect, in the internal affairs of other States;

(*d*) To terminate treaties and agreements that are incompatible with its sovereignty, independence, territorial integrity and inviolability, neutrality, and national unity;

(*e*) To refrain from the threat or use of force against the territorial integrity or political independence of any State, or in any other manner inconsistent with the purposes of the United Nations;

(*f*) To settle all disputes with other States by peaceful means;

(*g*) To refrain from using its territory or the territories of other States to impair the sovereignty, independence, and territorial integrity and inviolability of other States;

(*h*) To refrain from permitting the introduction or stationing of foreign forces, including military personnel, in any form whatsoever, in Cambodia, and to prevent the establishment or maintenance of foreign military bases, strong points or facilities in Cambodia, except pursuant to United Nations authorization for the implementation of the comprehensive political settlement.

Article 2

1. The other parties to this Agreement hereby solemnly undertake to recognize and to respect in every way the sovereignty, independence, territorial integrity and inviolability, neutrality and national unity of Cambodia.

2. To this end, they undertake:

(*a*) To refrain from entering into any military alliances or other military agreements with Cambodia that would be inconsistent with Cambodia's neutrality, without prejudice to Cambodia's right to acquire the necessary military equipment, arms, munitions and assistance to enable it to exercise its inherent right of self-defence and to maintain law and order;

(*b*) To refrain from interference in any form whatsoever, whether direct or indirect, in the internal affairs of Cambodia;

(*c*) To refrain from the threat or use of force against the territorial integrity or political independence of Cambodia, or in any other manner inconsistent with the purposes of the United Nations;

(*d*) To settle all disputes with Cambodia by peaceful means;

(*e*) To refrain from using their territories or the territories of other States to impair the sovereignty, independence, territorial integrity and inviolability, neutrality and national unity of Cambodia;

(*f*) To refrain from using the territory of Cambodia to impair the sovereignty, independence and territorial integrity and inviolability of other States;

(*g*) To refrain from the introduction or stationing of foreign forces, including military personnel, in any form whatsoever, in Cambodia and from establishing or maintaining military bases, strong points or facilities in Cambodia, except pursuant to United Nations authorization for the implementation of the comprehensive political settlement.

Article 3

1. All persons in Cambodia shall enjoy the rights and freedoms embodied in the Universal Declaration of Human Rights and other relevant international human rights instruments.

2. To this end,

(*a*) Cambodia undertakes:

– to ensure respect for and observance of human rights and fundamental freedoms in Cambodia ;

– to support the right of all Cambodian citizens to undertake activities that would promote and protect human rights and fundamental freedoms;

– to take effective measures to ensure that the policies and practices of the past shall never be allowed to return;

– to adhere to relevant international human rights instruments;

(*b*) The other parties to this Agreement undertake to promote and encourage respect for and observance of human rights and fundamental freedoms in Cambodia as embodied in the relevant international instruments in order, in particular, to prevent the recurrence of human rights abuses.

3. The United Nations Commission on Human Rights should continue to monitor closely the human rights situation in Cambodia, including, if necessary, by the appointment of a Special Rapporteur who would report his findings annually to the Commission and to the General Assembly.

Article 4

The parties to this Agreement call upon all other States to recognize and respect in every way the sovereignty, independence, territorial integrity and inviolability, neutrality and national unity of Cambodia and to refrain from any action inconsistent with these principles or with other provisions of this Agreement.

Article 5

1. In the event of a violation or threat of violation of the sovereignty, independence, territorial integrity and inviolability, neutrality or national unity of Cambodia, or of any of the other commitments herein, the parties to this Agreement undertake to consult immediately with a view to adopting all appropriate steps to ensure respect for these commitments and resolving any such violations through peaceful means.

2. Such steps may include, *inter alia*, reference of the matter to the Security Council of the United Nations or recourse to the means for the peaceful settlement of disputes referred to in Article 33 of the Charter of the United Nations.

3. The parties to this Agreement may also call upon the assistance of the co-chairmen of the Paris Conference on

Cambodia.

4. In the event of serious violations of human rights in Cambodia, they will call upon the competent organs of the United Nations to take such other steps as are appropriate for the prevention and suppression of such violations in accordance with the relevant international instruments.

Article 6

This Agreement shall enter into force upon signature.

Article 7

This Agreement shall remain open for accession by all States. The instruments of accession shall be deposited with the Governments of the French Republic and the Republic of Indonesia. For each State acceding to this Agreement, it shall enter into force on the date of deposit of its instrument of accession.

Article 8

The original of this Agreement, of which the Chinese, English, French, Khmer and Russian texts are equally authentic, shall be deposited with the Governments of the French Republic and the Republic of Indonesia, which shall transmit certified true copies to the Governments of the other States participating in the Paris Conference on Cambodia and to the Secretary-General of the United Nations.

. . .

Source: UN document A/46/608, S/23177, 30 Oct. 1991, pp. 48–54.

DECLARATION ON THE REHABILITATION AND RECONSTRUCTION OF CAMBODIA

[23 October 1991]

1. The primary objective of the reconstruction of Cambodia should be the advancement of the Cambodian nation and people, without discrimination or prejudice, and with full respect for human rights and fundamental freedom for all. The achievement of this objective requires the full implementation of the comprehensive political settlement.

2. The main responsibility for deciding Cambodia's reconstruction needs and plans should rest with the Cambodian people and the government formed after free and fair elections. No attempt should be made to impose a development strategy on Cambodia from any outside source or deter potential donors from contributing to the reconstruction of Cambodia.

3. International, regional and bilateral assistance to Cambodia should be coordinated as much as possible, complement and supplement local resources and be made available impartially with full regard for Cambodia's sovereignty, priorities, institutional means and absorptive capacity.

4. In the context of the reconstruction effort, economic aid should benefit all areas of Cambodia, especially the more disadvantaged, and reach all levels of society.

5. The implementation of an international aid effort would have to be phased in over a period that realistically acknowledges both political and technical imperatives. It would also necessitate a significant degree of co-operation between the future Cambodian Government and bilateral, regional and international contributors.

6. An important role will be played in rehabilitation and reconstruction by the United Nations system. The launching of an international reconstruction plan and an appeal for contributions should take place at an appropriate time, so as to ensure its success.

7. No effective programme of national reconstruction can be initiated without detailed assessments of Cambodia's human, natural and other economic assets. It will be necessary for a census

to be conducted, developmental priorities identified, and the availability of resources, internal and external, determined.

To this end there will be scope for sending to Cambodia fact-finding missions from the United Nations system, international financial institutions and other agencies, with the consent of the future Cambodian Government.

8. With the achievement of the comprehensive political settlement, it is now possible and desirable to initiate a process of rehabilitation, addressing immediate needs, and to lay the groundwork for the preparation of medium- and long-term reconstruction plans.

9. For this period of rehabilitation, the United Nations Secretary-General is requested to help co-ordinate the programme guided by a person appointed for this purpose.

10. In this rehabilitation phase, particular attention will need to be given to food security, health, housing, training, education, the transport network and the restoration of Cambodia's existing basic infrastructure and public utilities.

11. The implementation of a longer-term international development plan for reconstruction should await the formation of a government following the elections and the determination and adoption of its own policies and priorities.

12. This reconstruction phase should promote Cambodian entrepreneurship and make use of the private sector, among other sectors, to help advance self-sustaining economic growth. It would also benefit from regional approaches, involving, *inter alia*, institutions such as the Economic and Social Commission for Asia and the Pacific (ESCAP) and the Mekong Committee, and Governments within the region; and from participation by non-governmental organizations.

13. In order to harmonize and monitor the contributions that will be made by the international community to the re-construction of Cambodia after the formation of a government following the elections, a consultative body, to be called the International Committee on the Reconstruction of Cambodia (ICORC), should be set up at an appropriate time and be open to potential donors and other relevant parties. The United Nations Secretary-General is requested to make special arrangements for the United Nations system to support ICORC in its work, notably in ensuring a smooth transition from the rehabilitation to reconstruction phases.

_____

Source: UN document A/46/608, S/23177, 30 Oct. 1991, pp. 55–57.

CONSTITUTION OF THE KINGDOM OF CAMBODIA

24 September 1993

Preamble

WE, THE PEOPLE OF CAMBODIA

Accustomed to having been an outstanding civilization, a prosperous, large, flourishing and glorious nation, with high prestige radiating like a diamond,

Having declined grievously during the past two decades, having gone through suffering and destruction, and having been weakened terribly,

Having awakened and resolutely rallied and determined to unite for the consolidation of national unity, the preservation and defense of Cambodia's territory and precious sovereignty and the fine Angkor civilization, and the restoration of Cambodia into an 'Island of Peace' based on a multi-party liberal democratic regime guaranteeing human rights, abiding by law, and having high responsibility for the nation's future destiny of moving toward perpetual progress, development, prosperity, and glory,

WITH THIS RESOLUTE WILL

WE inscribe the following as the Constitution of the Kingdom of Cambodia:

Chapter I. Sovereignty

Article 1

Cambodia is a Kingdom with a King who shall rule according to the Constitution and to the principles of liberal democracy and pluralism.

The Kingdom of Cambodia shall be an independent, sovereign, peaceful, permanently neutral and non-aligned country.

Article 2

The territorial integrity of the Kingdom of Cambodia shall absolutely not be violated within its borders as defined in the 1/100 000 scale map made between the years 1933–1953 and internationally recognized between the years 1963–1969.

Article 3

The Kingdom of Cambodia is an indivisible State.

Article 4

The motto of the Kingdom of Cambodia is: 'Nation, Religion, King'.

Article 5

The official language and script are Khmer.

Article 6

Phnom Penh is the capital of the Kingdom of Cambodia.

The national flag, anthem and coat-of-arms shall be defined in Annexes I, II and III [not reproduced here].

Chapter II. The King

Article 7

The King of Cambodia shall reign but shall not govern.

The King shall be the Head of State for life.

The King shall be inviolable.

Article 8

The King of Cambodia shall be a symbol of unity and eternity of the nation.

The King shall be the guarantor of the national independence, sovereignty, and territorial integrity of the Kingdom of Cambodia, the protector of rights and freedom for all citizens and the guarantor of international treaties.

Article 9

The King shall assume the august role of arbitrator to ensure the faithful execution of public powers.

Article 10

The Cambodian monarchy shall be an appointed regime.

The King shall not have the power to appoint a heir to the throne.

Article 11

If the King cannot perform His normal duties as Head of State due to His serious illness as certified by doctors chosen by the President of the Assembly and the Prime Minister, the President of the Assembly shall perform the duties of Head of State as 'Regent'.

Article 12

In case of the death of the King, the President of the Assembly shall take over the responsibility as Acting Head of State in the capacity of Regent of the Kingdom of Cambodia.

Article 13

Within a period of not more than seven days, the new King of the Kingdom of Cambodia shall be chosen by the Royal Council of the Throne.

The Royal Council of the Throne shall consist of:

– The President of the National Assembly
– The Prime Minister
– Samdech the Chiefs of the Orders of Mohanikay and Thammayut
– The First and Second Vice-Presidents of the Assembly.

The organization and functioning of the Council of the Throne shall be determined by law.

Article 14

The King of Cambodia shall be a member of the Royal family, of at least 30 years old, descending from the blood line of King Ang Duong, King Norodom or King Sisowath.

Upon enthronement, the King shall take the oath of allegiance as stipulated in Annex IV [not reproduced here].

Article 15

The wife of the reigning King shall have the royal title of Queen of Cambodia.

Article 16

The Queen of the Kingdom of Cambodia shall not have the right to engage in politics, to assume the role of Head of State or Head of Government, or to assume other administrative or political roles.

The Queen of the Kingdom of Cambodia shall exercise activities that serve the social, humanitarian, religious interests, and shall assist the King with protocol and diplomatic functions.

Article 17

The provision as stated in the first clause of Article 7, 'the King of Cambodia shall reign but shall not govern', absolutely shall not be amended.

Article 18

The King shall communicate with the Assembly by royal messages. These royal messages shall not be subjected to discussion by the National Assembly.

Article 19

The King shall appoint the Prime Minister and the Council of Ministers according to the procedure stipulated in article 100.

Article 20

The King shall grant an audience twice a month to the Prime Minister and the Council of Ministers to hear their reports on the State of the Nation.

Article 21

Upon proposals by the Council of Ministers, the King shall sign decrees (Kret) appointing, transferring or ending the mission of high civil and military officials, ambassadors and Envoys Extraordinary and Plenipotentiary.

Upon proposals by the Supreme Council of the Magistracy, the King shall sign decrees (kret) appointing, transferring or removing judges.

Article 22

When the nation faces danger, the King shall make a proclamation to the people putting the country in a state of emergency after agreement with the Prime Minister and the President of the Assembly.

Article 23

The King is the Supreme Commander of the Royal Khmer Armed Forces. The Commander-in-Chief of the Royal Khmer Armed Forces shall be appointed to command the Royal Khmer Armed Forces.

Article 24

The King shall serve as Chairman of the Supreme Council of National Defense to be established by law.

The King shall declare war after approval of the National Assembly.

Article 25

The King shall receive letters of credentials from ambassadors or envoys extraordinary and plenipotentiary of foreign countries accredited to the Kingdom of Cambodia.

Article 26

The King shall sign and ratify international treaties and conventions after a vote of approval by the National Assembly.

Article 27

The King shall have the right to grant partial or complete amnesty.

Article 28

The King shall sign the law promulgating the Constitution, laws (Kram) adopted by the National Assembly, and sign decrees (Kret) presented by the Council of Ministers.

Article 29

The King shall establish and confer national medals proposed by the Council of Ministers.

The King shall confer civil and military ranks as determined by law.

Article 30

In the absence of the King, the President of the Assembly shall assume the duties of Acting Head of State.

Chapter III. The Rights and Obligations of Khmer Citizens

Article 31

The Kingdom of Cambodia shall recognize and respect human rights as stipulated in the United Nations Charter, the Universal Declaration of Human Rights, the covenants and conventions related to human rights, women's and children's rights.

Every Khmer citizen shall be equal before the law, enjoying the same rights, freedom and fulfilling the same obligations regardless of race, colour, sex, language, religious belief, political tendency, birth origin, social status, wealth or other status.

The exercise of personal rights and freedom by any individual shall not adversely affect the rights and freedom of others. The exercise of such rights and freedom shall be in accordance with the law.

Article 32

Every Khmer citizen shall have the right to life, personal freedom and security.

There shall be no capital punishment.

Article 33

Khmer citizens shall not be deprived of their nationality, exiled or arrested and deported to any foreign country unless there is a mutual agreement on extradition.

Khmer citizens residing abroad enjoy the protection of the State.

The Khmer nationality shall be determined by a law.

Article 34

Khmer citizens of either sex shall enjoy the right to vote and to stand as candidates for the election.

Citizens of either sex of at least eighteen years old, have the right to vote.

Citizens of either sex of at least 25 years old, have the right to stand as candidates for the election.

Provisions restricting the right to vote and to stand for the election shall be defined in the Electoral Law.

Article 35

Khmer citizens of either sex shall have the right to participate actively in the political, economic, social and cultural life of the nation.

Any suggestions from the people shall be given full consideration by the organs of the State.

Article 36

Khmer citizens of either sex shall have the right to choose any employment according to their ability and to the needs of the society.

Khmer citizens of either sex shall receive equal pay for equal work.

The work by housewives in the home shall have the same value as what they can receive when working outside the home.

Every Khmer citizen shall have the right to obtain social security and other social benefits as determined by law.

Khmer citizens of either sex shall have the right to form and to be members of trade unions.

The organization and conduct of trade unions shall be determined by law.

Article 37

The right to strike and to non-violent demonstration shall be implemented in the framework of a law.

Article 38

The law guarantees there shall be no physical abuse against any individual.

The law shall protect the life, honor and dignity of the citizens.

The prosecution, arrest, or detention of any person shall not be done except in accordance with the law.

Coercion, physical ill-treatment or any other mistreatment that imposes additional punishment on a detainee or prisoner shall be prohibited. Persons who commit, participate or conspire in such acts shall be punished according to the law.

Confessions obtained by physical or mental force shall not be admissible as evidence of guilt.

Any case of doubt shall be resolved in favor of the accused.

The accused shall be considered innocent until the court has judged finally on the case.

Every citizen shall enjoy the right to defense through judicial recourse.

Article 39

Khmer citizens shall have the right to denounce, make complaints or file claims against any breach of the law by State and social organs or by members of such organs committed during the course of their duties. The settlement of complaints and claims shall reside under the competence of the courts.

Article 40

Citizens' freedom to travel, far and near, and legal settlement shall be respected.

Khmer citizens shall have the right to travel and settle abroad and return to the country.

The right to privacy of residence and to the secrecy of correspondence by mail, telegram, fax, telex and telephone shall be guaranteed.

Any search of the house, material and body shall be in accordance with the law.

Article 41

Khmer citizens shall have freedom of expression, press, publication and assembly. No one shall exercise this right to infringe upon the rights of others, to affect the good traditions of the society, to violate public law and order and national security.

The regime of the media shall be determined by law.

Article 42

Khmer citizens shall have the right to establish associations and political parties. These rights shall be determined by law.

Khmer citizens may take part in mass organizations for mutual benefit to protect national achievements and social order.

Article 43

Khmer citizens of either sex shall have the right to freedom of belief.

Freedom of religious belief and worship shall be guaranteed by the State on the condition that such freedom does not affect other religious beliefs or violate public order and security.

Buddhism shall be the State religion.

Article 44

All persons, individually or collectively, shall have the right to ownership. Only Khmer legal entities and citizens of Khmer nationality shall have the right to own land.

Legal private ownership shall be protected by law.

The right to confiscate possessions from any person shall be exercised only in the public interest as provided for under law and shall require fair and just compensation in advance.

Article 45

All forms of discrimination against women shall be abolished.

The exploitation of women in employment shall be prohibited.

Men and women are equal in all fields especially in marriages and matters of the family.

Marriage shall be conducted according to conditions determined by law based on the principle of mutual consent between one husband and one wife.

Article 46

The commerce of human beings, exploitation by prostitution and obscenity which affect the reputation of women shall be prohibited.

A woman shall not lose her job because of pregnancy. Women shall have the right to take maternity leave with full pay and with no loss of seniority or other social benefits.

The State and society shall provide opportunities to women, especially to those living in rural areas without adequate social support, so they can get employment, medical care, and send their children to school, and to have decent living conditions.

Article 47

Parents shall have the duty to take care of and educate their children to become good citizens.

Children shall have the duty to take good care of their elderly mother and father according to Khmer traditions.

Article 48

The State shall protect the rights of the children as stipulated in the Convention on Children, in particular, the right to life, education, protection during wartime, and from economic or sexual exploitation.

The State shall protect children from acts that are injurious to their educational opportunities, health and welfare.

Article 49

Every Khmer citizen shall respect the Constitution and laws.

All Khmer citizens shall have the duty to take part in the national reconstruction and to defend the homeland. The duty to defend the country shall be determined by law.

Article 50

Khmer citizens of either sex shall respect the principles of national sovereignty, liberal multi-party democracy.

Khmer citizens of either sex shall respect public and legally acquired private properties.

Chapter IV. On Policy

Article 51

The Kingdom of Cambodia adopts a policy of Liberal Democracy and Pluralism.

The Cambodian people are the masters of their own country.

All powers belong to the people. The people exercise these powers through the National Assembly, the Royal Government and the Judiciary.

The Legislative, Executive, and the Judicial powers shall be separate.

Article 52

The Royal Government of Cambodia shall protect the independence, sovereignty, territorial integrity of the Kingdom of Cambodia, adopt the policy of national reconciliation to insure national unity, and preserve the good national traditions of the country. The Royal Government of Cambodia shall preserve and protect the law and ensure public order and security. The State shall give priority to endeavours which improve the welfare and standard of living of citizens.

Article 53

The Kingdom of Cambodia adopts a policy of permanent neutrality and non-alignment. The Kingdom of Cambodia follows a policy of peaceful co-existence with its neighbors and with all other countries throughout the world.

The Kingdom of Cambodia shall not invade any country, nor interfere in any other country's internal affairs, directly or indirectly, and shall solve any problems peacefully with due respect for mutual interests.

The Kingdom of Cambodia shall not join in any military alliance or military pact which is incompatible with its policy of neutrality.

The Kingdom of Cambodia shall not permit any foreign military base on its territory and shall not have its own military base abroad, except within the framework of a United Nations request.

The Kingdom of Cambodia reserves the right to receive foreign assistance in military equipment, armaments, ammunitions, in training of its armed forces, and other assistance for self-defense and to maintain public order and security within its territory.

Article 54

The manufacturing, use, storage of nuclear, chemical or biological weapons shall be absolutely prohibited.

Article 55

Any treaty and agreement incompatible with the independence, sovereignty, territorial integrity, neutrality and national unity of the Kingdom of Cambodia shall be annulled.

Chapter V. Economy

Article 56

The Kingdom of Cambodia shall adopt market economy system. The preparation and process of this economic system shall be determined by law.

Article 57

Tax collection shall be in accordance with the law. The national budget shall be determined by law.

The management of the monetary and financial system shall be defined by law.

Article 58

State property notably comprises land, mineral resources, mountains, sea, underwater, continental shelf, coastline, airspace, islands, rivers, canals, streams, lakes, forests, natural resources, economic and cultural centers, bases for national defense and other facilities determined as State property.

The control, use and management of State properties shall be determined by law.

Article 59

The State shall protect the environment and balance of abundant natural resources and establish a precise plan of management of land, water, air, wind, geology, ecologic system, mines, energy, petrol and gas, rocks and sand, gems, forests and forestrial [sic] products, wildlife, fish and aquatic resources.

Article 60

Khmer citizens shall have the right to sell their own products. The obligation to sell products to the State, or the temporary use of private or State properties shall be prohibited unless authorized by law under special circumstances.

Article 61

The State shall promote economic development in all sectors and remote areas, especially in agriculture, handicrafts, industry, with attention to policies of water, electricity, roads and means of transport, modern technology and a system of credit.

Article 62

The State shall pay attention and help solve production matters, protect the price of products for farmers and crafters [sic], and find marketplace for them to sell their products.

Article 63

The State shall respect market management in order to guarantee a better standard of living for the people.

Article 64

The State shall ban and severely punishes those who import, manufacture, sell illicit drugs, counterfeit and expired goods which affect the health and life of the consumer.

Chapter VI. Education, Culture, Social Affairs

Article 65

The State shall protect and upgrade citizens' rights to quality education at all levels and shall take necessary steps for quality education to reach all citizens.

The State shall respect physical education and sports for the welfare of all Khmer citizens.

Article 66

The State shall establish a comprehensive and standardized educational system throughout the country that shall guarantee the principles of educational freedom and equality to ensure that all citizens have equal opportunity to earn a living.

Article 67

The State shall adopt an educational program according to the principle of modern pedagogy including technology and foreign languages.

The State shall control public and private schools and classrooms at all levels.

Article 68

The State shall provide free primary and secondary education to all citizens in public schools.

Citizens shall receive education for at least 9 years.

The State shall disseminate and develop the Pali schools and the Buddhist Institute.

Article 69

The State shall preserve and promote national culture.

The State shall protect and promote the Khmer language as required.

The State shall preserve ancient monuments, artifacts and restore historic sites.

Article 70

Any offense affecting cultural and artistic heritage shall carry a severe punishment.

Article 71

The perimeter of the national heritage sites as well as heritage that has been classified as world heritage, shall be considered neutral zones where there shall be no military activity.

Article 72

The health of the people shall be guaranteed. The State shall give full consideration to disease prevention and medical treatment. Poor citizens shall receive free medical consultation in public hospitals, infirmaries and maternities.

The State shall establish infirmaries and maternities in rural areas.

Article 73

The State shall give full consideration to children and mothers. The State shall establish nurseries, and help support women and children who have inadequate support.

Article 74

The State shall assist the disabled and the families of combatants who sacrificed their lives for the nation.

Article 75

The State shall establish a social security system for workers and employees.

Chapter VII. The Assembly

Article 76

The Assembly consists of at least 120 members.

The deputies shall be elected by a free, universal, equal, direct and secret ballot.

The deputies may be re-elected.

Khmer citizens able to stand for election shall be the Khmer citizens of either sex who have the right to vote, at least 25 years of age, and who have Khmer nationality at birth.

Preparation for the election, procedure and electoral process shall be determined by an Electoral Law.

Article 77

The deputies in the Assembly shall represent the entire Khmer people, not only Khmers from their constituencies.

Any imperative mandate shall be nullified.

Article 78

The legislative term of the Assembly shall be 5 years and terminates on the day when the new Assembly convenes.

The Assembly shall not be dissolved before the end of its term except when the Royal Government is twice deposed within a period of twelve months. In this case, following a proposal from the Prime Minister and the approval of the Assembly President, the King shall dissolve the Assembly.

The election of a new Assembly shall be held no later than 60 days from the date of dissolution. During this period, the Royal Government shall only be empowered to conduct routine business.

In times of war or other special circumstances where an election cannot be held, the Assembly may extend its term for one year at a time, upon the request of the King.

Such an extension shall require at least a two-thirds vote of the entire Assembly.

Article 79

The Assembly mandate shall be incompatible with the holding of any active public function and of any membership in other institutions provided for in the Constitution, except when the Assembly member(s) is (are) required to serve in the Royal Government.

In these circumstances, the said Assembly member(s) shall retain the usual Assembly membership but shall not hold any position in the Permanent Standing Committee and in other Assembly commissions.

Article 80

The deputies shall enjoy parliamentary immunity.

No Assembly member shall be prosecuted, detained or arrested because of opinions expressed during the exercise of his (her) duties.

The accusation, arrest, or detention of a member of Assembly shall be made only with the permission of the Assembly or by the Standing Committee of the Assembly between sessions, except in case of *flagrante delicto*. In that case, the competent authority shall immediately report to the Assembly or to the Standing Committee for decision.

The decision made by the Standing Committee of the Assembly shall be submitted to the Assembly at its next session for approval by a 2/3 majority vote of the Assembly members.

In any case, detention or prosecution of a deputy shall be suspended by a 3/4 majority vote of the Assembly members.

Article 81

The Assembly shall have an autonomous budget to conduct its function.

The deputies shall receive a remuneration.

Article 82

The Assembly shall hold its first session no later than sixty days after the election upon notice by the King.

Before taking office, the Assembly shall decide on the validity of each member's mandate and vote separately to choose a President, Vice-Presidents and members of each Commission by a 2/3 majority vote.

All Assembly members must take the oath before taking office according to the text contained in Annex [V] [not reproduced here].

Article 83

The Assembly shall hold its ordinary sessions twice a year.

Each session shall last at least 3 months. If there is a proposal from the King or the Prime Minister, or at least 1/3 of the Assembly members, the Assembly Standing Committee shall call an extraordinary session of the Assembly.

In this case, the agenda with the conditions of the extraordinary session, shall be disseminated to the population as well as the date of the meeting.

Article 84

Between the Assembly sessions, the Assembly Standing Committee shall manage the work of the Assembly.

The Permanent Standing Committee of the Assembly consists of the President of the Assembly, the Vice-Presidents, and the Presidents of Assembly commissions.

Article 85

The Assembly sessions shall be held in the royal capital of Cambodia in the Assembly Hall, unless stipulated otherwise in the summons, due to special circumstances.

Except where so stipulated and unless held at the place and date as stipulated, any meeting of the Assembly shall be considered as illegal and void.

Article 86

If the country is in a state of emergency, the Assembly shall meet every day continuously. The Assembly has the right to terminate this state of emergency whenever the situation permits.

If the Assembly is not able to meet because of circumstances such as the occupation by foreign forces the declaration of the state of emergency must be automatically extended.

During the state of emergency, the Assembly shall not be dissolved.

Article 87

The President of the Assembly shall chair the Assembly sessions, receive draft bills and resolutions adopted by the Assembly, ensure the implementation of the Internal Rules of Procedure and manage the Assembly relations with foreign countries.

If the President is unable to perform his/her duties due to illness or to fulfill the functions of Head of State *ad interim* or as a Regent, or is on a mission abroad, a Vice-President shall replace him.

In case of resignation or death of the President or the Vice-President(s), the Assembly shall elect a new President or Vice-President(s).

Article 88

The Assembly sessions shall be held in public.

The Assembly shall meet in closed session at the request of the President or of at least 1/10 of its members, of the King or of the Prime Minister.

The Assembly meeting shall be considered as valid provided there is a quorum of 7/10 of all members.

Article 89

Upon the request by at least 1/10 of its members, the Assembly shall invite a high ranking official to clarify important special issues.

Article 90

The Assembly shall be the only organ to hold legislative power. This power shall not be transferable to any other organ or any individual.

The Assembly shall approve the national budget, the State Planning, the Loans, the Lending and the creation, changes or annulment of tax.

The Assembly shall approve Administrative Accounts.

The Assembly shall approve the law on amnesty.

The Assembly shall approve or annul

treaties or international conventions.

The Assembly shall approve law on the declaration of war.

The adoption of the above-mentioned clauses shall be decided by a simple majority of the entire Assembly membership.

The Assembly shall pass a vote of confidence in the Royal Government by a 2/3 majority of all members.

Article 91

The deputies and the Prime Minister shall have the right to initiate legislation.

The deputies shall have the right to propose any amendments to the laws, but, the proposals shall be unacceptable if they aim at reducing public income or increasing the burden on the people.

Article 92

Laws adopted by the Assembly which run counter to the principles of preserving national independence, sovereignty, territorial integrity, and affect the political unity or the administration of the nation shall be annulled. The Constitutional Council is the only organ which shall decide upon this annulment.

Article 93

Any law approved by the Assembly and signed by the King for its promulgation, shall go into effect in Phnom Penh 10 days after signing and throughout the country 20 days after its signing.

Laws that are stipulated as urgent shall take effect immediately throughout the country after promulgation.

All laws promulgated by the King shall be published in the *Journal Officiel* and published throughout the country in accordance with the above schedule.

Article 94

The Assembly shall establish various necessary commissions. The organization and functioning of the Assembly shall be determined by the Assembly Internal Rules of Procedure.

Article 95

In case of death, resignation, or dismissal of an Assembly deputy at least 6 months before the end of the mandate, a replacement shall be appointed in accordance with the Internal Rules of Procedure of the National Assembly and the Electoral Law.

Article 96

The deputies have the right to put a motion against the Royal Government. The motion shall be submitted in writing through the President of the Assembly.

The replies shall be given by one or several ministers depending on the matters related to the accountability of one or several ministers. If the case concerns the overall policy of the Royal Government, the Prime Minister shall reply in person.

The explanations by the ministers or by the Prime Minister shall be given verbally or in writing.

The explanations shall be provided within 7 days after the day when the question is received.

In case of verbal reply, the President of the Assembly shall decide whether to hold an open debate or not. If there is no debate, the answer of the minister or the Prime Minister shall be considered final. If there is a debate, the questioner, other speakers, the ministers, or the Prime Minister may exchange views within the timeframe not exceeding one session.

The Assembly shall establish one day each week for questions and answers. There shall be no vote during any session reserved for this purpose.

Article 97

The Assembly commissions may invite any minister to clarify certain issues under his/her field of responsibility.

Article 98

The Assembly shall dismiss a member or members of the Royal Government or the whole Cabinet by the adoption of a motion of censure by 2/3 majority of the entire Assembly.

The motion of censure shall be proposed to the Assembly by at least 30 Assembly members in order for the entire Assembly to decide.

Chapter VIII. The Royal Government

Article 99

The Council of Ministers is the Royal Government of Cambodia.

The Council of Ministers shall be led by one Prime Minister assisted by Deputy Prime Ministers, and by State Ministers, Ministers, and State Secretaries as members.

Article 100

At the recommendation of the President and with the agreement of both Vice-Presidents of the Assembly, the King shall designate a dignitary from among the representatives of the winning party to form the Royal Government. This designated dignitary shall lead his colleagues who shall be members of the Assembly or members of the political parties represented in the Assembly, to ask for a vote of confidence from the Assembly.

After the Assembly has given its vote of confidence, the King shall issue a Royal decree (Kret) appointing the entire Council of Ministers.

Before taking office, the Council of Ministers shall take an oath as stipulated in Annex 6 [*sic*. Not reproduced here].

Article 101

The functions of members of the Royal Government shall be incompatible with professional activities in trade or industry and with the holding of any position in the public service.

Article 102

Members of the Royal Government shall be collectively responsible to the Assembly for the overall policy of the Royal Government.

Each member of the Royal Govern-

ment shall be individually responsible to the Prime Minister and the Assembly for his/her own conduct.

Article 103

Members of the Royal Government shall not use the orders, written or verbal, of anyone as grounds to exonerate themselves from their responsibility.

Article 104

The Council of Ministers shall meet every week in plenary session or in a working session.

The Prime Minister shall chair the plenary sessions.

The Prime Minister may assign a Deputy Prime Minister to preside over the working sessions.

Minutes of the Council of Ministers' meetings shall be forwarded to the King for His information.

Article 105

The Prime Minister shall have the right to delegate his power to a Deputy Prime Minister or to any member of the Royal Government.

Article 106

If the post of Prime Minister is permanently vacant, a new Council of Ministers shall be appointed under the procedure stipulated in this Constitution. If the vacancy is temporary, an acting Prime Minister shall be provisionally appointed.

Article 107

Each member of the Royal Government shall be punished for any crimes or misdemeanors that he/she has committed in the course of his/her duty.

In such cases and when he/she has committed serious offenses in the course of his/her duty, the Assembly shall decide to file charges against him/her with the competent court.

The Assembly shall decide on such matters through a secret vote by a simple majority thereof.

Article 108

The organization and functioning of the Council of Ministers shall be determined by law.

Chapter IX. The Judiciary

Article 109

The Judicial power shall be an independent power.

The Judiciary shall guarantee and uphold impartiality and protect the rights and freedoms of the citizens.

The Judiciary shall cover all lawsuits including administrative ones.

The authority of the Judiciary shall be granted to the Supreme Court and to the lower courts of all sectors and levels.

Article 110

Trials shall be conducted in the name of the Khmer citizens in accordance with the legal procedures and laws in force.

Only judges shall have the right to adjudicate. A judge shall fulfill this duty with strict respect for the laws, wholeheartedly, and conscientiously.

Article 111

Judicial power shall not be granted to the legislative or executive branches.

Article 112

Only the Department of Public Prosecution shall have the right to file criminal suits.

Article 113

The King shall be the guarantor of the independence of the Judiciary. The Supreme Council of the Magistracy shall assist the King in this matter.

Article 114

Judges shall not be dismissed. The Supreme Council of the Magistracy shall take disciplinary actions against any delinquent judges.

Article 115

The Supreme Council of the Magistracy shall be establish [*sic*] by an organic law which shall determine its composition and functions.

The Supreme Council of the Magistracy shall be chaired by the King. The King may appoint a representative to chair the Supreme Council of the Magistracy.

The Supreme Council of the Magistracy shall make proposals to the King on the appointment of judges and prosecutors to all courts.

The Supreme Council of the Magistracy shall meet under the chairmanship of the President of the Supreme Court or the General Prosecutor of the Supreme Court to decide on disciplinary actions against judges or prosecutors.

Article 116

The statutes of judges and prosecutors and the functioning of the Judiciary shall be defined in separate laws.

Chapter X. The Constitutional Council

Article 117

The Constitutional Council shall have the duty to safeguard respect for the Constitution, to interpret the Constitution, and the laws passed by the Assembly.

The Constitutional Council shall have the right to examine and decide on contested cases involving the election of Assembly members.

Article 118

The Constitutional Council shall consist of nine members with a nine-year mandate. 1/3 of the members of the Council shall be replaced every three years. 3 members shall be appointed by the King, 3 members by the Assembly and 3 others by the Supreme Council of the Magistracy.

The Chairman shall be elected by the members of the Constitutional Council. He/she shall have a deciding vote in cases of equal vote.

Article 119

Members of the Constitutional Council shall be selected among the dignitaries with a higher-education degree in law, administration, diplomacy or economics and who have considerable work experience.

Article 120

The function of a Constitutional Council member shall be incompatible with that of a member of the Royal Government, member of the Assembly, President or Vice-President of a political party, President or Vice-President of a trade union or in-post judges.

Article 121

The King, the Prime Minister, the President of the Assembly, or 1/10 of the Assembly members shall forward draft bills to the Constitutional Council for examination before their promulgation.

The Assembly Rules of Procedure and various organizational laws shall be forwarded to the Constitutional Council before their promulgation.

The Constitutional Council shall decide within no more than thirty days whether the laws and the Internal Rules of Procedure are constitutional.

Article 122

After a law is promulgated, the King, the Prime Minister, the President of the Assembly, 1/10 of the Assembly members or the courts, may ask the Constitutional Council to examine the constitutionality of that law.

Citizens shall have the right to appeal against the constitutionality of laws through their representatives or the President of the Assembly as stipulated in the above paragraph.

Article 123

Provisions in any article ruled by the Constitutional Council as unconstitutional shall not be promulgated or implemented.

The decision of the Council is final.

Article 124

The King shall consult with the Constitutional Council on all proposals to amend the Constitution.

Article 125

An organic law shall specify the organization and operation of the Constitutional Council.

Chapter XI. The Administration

Article 126

The territory of the Kingdom of Cambodia shall be divided into provinces and municipalities.

Provinces shall be divided into districts (srok) and districts into communes (khum).

Municipalities shall be divided into Khan and Khan into Sangkat.

Article 127

Provinces, municipalities, districts, khan, khum and sangkat shall be governed in accordance with organic law.

Chapter XII. The National Congress

Article 128

The National Congress shall enable the people to be directly informed on various matters of national interests and to raise issues and requests for the State authority to solve.

Khmer citizens of both sexes shall have the right to participate in the National Congress.

Article 129

The National Congress shall meet once a year in early December at the convocation of the Prime Minister.

It shall proceed under the chairmanship of the King.

Article 130

The National Congress shall adopt recommendations for consideration by State authorities and the Assembly.

The organization and operation of the

National Congress shall be defined by a law.

Chapter XIII. Effects, Revision and Amendments of the Constitution

Article 131

This Constitution shall be the supreme law of the Kingdom of Cambodia.

Laws and decisions by the State institutions shall have to be in strict conformity with the Constitution.

Article 132

The initiative to review or to amend the Constitution shall be the prerogative of the King, the Prime Minister, the President of the Assembly at the suggestion of 1/4 of all the Assembly members.

Revision or amendments shall be enacted by a Constitutional law passed by the Assembly with a 2/3 majority vote.

Article 133

Revision or amendments shall be prohibited when the country is in the state of emergency, as outlined in article 86.

Article 134

Any revision or amendment affecting the system of liberal and pluralistic democracy and the regime of Constitutional Monarchy shall be prohibited.

Chapter XIV. Transitional Provisions

Article 135

This Constitution, after its adoption, shall be declared in force immediately by the Head of State of Cambodia.

Article 136

After the entry into force of this Constitution, the Constituent Assembly shall become the National Assembly.

The Internal Rules of Procedure of the Assembly shall come into force after adoption by the Assembly.

In the case where the Assembly is not yet functional, the President, the First and Second Vice-Presidents of the Constituent Assembly shall participate in the discharge of duties in the Throne Council if so required by the situation in the country.

Article 137

After this Constitution takes effect, the King shall be selected in accordance with conditions stipulated in articles 13 and 14.

Article 138

After this Constitution takes effect, and during the first legislature, the King of the Kingdom of Cambodia shall appoint a First Prime Minister and a Second Prime Minister to form the Royal Government after securing the consent of the President and the two Vice-Presidents of the Assembly.

The Co-Presidents existing before the adoption of this Constitution shall participate as members of the Committee and in the Throne Council as stipulated in articles 11 and 13 above.

Article 139

Laws and standard documents in Cambodia that safeguard State properties, rights, freedom and legal private properties and in conformity with the national interests, shall continue to be effective until altered or abrogated by new texts, except those provisions that are contrary to the spirit of this Constitution.

This Constitution was adopted by the Constitutional [*sic*] Assembly in Phnom Penh on 21 September 1993 at its 2nd Plenary session.

Phnom Penh, 21 September, 1993.
The President,
Signed: SON SANN

Source: Constitution of the Kingdom of Cambodia, 1993. 1, 22 pp. + Annexes and list of members of the Drafting Committee. Supplied by the Embassy of the Kingdom of Cambodia in Paris.

Chronology, 1970–94

1970

19 Mar.   Prince Sihanouk overthrown by Lon Nol; civil war between the Khmer Rouge and Phnom Penh Government escalates

1975

17 Apr.   Khmer Rouge takes power in Phnom Penh; Democratic Kampuchea established

1978–79

25 Dec.–7 Jan.   Vietnamese invasion of Cambodia; pro-Vietnamese government installed in Phnom Penh

1981

13 June   International Conference on Kampuchea, New York, fails to reach a settlement

1988

25–27 July   Informal Meeting on Cambodia

1989

6 Jan.   Announcement of complete Vietnamese withdrawal before end of September 1989

19–21 Feb.   Second Jakarta Informal Meeting

30 July–30 Aug.   International Conference on Cambodia, Paris

27 Sep.   Viet Nam claims withdrawal complete

1990

6–28 Feb.   Third Jakarta Informal Meeting

1991

30 Sep.   Secretary-General recommends UN deploy advance mission in Cambodia

23 Oct.   International Conference on Cambodia resumed in Paris and Peace Accords signed

16 Oct.   Security Council authorizes establishment of UN Advance Mission in Cambodia (UNAMIC)

31 Oct.   Security Council requests Secretary-General to prepare detailed plan for implementation of Paris Accords

9 Nov.   UNAMIC formally established in Phnom Penh

27 Nov.	Near-lynching of Khmer Rouge leader Khieu Samphan

1992

8 Jan.	Security Council expands UNAMIC mandate to include training in mine clearance and initiation of mine-clearance programme
19 Feb.	Report by UN Secretary-General to Security Council on Cambodia, setting out modalities for establishing UNTAC
28 Feb.	UNTAC established by the Security Council
15 Mar.	Yasushi Akashi, head of UNTAC, arrives in Phnom Penh
30 Mar.	UNHCR's repatriation of refugees from Thailand begins
1 Apr.	UNTAC submits Electoral Law to SNC
20 Apr.	SNC ratifies International Convenants on Civil and Political Rights and on Economic, Social and Cultural Rights
1 May	First Progress Report of the Secretary-General on UNTAC to Security Council
9 May	UNTAC announces phase II of cease-fire will begin on 13 June
5 June	SNC adopts laws enshrining rights of freedom of association and of assembly
10 June	SNC establishes Cambodian Mine Action Centre
13 June	Phase II of cease-fire begins
22 June	Ministerial Conference on the Rehabilitation and Reconstruction of Cambodia, Tokyo
15 July	UNTAC civil administration offices established in all 21 provinces
21 July	Security Council approves efforts of Secretary-General to continue implementing Paris Accords
5 Aug.	SNC adopts Electoral Law
12 Aug.	Electoral Law promulgated
15 Aug.	Registration of political parties begins
10 Sep.	SNC agrees to accede to the Convention against Torture and Other Cruel, Inhuman or Degrading Treatment or Punishment; International Convention on the Elimination of All Forms of Discrimination against Women; Convention on the Rights of the Child; Convention and Protocol relating to the Status of Refugees

	SNC approves set of principles relating to Cambodia's legal system, penal law and penal procedure
21 Sep.	Second Progress Report on UNTAC to Security Council
22 Sep.	SNC declares country-wide moratorium on export of logs
5 Oct.	Voter registration begins
13 Oct.	Security Council accepts Secretary-General's recommendation to proceed with elections
9 Nov.	Radio UNTAC begins broadcasting
30 Nov.	Security Council imposes non-mandatory embargo on petroleum supplies to Khmer Rouge

1993

6 Jan.	UNTAC establishes procedures for prosecuting human rights violators
25 Jan.	Third progress report on UNTAC to Security Council
27 Jan.	20 political parties register for election
28 Jan.	SNC agrees that elections for Constituent Assembly be held 23–25 May 1993
	Prince Sihanouk tells SNC that presidential election should be held after adoption of new constitution
31 Jan.	Voting rolls close
10 Feb.	SNC adopts moratorium on export of minerals and gems
25 Feb.	Informal meeting of international aid donors in Phnom Penh
28 Feb.	Moratorium on export of minerals and gems takes effect
4 Apr.	Khmer Rouge officially announces it will not participate in elections
7 Apr.	Official election campaign starts
3 May	Khmer Rouge attacks Siem Reap near Angkor Wat
	Fourth Progress Report on UNTAC to Security Council
23–28 May	Voting period
29 May	Yasushi Akashi declares elections 'free and fair' and counting proceeds
14 June	Prince Sihanouk reinstated as Head of State by Constituent Assembly at its inaugural session
15 June	Security Council endorses election result
1 July	Provisional Government accepted by Constituent Assembly

2 July	Provisional Government sworn in
8–9 Sep.	First meeting of International Committee on the Reconstruction of Cambodia, Paris
21 Sep.	Draft constitution ratified
24 Sep.	King Sihanouk enthroned and signs constitution into law
	Constituent Assembly becomes National Assembly
	Provisional Government becomes new Cambodian Government
	SNC formally hands back sovereignty to new Government
26 Sep.	·Yasushi Akashi leaves Phnom Penh, formally ending the UN operation
30 Sep.	Withdrawal of CivPols completed
15 Nov.	Military withdrawal completed
30 Nov.	Mine clearance and training unit departs
Dec.	National Assembly passes the National Programme to Rehabilitate and Develop Cambodia
31 Dec.	Withdrawal of all UNTAC personnel completed

1994

Feb.–Mar.	Continued KR military activity. Victories for government forces at Anlong Veng and Pailin
10–11 Mar.	Second meeting of International Committee on Reconstruction of Cambodia, in Tokyo
May	KR retakes Anlong Veng and Pailin
May–June	Inconclusive talks between the Government and the KR
June	KR office in Phnom Penh closed
	Sihanouk proposes to take over power and form a government of national unity: proposal rejected by Hun Sen and Ranariddh
July	Coup attempt by CPP hardliners
	Kidnapping of three foreign hostages by KR
	KR outlawed by the National Assembly
	KR announces formation of a provisional government of national unity in Preah Vihear province
Sep.	Murder of three foreign hostages by the KR
Oct.	Resignation of the Finance Minister, Sam Rainsy
	Resignation of the Foreign Minister, Prince Norodom Sirivudh

Bibliography

Books

Aitkin, S., Getting the message about mines: towards a national public information strategy and program on mines and mine safety, vol. 1: Report (UNESCO, Phnom Penh, Sep. 1993).

Asia Watch, *Political Control, Human Rights, and the UN Mission in Cambodia* (Asia Watch: New York, Sep. 1992).

Asia Watch, *Khmer Abuses Along the Thai–Cambodian Border* (Asia Watch Committee: Washington, DC, 1989).

Asia Watch and Physicians for Human Rights, *Land Mines in Cambodia: The Coward's War* (New York, Sep. 1991).

Australian Department of Foreign Affairs and Trade, *Cambodia: An Australian Peace Proposal* (Australian Government Printing Service: Canberra, Feb. 1990).

Axell, K. (ed.), Uppsala University, Department of Peace and Conflict Research, *States in Armed Conflict 1992*, Report no. 36 (Uppsala, 1993).

Berdal, M., Institutt for forsvarsstudier, *United Nations Peacekeeping at a Crossroads*, IFS Info. no. 7, 1993 (IFS: Oslo, 1993).

Berdal, M., International Institute for Strategic Studies, *Whither UN Peacekeeping?* Adelphi Paper no. 281 (Brassey's: London, 1993).

Carney, T. and Tan Lian Choo (eds), Institute of Southeast Asian Studies, *Whither Cambodia? Beyond the Election* (ISEAS: Singapore, 1994).

Chandler, D. P., *A History of Cambodia*, 2nd edn (Westview Press: Boulder, Colo., 1993).

Chandler, D. P., *Brother Number One: A Political Biography of Pol Pot* (Westview Press: Boulder, Colo., 1992).

Chopra, J., Mackinlay, J. and Minear, L., Norwegian Institute of International Affairs, *Report on the Cambodian Peace Process*, Research Report no. 165 (NIIA: Oslo, Feb. 1993).

Daniel, D., US Naval War College, Centre for Naval War Studies, *Issues and Considerations in UN Gray Area and Enforcement Operations*, Strategic Research Department Research Memorandum 4-94 (US Naval War College: Newport, R.I., 1994).

Evans, G., *Cooperating for Peace: The Global Agenda for the 1990s and Beyond* (Allen & Unwin: Sydney, 1993).

Evans, G. and Grant, B., *Australia's Foreign Relations in the World of the 1990s* (Melbourne University Press: Carlton, 1991).

Fernando, J. B., *The Inability to Prosecute: Courts and Human Rights in Cambodia and Sri Lanka* (Future Asia Link: Hong Kong, 1993).

Fetherston, A. B., University of Bradford, Department of Peace Studies, *Toward A Theory of United Nations Peacekeeping*, Peace Research Report no. 31 (University of Bradford: Bradford, Feb. 1993).

Heder, S. R., Australian National University, Research School of Pacific Studies, Strategic and Defence Studies Centre, *Reflections on Cambodian Political History: Backgrounder to Recent Developments*, Working Paper no. 239 (SDSC: Canberra, 1991).

Kevin, A. C., Australian National University, Research School of Pacific Studies, Strategic and Defence Studies Centre, *Southeast Asia Beyond the Cambodia Settlement, Sources of Political and Economic Tensions and Conflict, Trends in Defence Spending, and Options for Cooperative Engagement*, Working Paper no. 213 (SDSC: Canberra, 1990).

Klintworth, G., Australian National University, Research School of Pacific Studies, Strategic and Defence Studies Centre, *Cambodia and Peace-keeping: 1990*, Working Paper no. 210 (SDSC: Canberra, 1990).

Klintworth, G., Australian National University, Research School of Pacific Studies, Strategic and Defence Studies Centre, *Cambodia's Past, Present and Future*, Working Paper no. 268 (SDSC: Canberra, 1990).

Ledgerwood, J. L., East-West Center, 'UN peacekeeping missions: the lessons from Cambodia', Asia Pacific Issues no. 11 (East–West Center: Honolulu, Mar. 1994).

Mahmud, T. (Col), *The Peacekeepers: 2 AK in Cambodia* (2 AK Regiment: Lahore, 1993).

Morgan Stanley, International Investment Research, *Cambodia: Dark History, Brighter Future*, Letters from Asia no. 6 (Morgan Stanley: Tokyo &c., 1994).

Munck, G. L. and Kumar, C., University of Illinois at Urbana-Champaign, Program in Arms Control, Disarmament, and International Security, *Conflict Resolution through International Intervention: A Comparative Study of Cambodia and El Salvador*, Occasional Paper (ACDIS: Urbana, Ill., Apr. 1993).

Osborne, M., *Sihanouk: Prince of Light, Prince of Darkness* (Allen & Unwin: Sydney, 1994).

Snitwongse, K., Australian National University, Research School of Pacific Studies, Strategic and Defence Studies Centre, *Southeast Asia Beyond a Cambodia Settlement: Conflict or Cooperation?*, Working Paper no. 223 (SDSC: Canberra, 1990).

UN, *The United Nations in Cambodia : A Vote for Peace* (United Nations: New York, 1994).

UN, *United Nations Peace-keeping* (United Nations: New York, 31 May 1993).

UN, *Yearbook of the United Nations 1992* (United Nations: New York, 1993).

United Nations Institute for Training and Research (UNITAR), *A Peace-keeping Training Manual*, 2nd draft (United Nations: New York, 1994).

United Nations Institute for Training and Research (UNITAR), UNITAR Video Training Package on Peace-keeping Operations, multimedia package (UNITAR: Geneva, 1994).

Wurmser, D., *et al.*, *The Professionalization of Peacekeeping* (US Institute of Peace: Washington, DC, Aug. 1993).

Articles

Abuza, Z., 'The Khmer Rouge quest for economic independence', *Asian Survey*, vol. 33, no. 10 (Oct. 1993).

Adolph, R. B., Jr (Lt-Col), 'UN military civil action in Cambodia', *Special Warfare*, vol. 7, no. 3 (July 1994).

Akashi, Y., 'The challenges faced by UNTAC', *Japan Review of International Affairs*, summer 1993.

Alagappa, M., 'The Cambodian conflict: changing interests of external actors and implications for conflict resolution', *Pacific Review*, fall 1990.

Amer, R., 'The United Nations' peacekeeping operation in Cambodia: overview and assessment', *Contemporary Southeast Asia*, vol. 15, no. 2 (Sep. 1993).

Asia Watch, 'Cambodia: human rights before and after the elections', *Asia Watch*, vol. 5, no. 10 (May 1993).

Asia Watch, 'An exchange on human rights and peace-keeping in Cambodia', *Asia Watch*, vol. 5, no. 14 (23 Sep. 1993).

Awanohara, S., 'Budget blues', *Far Eastern Economic Review*, 27 Feb. 1993.

Ayling, S. (Lt-Col), 'UNTAC: the ambitious mission', ed. H. Smith, Australian Defence Force Academy, Australian Defence Studies Centre, *Peacekeeping: Challenges for the Future* (ADSC: Canberra, 1993).

Barrington, K., 'Pay dispute undermines UNTAC morale', *Phnom Penh Post*, 12–25 Mar. 1993.

Becker, E., 'Sihanouk's turnabouts don't serve Cambodians', *International Herald Tribune*, 9 Feb. 1989.

de Beer, P., 'Khmer Rouge threat to UN peace process', *Guardian Weekly*, 21 June 1992.

de Beer, D., Netherlands Institute of International Relations, 'Observing the elections in Angola (September 1992) and in Cambodia (May 1993)', ed. D. A. Leurdijk *et al.*, *Case Studies in Second Generation United Nations Peacekeeping*, Clingendael Paper (NIIR: The Hague, Jan. 1994).

Birgisson, K. Th., 'United Nations Yemen Observation Mission', ed. W. J. Durch, *The Evolution of UN Peacekeeping: Case Studies and Comparative Analysis* (St Martin's Press for The Henry L. Stimson Center: Washington, DC, 1993).

Branegan, J., 'Cambodia: up against a wall', *Time* (Australia), 29 June 1992.

Branigin, W., 'Bulgarians put crimp in UN peacekeeping mission', *Washington Post,* 30 Oct. 1993.

Branigin, W. 'Curtain falls in Cambodia: a UN success, with flaws', *International Herald Tribune,* 27 Sep. 1993.

Branigin, W., 'UN Cambodian force is malfunctioning', *International Herald Tribune,* 5 Oct. 1992.

Brown, J. C., 'FUNCINPEC's evaporating mandate', *Phnom Penh Post,* 25 Mar.–7 Apr. 1994.

Burslem, C., 'When the office is a minefield', *Phnom Penh Post,* 13–26 Aug. 1993.

Cambodia: recent developments, Statement by Peter Tomsen, Deputy Assistant Secretary for East Asian and Pacific Affairs, before the Subcommittee on Asia and the Pacific of the House Foreign Affairs Committee, US Congress, Washington DC, 11 May 1994. Reproduced in *US Department of State Dispatch*, vol. 5, no. 21 (23 May 1994).

Cambodian Mine Action Centre, Phnom Penh, *CMAC Bulletin*, vol. 1, no. 1 (21 Apr. 1993).

Chanda, N., 'Cambodia: UN divisions', *Far Eastern Economic Review,* 23 July 1992.

Chandler, D., 'The tragedy of Cambodian history revisited', *SAIS Review,* vol. 14, no. 2 (summer–fall 1994).

Cummings-Bruce, N., '"Futile" bill to ban Khmer Rouge', *The Guardian,* 6 July 1994.

Curran, B., 'Whither the Throne?', *Phnom Penh Post,* 3–16 Dec. 1993.

Davies, R., 'Blue berets, green backs, what was the impact?', *Phnom Penh Post,* 22 Oct.–4 Nov. 1993.

Deron, F., 'Cambodian factions reach agreement', *Le Monde,* republished in *Guardian Weekly,* 28 July 1991.

Dobbie, C., 'A concept for post-cold war peacekeeping', *Survival,* vol. 36, no. 3 (autumn 1994).

Doyle, M. W., 'UNTAC: sources of success and failure', ed. H. Smith, Australian Defence Force Academy, Australian Defence Studies Centre, *International Peacekeeping: Building on the Cambodian Experience* (ADSC: Canberra, 1994).

Durch, W. J., 'The UN Operation in the Congo: 1960–64', ed. W. J. Durch, *The Evolution of UN Peacekeeping: Case Studies and Comparative*

Analysis (St Martin's Press for The Henry L. Stimson Center: Washington DC, 1993).

Durch, W. J., 'The UN Temporary Executive Authority', ed. W. J. Durch, *The Evolution of UN Peacekeeping: Case Studies and Comparative Analysis* (St Martin's Press for The Henry L. Stimson Center: Washington, DC, 1993).

Eaton, C., 'The role of police in institution building', ed. H. Smith, Australian Defence Force Academy, Australian Defence Studies Centre, *International Peacekeeping: Building on the Cambodian Experience* (ADSC: Canberra, 1994).

Etcheson, C., 'Pol Pot and the art of war', *Phnom Penh Post*, 13–26 Aug. 1993.

Evans, G., 'The comprehensive political settlement to the Cambodia conflict: an exercise in cooperating for peace', ed. H. Smith, Australian Defence Force Academy, Australian Defence Studies Centre, *International Peacekeeping: Building on the Cambodian Experience* (ADSC: Canberra, 1994).

Evans, G., 'Conflict of interests', *The Bulletin* (Sydney), 18 May 1993.

Evans, G., 'Peacekeeping in Cambodia: lessons learned', *NATO Review*, vol. 42, no. 4 (Aug. 1994).

Farris, K., 'UN peacekeeping in Cambodia: on balance, a success', *Parameters,* vol. 24, no. 1 (1994).

Findlay, T., 'Multilateral conflict prevention, management and resolution', *SIPRI Yearbook 1994* (Oxford University Press: Oxford, 1994), chapter 1.

Findlay, T., 'The Cambodian election', *Current Affairs Bulletin*, vol. 70, no. 2 (July 1993).

Findlay, T., 'UNTAC—lessons to be learned?', *International Peacekeeping*, vol. 1, no. 1 (Jan.–Feb. 1994).

Fortuna, V. P., 'United Nations Transition Assistance Group', ed. W. J. Durch, *The Evolution of UN Peacekeeping: Case Studies and Comparative Analysis* (St Martin's Press for The Henry L. Stimson Center: Washington, DC, 1993).

Friedland, J., 'Someone to trust: Cambodia's free-market plan wins over donors', *Far Eastern Economic Review*, 24 Mar. 1994.

Frost, F., Institute of Southeast Asian Studies, 'Cambodia: from UNTAC to Royal Government', *Southeast Asian Affairs 1994* (ISEAS: Singapore, 1994).

Griffith, A., 'World needs benefit of a success in Cambodia', *Canberra Times*, 15 Mar. 1993.

Harris, B., 'Gloomy PM warns of more fighting', *Phnom Penh Post*, 3–16 June 1994.

Hayes, M., 'UN advance team sets stage for elections', *Phnom Penh Post*, 24 July 1992.

Hornik, R., 'Cambodia: the people take charge', *Time* (Australia), 7 June 1993.

Hornik, R., 'Sympathy for the devil', *Time* (Australia), 21 Sep. 1992.

Jackson, K. D., 'Introduction: the Khmer Rouge in context', ed. K. D. Jackson, *Cambodia 1975–1978: Rendezvous with Death* (Princeton University Press: Princeton, N.J., 1989).

Jeldres, J. A., 'The UN and the Cambodian transition', *Journal of Democracy*, vol. 4, no. 4 (Oct. 1993).

Jennar, R. M., 'UNTAC: "international triumph" in Cambodia?', *Security Dialogue*, vol. 25, no. 2 (1994).

Kiernan, B., 'The Cambodian crisis, 1990–1992: the UN plan, the Khmer Rouge, and the state of Cambodia', *Bulletin of Concerned Asian Scholars*, vol. 24, no. 2 (Apr.–June 1992).

Koh, T. T. B., 'The Paris Conference on Cambodia: a multilateral negotiation that "failed"', *Negotiation Journal*, vol. 6, no. 1 (Jan. 1990).

Lao, M. H., 'Obstacles to peace in Cambodia', *Pacific Review*, vol. 6, no. 4 (1993).

Leifer, M., 'Cambodia: the obstacle is in Beijing', *International Herald Tribune*, 16 Aug. 1988.

Lithgow, S., 'Cambodia: an early retrospect', ed. C. Bell, Australian National University, Research School of Pacific Studies, Strategic and Defence Studies Centre, *The United Nations and Crisis Management: Six Studies*, Canberra Papers on Strategy and Defence no. 104 (SDSC: Canberra, 1994).

Lizée, P., 'Peacekeeping, peace building and the challenge of conflict resolution in Cambodia', ed. D. A. Charters, University of New Brunswick, Centre for Conflict Studies, *Peacekeeping and the Challenge of Civil Conflict Resolution* (CCS: Fredericton, 1991).

McAulay, P., 'Civilian police and peacekeeping: challenges in the 1990s', ed. H. Smith, Australian Defence Force Academy, Australian Defence Studies Centre, *Peacekeeping: Challenges for the Future* (ADSC: Canberra, 1994).

Mackinlay, J., 'Defining a role beyond peacekeeping', ed. W. H. Lewis, National Defense University, Institute for National Strategic Studies, *Military Implications of United Nations Peacekeeping Operations*, McNair Paper no. 17 (INSS: Washington, DC, June 1993).

Mackinlay, J., 'Improving multifunctional forces', *Survival*, vol. 36, no. 3 (autumn 1994).

Mackinlay, J., 'Successful intervention', *Internationale Spectator*, Nov. 1993.

Mackinlay, J. and Chopra, J., 'Second generation multinational operations', *Washington Quarterly*, summer 1992.

McLean, L., 'Civil administration in transition: public information and the neutral political/electoral environment', ed. H. Smith, Australian Defence Force Academy, Australian Defence Studies Centre, *International Peacekeeping: Building on the Cambodian Experience* (ADSC: Canberra, 1994).

McNulty, S., 'Blue helmets, peacekeeping and a few sidelines', Associated Press report from Phnom Penh, 13 Dec. 1993.

Magstad, M. K., 'UN workers in Cambodia give ultimatum', *Washington Post,* 16 Apr. 1993.

Maley, M., 'Reflections on the electoral process in Cambodia', ed. H. Smith, Australian Defence Force Academy, Australian Defence Studies Centre, *International Peacekeeping: Building on the Cambodian Experience* (ADSC: Canberra, 1994).

Mallet, V., 'Khmer Rouge keeps the world guessing', *Financial Times*, 27 May 1993.

Michaels, M., 'Blue-helmet blues', *Time* (Australia), 15 Nov. 1993.

Moreau, R., 'Disillusioned, demoralized and defecting', *The Bulletin* (Sydney), 28 Sep. 1993.

Moser-Phoungsuwan, Y., 'Cambodia article', *APRA Newsletter,* no. 5 (Sep./Oct. 1994).

Munthit, K., 'Cambodia chooses Franco-phone path', *Phnom Penh Post*, 13–26 Aug. 1993.

Murdoch, L., 'The spoils of peace', *Good Weekend* (Sydney), Apr. 1993.

Peang-Meth, A., 'The United Nations peace plan, the Cambodian conflict and the future of Cambodia', *Contemporary Southeast Asia*, vol. 14, no. 1 (June 1992).

Pilger, J., 'Cambodia: return to year zero', *New Internationalist*, no. 242 (Apr. 1993).

Pilger, J., 'Peace in our time?', *New Statesman and Society,* 27 Nov. 1992.

Pilger, J., 'The return to year zero', *The Bulletin* (Sydney), 11 May 1993.

Plunkett, M., 'The establishment of the rule of law in post-conflict peace-keeping', ed. H. Smith, Australian Defence Force Academy, Australian Defence Studies Centre, *International Peacekeeping: Building on the Cambodian Experience* (ADSC: Canberra, 1994).

Prasso, S., 'Cambodia: a heritage of violence', *World Policy Journal,* vol. 11, no. 3 (fall 1994).

Randall, S. J., Canadian Institute of International Affairs, 'Peacekeeping in the post-cold war era: the United Nations and the 1993 Cambodian elections', *Behind the Headlines*, vol. 51, no. 3 (CIIA: Toronto, 1994).

Ratner, S. R., 'The Cambodia settlement agreements', *American Journal of International Law*, vol. 87, no. 1 (Jan. 1993).

Ratner, S. R., 'The United Nations in Cambodia: a model for resolution of internal conflicts?', ed. L. F. Damrosch, *Enforcing Restraint: Collective Intervention in Internal Conflicts* (Council on Foreign Relations Press: New York, 1993).

Roberts, D., 'Democratic Kampuchea?', *Pacific Review*, vol. 7, no. 1 (1994).

Ross, J. D., 'Cambodia hasn't been rescued', *International Herald Tribune*, 24 May 1994.

Rowley, K., 'UN has an active option open to it in Cambodia', *Canberra Times*, 29 June 1992.

Sanderson, J. M. (Lt-Gen.), 'UNTAC: successes and failures', ed. H. Smith, Australian Defence Force Academy, Australian Defence Studies Centre, *International Peacekeeping: Building on the Cambodian Experience* (ADSC: Canberra, 1994).

Schear, J. A., 'The case of Cambodia', eds D. Daniel and B. Hayes, *Beyond Traditional Peacekeeping* (Macmillan: London, forthcoming 1995).

Segal, G. and Berdal, M., 'The Cambodian dilemma', *Jane's Intelligence Review*, vol. 5, no. 3 (Mar. 1993).

Serrill, M. S., 'Cambodia: back to war', *Time* (Australia), 25 May 1993.

Shawcross, W., 'Cambodia: the UN's biggest gamble', *Time* (Australia), 28 Dec. 1992.

Shawcross, W., 'A new Cambodia', *New York Review of Books*, 12 Aug. 1993.

Shenon, P., 'A Japanese envoy's impossible job: keeping the peace in Cambodia', *New York Times*, 4 Oct. 1992.

Sheridan, G., 'Peace plan critics fail to see erosion of Khmer Rouge position', *The Australian*, 26 Jan. 1993.

Smith, C., 'Stop bashing Bulgabatt', letter to the editor, *Phnom Penh Post*, 19 Nov.–2 Dec. 1993.

Solarz, S., 'Cambodia and the international community', *Foreign Affairs*, spring 1990.

Thayer, C., 'Who will run Cambodia?', *Business Times*, 10 Feb. 1993.

Thayer, N., 'Budget law passed unanimously', *Phnom Penh Post*, 31 Dec. 1993–13 Jan 1994.

Thayer, N., 'Cambodia: shot to pieces', *Far Eastern Economic Review*, 20 May 1993.

Thayer, N., 'IMF to press over logs', *Phnom Penh Post*, 29 July–11 Aug. 1994.

Thayer, N., 'King talks of taking power', *Phnom Penh Post*, 17–30 June 1994.

Thayer, N., 'Murder with impunity', *Far Eastern Economic Review*, 18 Aug. 1994.

Thayer, N., 'No way home for KR defectors', *Phnom Penh Post*, 17–31 Dec. 1993.

Thayer, N., 'Shake-up in KR heirarchy', *Phnom Penh Post*, 28 Jan.–10 Feb. 1994.

Thayer, N., 'Sihanouk back at the helm', *Phnom Penh Post*, 28 June–1 July 1993.

Thayer, N., 'Split emerges in Core Group', *Phnom Penh Post*, 28 June–1 July 1993.

Thayer, N., 'Theatre of the absurd', *Far Eastern Economic Review*, 1 Sep. 1994.

Thayer, N.,'Unsettled land', *Far Eastern Economic Review*, 27 Feb. 1993.

Thayer, N. and Chanda, N., 'Cambodia: shattered peace', *Far Eastern Economic Review*, 11 Feb. 1993.

Thayer, N. and Tasker, R., 'The plot thickens', *Far Eastern Economic Review*, 21 July 1994.

Tomoda, S., 'Japan's search for a political role in Asia: the Cambodian peace settlement', *Japan Review of International Affairs*, vol. 6, no. 1 (spring 1992).

UN, Department of Public Information, *Background Note: United Nations Peace-keeping Operations* (United Nations: New York, Jan. 1993).

UN, *United Nations Focus: Cambodia: Cambodia Election Results*, July 1993.

UN, *United Nations Focus: Cambodia: United Nations Transitional Authority in Cambodia*, New York, Feb. 1993, Mar. 1993 and Apr. 1993.

UN, *United Nations Peacekeeping Operations Information Notes: UNTAC*, New York, 31 Oct. 1993.

UNHCR, *Information Bulletin*, Phnom Penh, nos 7 (Oct. 1993) and 8 (Mar. 1993).

UNTAC Electoral Component, Phnom Penh, *Free Choice: Electoral Component Newsletter*, nos 10 (18 Dec. 1992), 11 (15 Jan. 1993) and 15 (12 Mar. 1993).

UNTAC XII, Information/Education Division, *Brief*, nos 13 (23 Dec. 1992), 16 (25 Jan. 1993) and 31 (20 May 1993).

Vickery, M., Institute of Southeast Asian Studies, 'The Cambodian People's Party: where has it come from, where is it going?', *Southeast Asian Affairs 1994* (ISEAS: Singapore, 1994).

Wurst, J., 'Mozambique: peace and more', *World Policy Journal*, vol. 11, no. 3 (fall 1994).

Wurst, J., 'Ten million tragedies, one step at a time', *Bulletin of the Atomic Scientists*, July/Aug. 1993.

Zartman, I. W., 'Regional conflict resolution', ed. V. A. Kremenyuk, Processes of International Negotiations (PIN) Project, *International Negotiation: Analysis, Approaches, Issues* (Jossey-Bass: San Francisco, Calif. and Oxford, 1991).

Documents

1990

UN, The situation in Kampuchea: Question of peace, stability and co-operation in South-East Asia, Letter dated 90/05/29 from the representatives of China, France, the Union of Soviet Socialist Republics, the United Kingdom of Great Britain and Northern Ireland and the United States of America to the United Nations addressed to the Secretary-General, UN document A/45/293, S/21318, 29 May 1990.

UN, The situation in Kampuchea: Question of peace, stability and co-operation in South-East Asia, Letter dated 90/07/19 from the representatives of China, France, the Union of Soviet Socialist Republics, the United Kingdom of Great Britain and Northern Ireland and the United States of America to the United Nations addressed to the Secretary-General, UN document A/45/353, S/21404, 23 July 1990.

Statement by the Permanent Five of 28 Aug. 1990, published as an Annex to UN, The situation in Kampuchea: Question of peace, stability and co-operation in South-East Asia, Letter dated 90/08/30 from the permanent representatives of China, France, the Union of Soviet Socialist Republics, the United Kingdom of Great Britain and Northern Ireland and the United States of America to the United Nations addressed to the Secretary-General, UN document A/45/472, S/21689, 31 Aug. 1990.

UN, The situation in Kampuchea: Letter dated 90/09/11 from the permanent representatives of France and Indonesia to the United Nations addressed to the Secretary-General, UN document A/45/490, S/21732, 17 Sep. 1990.

UN, Letter dated 90/10/01 from the permanent representatives of China, France, the Union of Soviet Socialist Republics, the United Kingdom of Great Britain and Northern Ireland and the United States of America to the United Nations addressed to the Secretary-General, UN document S/21835, 2 Oct. 1990.

UN, The situation in Cambodia: Question of peace, stability and co-operation in South-East Asia, Letter dated 90/10/18 from the permanent representatives of China, France, the Union of Soviet Socialist Republics, the United Kingdom of Great Britain and Northern Ireland and the United States of America to the United Nations addressed to the Secretary-General, UN document A/45/671, S/21908, 25 Oct. 1990.

1991

UN, The situation in Cambodia. Letter dated 91/01/08 from the permanent representatives of France and Indonesia to the United Nations addressed to the Secretary-General, UN document A/46/61, S/22059, 11 Jan. 1991.

UN, The situation in Cambodia. Letter dated 91/02/21 from the representatives of France and Indonesia to the United Nations addressed to the Secretary-General, UN document A/46/112, S/22344, 8 Mar. 1991.

UN, The situation in Cambodia. Letter dated 91/04/22 from the permanent representatives of France and Indonesia to the United Nations addressed to the Secretary-General, UN document A/46/161, S/22552, 29 Apr. 1991.

UN, The situation in Cambodia. Letter dated 91/06/24 from the Chargé d'affaires a.i. of the permanent mission of Cambodia to the United Nations addressed to the Secretary-General, UN document A/46/267, S/22733, 24 June 1991.

UN, The situation in Cambodia. Letter dated 91/06/25 from the Chargé d'affaires a.i. of the permanent mission of Cambodia to the United Nations addressed to the Secretary-General, UN document A/46/269, S/22736, 25 June 1991.

UN, The situation in Cambodia. Letter dated 91/06/26 from the Chargé d'affaires a.i. of the permanent mission of Cambodia to the United Nations addressed to the Secretary-General, UN document A/46/271, S/22740, 26 June 1991.

UN, The situation in Cambodia. Letter dated 91/07/18 from the President of the Supreme National Council of Cambodia addressed to the Secretary-General, UN document A/46/310, S/22808, 18 July 1991.

UN, The situation in Cambodia. Letter dated 91/09/03 from the representatives of China, France, Indonesia, the Union of Soviet Socialist Republics, the United Kingdom of Great Britain and Northern Ireland and the United States of America to the United Nations addressed to the Secretary-General, UN document A/46/418, S/23011, 4 Sep. 1991.

UN, The situation in Cambodia. Letter dated 91/09/24 from the permanent representatives of China, France, Indonesia, the Union of Soviet Socialist Republics, the United Kingdom of Great Britain and Northern Ireland and the United States of America to the United Nations addressed to the Secretary-General, UN document A/46/508, S/23087, 27 Sep. 1991.

Agreement on a Comprehensive Political Settlement of the Cambodia Conflict. Published as an annex to UN document A/46/608, S/23177, 30 Oct. 1991.

Agreement Concerning the Sovereignty, Independence, Territorial Integrity and Inviolability, Neutrality and National Unity of Cambodia. Published as an annex to UN document A/46/608, S/23177, 30 Oct. 1991.

Declaration on the Rehabilitation and Reconstruction of Cambodia. Published as an annex to UN document A/46/608, S/23177, 30 Oct. 1991.

Final Act of the Paris Conference on Cambodia. Published as an annex to UN document A/46/608, S/23177, 30 Oct. 1991.

Cambodian peace negotiations: prospects for a settlement, Hearings before the Subcommittee on East Asian and Pacific Affairs of the Committee on Foreign Relations, US Senate, 101st Congress (US Government Printing Office: Washington, DC, 1991).

Effects of the Continued Diplomatic Stalemate in Cambodia, Hearing before the Subcommittee on East Asian and Pacific Affairs of the Committee on Foreign Relations, US Senate, 102nd Congress (US Government Printing Office: Washington, DC, 11 Apr. 1991). Statement of Richard H. Solomon. Reproduced in *East Asia and Pacific Wireless File* (United States Information Service, Canberra), 11 Apr. 1991.

1992

UN, An Agenda for Peace, Report of the Secretary-General pursuant to the statement adopted by the Summit Meeting of the Security Council, 31 Jan. 1992, UN document A/47/277, S/24111, United Nations, New York, 1992.

UN, Report of the Secretary-General on Cambodia, UN document S/23613, 19 Feb. 1992.

UN, Report of the Secretary-General on Cambodia: addendum, UN document S/23613/Add.1., 26 Feb. 1992.

UN, First progress report of the Secretary-General on the United Nations Transitional Authority in Cambodia, UN document S/23870, 1 May 1992.

UN, Special report of the Secretary-General on the United Nations Transitional Authority in Cambodia, UN document S/24090, 12 June 1992.

UN, Financing of the United Nations Transitional Authority in Cambodia. Letter dated 92/06/24 from the permanent representative of Japan to the United Nations addressed to the Secretary-General, UN document A/47/285, S/24183, 25 June 1992.

UN, UNTAC Cambodia: United Nations Transitional Authority in Cambodia, UN document DPI/1218-92542, June 1992.

UN, Second special report of the Secretary-General on the United Nations Transitional Authority in Cambodia, UN document S/24286, 14 July 1992.

UN, Second progress report of the Secretary-General on the United Nations Transitional Authority in Cambodia, UN document S/24578, 21 Sep. 1992.

UN, Report of the Secretary-General on the implementation of Security Council Resolution 783 (1992), UN document S/24800, 15 Nov. 1992.

UNTAC Economic Adviser's Office, Impact of UNTAC on Cambodia's economy, Phnom Penh, 21 Dec. 1992.

Cambodian Mine Action Centre, Cambodia's future (CMAC: Phnom Penh [late 1992]).

1993

UN, The right of peoples to self-determination and its application to peoples under colonial or alien domination or foreign occupation: Situation in Cambodia, Report of the Secretary-General, UN document E/CN.4/1993/19, 14 Jan. 1993.

UN, Third progress report of the Secretary-General on the United Nations Transitional Authority in Cambodia, UN document S/25124, 25 Jan. 1993.

UN, Report on the implementation of Security Council Resolution 792 (1992), UN document S/25289, 13 Feb. 1993.

Australian Minister for Foreign Affairs, Senator Gareth Evans, Statement on Cambodia, News Release M66, 24 Apr. 1993.

UN, Fourth progress report of the Secretary-General on the United Nations Transitional Authority in Cambodia, UN document S/25719, 3 May 1993.

UN, Report of the Secretary-General in pursuance of paragraph 6 of Security Council Resolution 810 (1993), UN document S/25784, 15 May 1993.

UN, Note by the President of the Security Council, UN document S/25822, 22 May 1993.

UNTAC, Statement by the Director of UNTAC Human Rights Component on political violence, Phnom Penh, 23 May 1993.

UN, Report of the Secretary-General on the conduct and results of the elections in Cambodia, UN document S/25913, 10 June 1993.

UN Research Institute for Social Development (UNRISD), The social consequences of the peace process in Cambodia, recommendations and findings from UNRISD Workshop, Geneva, 29–30 Apr. 1993 (UNRISD: Geneva, July 1993).

UN Peacekeeping: Observations on Mandates and Operational Capability, Statement of Frank C. Conahan, Assistant Comptroller General, National Security and International Affairs Division, Testimony before the Subcommittee on Terrorism, Narcotics, and International Operations, Committee on Foreign Relations, US Senate, 9 June 1993, GAO/T-NSIAD-93-15.

UN, Report of the Secretary-General pursuant to paragraph 7 of Resolution 840 (1993), UN document S/26090, 16 July 1993.

UN, Letter dated 26 July 1993 from the President of the Security Council addressed to the Secretary-General, UN document S/26150, 26 July 1993.

UN, Further report of the Secretary-General pursuant to paragraph 7 of Resolution 840 (1993), UN document S/26360, 26 Aug. 1993.

UN, United Nations Transitional Authority in Cambodia, UN document PS/DPI/16/Rev. 3, Oct. 1993. Published as part of UN, *United Nations Peace-keeping Operations Information Notes, 1993,* update no. 2, UN document DPI/1306/Rev. 2, Nov. 1993.

UN, Further report of the Secretary-General on the implementation of Security Council Resolution 745 (1992), UN document S/26529, 5 Oct. 1993.

UN, Further report of the Secretary-General pursuant to paragraph 7 of Resolution 840 (1993), UN document S/26546, 7 Oct. 1993.

UN, Further report of the Secretary-General pursuant to paragraph 7 of Resolution 840 (1993), UN document S/26649, 27 Oct. 1993.

UN, Letter dated 28 October 1993 from the Secretary-General addressed to the President of the Security Council, UN document S/26675, 1 Nov. 1993.

UN, Further report of the Secretary-General pursuant to paragraph 7 of Resolution 840 (1993), UN document S/26649/Add. 1, 3 Nov. 1993.

UN, Financing of the United Nations Transitional Authority in Cambodia: report of the Secretary-General, UN document A/48/701, 8 Dec. 1993.

Bulgarian Defence Ministry statement, Sofia, 13 Dec. 1993.

Constitution of the Kingdom of Cambodia, official English-language translation provided by the Royal Cambodian Embassy, Paris.

1994

UN, Human rights questions: human rights situations and reports of special rapporteurs and representatives. Situation of human rights in Cambodia. Note by the Secretary-General, UN document A/48/762, 7 Jan. 1994.

UN, Mid-term report of the Secretary-General on the United Nations Military Liaison Team in Cambodia, UN document S/1994/169, 14 Feb. 1994.

UN, Final report of the Secretary-General on the United Nations Military Liaison Team in Cambodia, UN document S/1994/645, 31 May 1994.

UN Security Council Resolutions

Resolution 668, UN document S/RES/668, 20 Sep. 1990.
Resolution 717, UN document S/RES/717, 16 Oct. 1991.
Resolution 718, UN document S/RES/718, 1 Nov. 1991.
Resolution 728, UN document S/RES/728, 8 Jan. 1992.
Resolution 745, UN document S/RES/745, 28 Feb. 1992.
Resolution 766, UN document S/RES/766, 21 July, 1992.
Resolution 783, UN document S/RES/783, 13 Oct. 1992.

Resolution 792, UN document S/RES/792, 30 Nov. 1992.
Resolution 810, UN document S/RES/810, 8 Mar. 1993.
Resolution 826, UN document S/RES/826, 20 May 1993.
Resolution 835, UN document S/RES/835, 2 June 1993.
Resolution 840, UN document S/RES/840, 15 June 1993.
Resolution 860, UN document S/RES/860, 27 Aug. 1993.
Resolution 880, UN document S/RES/880, 4 Nov. 1993.

UN General Assembly Resolutions

Resolution 45/3, UN document A/RES/45/3, 15 Oct. 1990.

Conference papers

Akashi, Y., 'The challenges of peace-keeping in Cambodia: lessons to be learned', Paper presented to School of International and Public Affairs, Columbia University, New York, 29 Nov. 1993.

Behar, N., 'Bulgarian peacekeeping prospects: new experiences and new dilemmas', Paper presented to the Friedrich-Ebert Stiftung/SIPRI conference on Challenges for the New Peacekeepers, Bonn, 21–22 Apr. 1994, p. 6.

'Executive summary', Institute for Policy Studies/UNITAR International Conference on UNTAC: debriefing and lessons, Singapore, 2–4 Aug. 1994.

Sanderson, J. M. (Lt-Gen.), 'Australia, the United Nations and the emerging world order', the 28th Alfred Deakin Lecture, Melbourne, 5 Sep. 1994.

Sanderson, J. M. (Lt-Gen.), 'Preparation for, deployment and conduct of peacekeeping operations: a Cambodia snapshot', Paper presented at a conference on UN Peacekeeping at the Crossroads, Canberra, 21–24 Mar. 1993.

Sanderson, J. M. (Lt-Gen.), 'A review of recent peacekeeping operations', Paper presented to the Pacific Armies Management Seminar (PAMS) XVIII Conference, Dacca, Jan. 1994.

Schear, J. A., 'Beyond traditional peacekeeping: the case of Cambodia', Paper presented to the Workshop on Beyond Traditional Peacekeeping, US Naval War College, Newport, R. I., 24 Feb. 1994.

Sturkey, D., 'Cambodia: issues for negotiation in a comprehensive settlement', Paper presented to the Fourth Asia–Pacific Roundtable on Confidence Building and Conflict Reduction in the Pacific, Kuala Lumpur, 17–20 June 1990.

Takahara, T., 'Combatting the specters of the past: the Japanese experience', Paper presented to the Friedrich-Ebert Stiftung/SIPRI conference on Challenges for the New Peacekeepers, Bonn, 21–22 Apr. 1994.

Takahara, T., 'Postwar pacifism in Japan and the new security environment: implications of participation in UN peacekeeping operations', Paper prepared for New York State Political Science Association 47th Annual Meeting, Hunter College, New York, 23–24 Apr. 1993.

Warner, N., 'Cambodia: lessons of UNTAC for future peacekeeping operations', Paper presented to an international seminar on UN Peacekeeping at the Crossroads, Canberra, 21–24 Mar. 1993.

Newspapers and journals consulted

The Age and Sunday Age (Melbourne)
Arms Control Today
Asian Recorder
The Australian
Bangkok Post
Beijing Review
The Bulletin (Sydney)
Canberra Times
Defense News
Disarmament Newsletter
East Asia and Pacific Wireless File (United States Information Service, Canberra)
Far Eastern Economic Review
Financial Times
The Guardian
The Independent
Insight (Australian Department of Foreign Affairs and Trade, Canberra)
International Defense Review
International Herald Tribune
Jane's Defence Weekly
Military and Arms Transfers News
The Nation (Bangkok)
New York Times
Phnom Penh Post
Sydney Morning Herald
Time (Australia)
Time (International)
The Times
UN Chronicle
Unity (United Nations Association of Australia, Canberra)
Washington Post

Index